First published by **Green Books Ltd** in 2008

Dartington Space, Dartington Hall, Totnes, Devon TQ9 6EN   edit@greenbooks.co.uk   www.greenbooks.co.uk

Reprinted 2011

Design & layout by **Christian Topf Design Ltd** (CTD) www.ctd-studio.co.uk

Illustrations by Christian Topf

Printed by Cambrian Printers, Aberystwyth, Wales, UK. Text printed on Pacesetter Silk FSC paper

Thank you to everyone below for your time and contributions to the making of this book:

UK: Cara Campbell, Jim Carfrae, Ian and Simone Pritchett of *Limetec*, *The Traditional Lime Company*, *Anglia Lime Company*, *Cornish Lime Company*, *Scottish Lime Centre*, Mike Wye and Associates, Rose of Jericho, *Masons Mortar*, *The Lime Centre*, *The Lime Firm*, Nigel and Joyce Gervis at *Calch-ty-Mawr*, Limeworks, SPAB (*Society for the Protection of Ancient Buildings*), Keith Hall of *Green Building Press*, Chris Lord-Smith of AECB (*Association for Environment Conscious Building*), Steven Laing of *Laing Masonry*, James Morris, Yantze, Ben Law, *Living Villages*, Matt Coleman, John at *Merchants House*, Alison Bunning, *The Green Building Store*, Dr. Mathew Hardy at *INTBAU*, Scott Mackie and all at the *National Trust Footprint Project*, *English Heritage*, Joanne Moss from the *Landmark Trust*, *Nutshell Paints*, Simon Dale.
Europe: Bruno Bengamra of *D'Ocres*, Carl Giskes and Martijn Hensius at *Tierrafino*, Claytec, Uta Herz at the *European Training Centre for Earth Building*, Titane Galer at *Craterre*.
USA: Paula and Robert Baker Laporte of *Eco-Nest*, *Crocker Ltd*, Bill and Athena Steene, Roxanne Swentzell and the *Poeh Gallery*, Tom and Satomi Lander, David Sheene, *Plants of the Southwest*, Felipe Ortega, Ojo Caliente, Francisco Uvina at *Cornerstones*, Mark at *Palo Santo Designs*, Len Brackett of *Eastwind Construction*, Ben and Jody of *Naturally Plaster*, Keely Meegan, Charlie Karuthers, Janice Vascot and *The Monastery of Christ in the Desert*, Carole Crews of *Gourmet Adobe*, Shaylor at *American Clay*, Will Powell, Hope Curtis, *Historic Santa Fe Centre*, Alan 'Mac' Watson, Kevin Manley, *Hopper Finishes*, Tony Atkin at *Atkin Olson Schade Architects*, *Yolo Paints*.
Morocco: Elie Mouyal, Quentin Wilbaux, Mr Bentbib, Malika, Montassir, Said Chaarawi.
New Zealand: Graeme North.
Japan: Tagawa Sangyo, Naito Yoshizo.

Photo credits: All photos by Katy Bryce and Adam Weismann except for: Back cover top, front piece, contents page, p.140, p.141 left, p.146, p.192 top, p.195 top: A. Mattern (American Clay); p.6 top left, p.32 bottom left, p.135 top right, bottom left: B. Bengamra; Front cover top middle, p.6, p.16 left, p.17 right, p.19 left and right, p.20 right, p.135 bottom right, p.149 middle, p.252 middle, middle: Claytec; Front cover top right, cover bottom middle, p.2, p.6 left & right, p.195 bottom right, p.195 right, p.198 top, p.205 middle, middle, p.252 middle right: Tierrafino; Cover bottom left, p.11, p.63, p.192 bottom left, p.246 middle: A. Brackett (www.ayabrackett.com); Back cover middle, p.12, p.14/15 top, p.142, p.156: T. Atkins; p.13 right: J. Morf; p.15 2nd from bottom, p.22: P. Baker-Laporte; p.17 left and middle, p.35, p.36, p.40 top left, top right, bottom middle, p.80 left, p.82, p.89 right, p.120, p.164: S. Mackie; p.18 middle, p.21 middle, p.132 left: Calch Ty Mawr; p.20 middle, p.206 bottom: Limetec; p.25, p.198 bottom, p.245, p.246 top and bottom, p.247, p.252 top left: Tagawa Sangyo; p.28: S. Dale; p.31, p.32 main picture and bottom right, p.40 top middle, bottom right, p.46/47, p.129 top right, p.135 top left, p.201: Living Villages; p.31 bottom: Phil G.; p.45, p.47 right, p.61 middle, middle, p.74 left, p.79 left, p.89 left, p.99 right, p.110: J. Haddow; Cover bottom right, p.54 top & middle, p.57 top, middle right & bottom left, p.58 top and bottom, p.61 top middle and middle right, p.62, p.107 right, p.173, p.205 bottom, p.209, p.211, p.212, p.214, p.215, p.223, p.224, p.225, p.252 top right : K. Manley; p. 54 bottom right, p. 57 middle, middle & bottom right: Landerland.com; p.61 top right, p.69 right, p.89 middle, p.90 left & middle, p.96 top and bottom right, p.104, p.129 bottom left: Scottish Lime Centre; p.69 third from left: J. Carfrae; p.90 right: Yantze; p.91 middle & right, p.206 top left: Landmark Trust; p.100: J. Orton; p.103: M. Wye; p.119: J. Morris (www.jamesmorris.info); p.126: B. Sargent; p.133 left: D. Sheen; p.145 back cover top, p. 217 top: B. Steen; p.186: Plants of the Southwest; Cover top left, p.195 left, p.242, p.243, p.244: C. Beyers; p.197: Craterre; Front cover centre, p.4 left, p.206 top right, p.234, p.238 top & bottom, p.240, p.241 top and bottom: C.Topf; p.226 right, p.228 bottom left: A. Bunning; p.228 top right and left: L. Dickson; p.232, p.233 C. Campbell; p.236, p.237: P. D. Marlow; Back cover bottom, p.192 top left, p195 bottom: Ben Tremper (www.bentremper.com).

using natural finishes

Lime- & earth-based plasters, renders & paints

a step-by-step guide

Adam Weismann & Katy Bryce

green books

Dedications

Phil Brown, Douglas Johnston, Peter Ellis and Ed Crocker – for your invaluable time and help with editing individual sections of this book.

Jeff Orton, Julie Haddow, Bill Sargent, Ed Crocker (again!), P. D. Marlow, Douglas Kent, Ian Prichett, Tom Woolley, Carina Beyers, Bruno Bengamra and Nobuyoshi Yukihara for your excellent interviews and written contributions.

Kelly Lerner, Barbara Jones and Bruce King for your help with the building design details diagrams in Chapter 2.

The Prince's Foundation for our scholarship to help fund our research travels to North Africa, Europe and USA.

Christian Topf for his outstanding design work on this book, and for his eternal patience with us.

Everyone at Green Books.

Contents

Introduction

Introduction

This book is about using 'natural' finishes based on lime and earth. These finishes can be defined as being 'natural' because they have undergone minimal processing, and contain no synthetic ingredients. The finishes that we describe in this book are plasters, renders, paints and washes. A plaster is applied internally, whereas a render is applied externally. A finish can be defined as a coating applied to the surface of a wall, which functions to give protection to the walls from the elements (external), and from the wear and tear of daily life. It can also beautify a space by providing colour and texture.

The raw materials – lime and earth – are versatile and adaptable. They have been used for finishing buildings for thousands of years, throughout the world. They have always been used simultaneously for the buildings of the wealthy and the buildings of ordinary folk. The techniques and recipes that we have included in this book are therefore not new: they are drawn from centuries of use and experience, and through this book we hope to pay respect to all those who have laid the foundations for this simple, yet highly effective, ancient know-how. We also hope to honour all those who in the last thirty years have worked tirelessly to resurrect these techniques. Through this work they have helped to turn them from lost arts into well-researched and documented materials and methods. This is enabling them to be used ever-increasingly by the mainstream building industry with confidence. They are now therefore well on their way to becoming the obvious choices for creating homes and structures that are life-enhancing to live in, kind to the environment and healthy for the building fabric itself.

The techniques presented in this book stem from two separate but inherently linked groups: the people of the 'green' building movement, that has been gently but powerfully emerging across the globe for the last thirty years, and the people involved in promoting the continued use of traditional lime and earth finishing and building techniques around the world. The bridge between these two bodies is that much of the philosophy behind the 'green' building movement has grown from the common-sense building principles of traditional architecture. These principles include:

- The local sourcing of materials, which supports the local economy, and also minimises the transport of materials over long distances.
- The use of naturally sourced, unadulterated materials, such as earth (clay), stone, lime, wood and reed.
- Building to fit into the surrounding land-scape and local ecology, so that buildings are site-specific and regionally distinct.
- Building by hand and with individual craftsmanship. This means that all buildings are unique to the hands that made them, instead of being the result of materials bought 'off-the-shelf'.
- The techniques used are simple, accessible and easy to learn. This means that self-build predominates, and that all members of the community – young and old, male and female – can be a part of the process in some way. This can encourage the development of community and encourage the philosophy that the process of building is just as, if not more important, than the end result.

Building to protect the environment
The 'green' building movement has grown as a direct response to an accelerated environmental imbalance. An imbalance precipitated by the

An external earth plaster makes this building blend into its natural surroundings in New Mexico, USA.

Industrial Revolution in the early nineteenth century. You will no doubt be aware of the undeniable link between CO_2 emissions and climate change. Globally, cement production contributes around 5% of all CO_2 emissions (source: *The Economist*, Jan 2008). Clearly, then, reducing the use of cement in building can play a significant part in reducing the negative impacts of the building industry on the environment.

Lime and earth-based finishes, used as alternatives to cement, can play a significant role in two ways. Firstly, as central components in all new-build finishes. Secondly, using lime and earth-based finishes (which are inherently softer and more porous than their cement counterparts), enables the use of low-impact, low-energy building materials. These are compatible in strength and porosity. Examples of such building materials include those made out of raw earth (cob, adobe, light clay and rammed earth), straw bales, hemp-lime and others. These building materials all produce less carbon emissions during their extraction, production and construction. Additionally, those materials based heavily on plant material, such as hemp, flax and straw, actually act to remove CO_2 from the atmosphere. Through the growth of the plant material, carbon dioxide is absorbed, converted into oxygen, and then released into the atmosphere. Buildings constructed out of these materials generally also have good in-built insulation values or 'thermal mass' (the ability to store heat), and can thus lower carbon emissions by minimising the need for heating a building.

Using lime- and earth-based finishes can also help restore balance to our planet in other ways. Though lime requires fairly large amounts of energy to produce (and requires quarrying), it has less impact than cement. The temperatures at which lime is fired are lower than those

The rich ochre lime finishes of this house
in France exude warmth and texture.
By *D'Ocres*, St. Antonin Noble Val, France.

needed for cement. Lime manufacturing has the potential to become a localised industry throughout the UK, and indeed around the world, although at present many local, small-scale limestone quarries and kilns are out of action. Additionally, all forms of building lime reabsorb much of the carbon dioxide released during their production, back into the structure as it dries and cures. Cement products are 'one direction only', meaning that they are unable to reabsorb any of the CO_2 released when they are fired. Lime is also recyclable and fully biodegradable. It can be crushed and then re-used as an aggregate in new mortars. Even when fully cured, it is soft enough to enable building units set in place or finished with lime to be dismantled, cleaned and re-used time and time again.

Raw earth-based finishes are exceptionally gentle on the planet. The clay-rich sub-soil that they are made with can be sourced on-site or locally, along with the other ingredients, aggregate and straw. They require no packaging, minimal processing, and can be eternally reused.

All the recipes and techniques used to create the simple, unadulterated finishes described in this book avoid the use of synthetic substances, and therefore eliminate the contamination of the ground, air and water. This avoids the poisoning of aquatic, animal, bird and human life that is a result of many of the conventional building materials being used today. By using lime- and earth-based finishes, as builders and homeowners, we can contribute to making changes that are environmentally and socially responsible.

Building to safeguard and enhance human health

Four significant changes have taken place since the end of World War II (1945), in the way we live, how we construct our buildings and the materials these buildings are constructed out of.

1. Westerners typically spend more time indoors than at any other time in history.
2. Building materials have become increasingly adulterated, with the use of chemical additives and synthetic products now making up most, if not all, of newly constructed buildings.
3. Buildings have become increasingly airtight.
4. Most modern buildings are made out of predominantly impervious materials (such as concrete and synthetic paints and varnishes), that are not 'breathable'. This means that they do not have the ability to regulate internal humidity, nor allow for the controlled movement of moisture and air through them. They can therefore potentially trap moisture within the fabric of the building. The presence of persistent dampness is unhealthy for the inhabitants, due to the possibility for mould and fungi to develop, and for the building itself, which, if left unchecked can lead to rotting and decay.

These changes have undoubtedly had an effect on our general health and well-being. Quantifiable evidence of this can be seen through the emergence of the increasingly common 'sick building syndrome', or 'multiple chemical sensitivities', which consist of a multitude of respiratory, immune system and skin disorders. They have developed in reaction to the inhalation and absorption of the noxious chemicals present in the building materials. This is made worse by the fact that they are often trapped inside poorly ventilated, tightly sealed, overheated buildings, inside which people are increasingly spending most of their time. The air inside such a building will be of poor quality, if not poisonous.

By using earth- and lime-based finishes, all of these conditions can be greatly improved, if not eliminated. They are free of harmful chemicals and toxins. They are permeable and breathable, and thus function to regulate internal humidity. This will help to protect the fabric of the building, and eliminate the potential for the growth of moulds and fungi. Lime finishes have antiseptic qualities, and earth-based finishes can even absorb pollutants and neutralize odours. Though not well researched at present, there also appears to be evidence that a sufficiently thick earth plaster is able to counteract the potentially damaging effects of electromagnetic radiation from electrical equipment such as mobile phones, computers and televisions. Earth-based finishes can also act as heat stores (thermal mass), absorbing heat and then re-radiating it as temperatures fall. Earth-based finishes have also been purported to influence the composition and type of ions in inside spaces, by encouraging the presence of small, negatively

These finishes are inherently dynamic and ever-changing. They are sensitive to the environment around them, and can respond to seasonal and daily changes in temperature and levels of humidity in the atmosphere. In this way, being inside a building made out of these materials can literally serve as an extension of ourself – breathing and respiring as we do.

The textures of finishes made out of lime and earth encourage people to touch their soft, cool or warm surfaces. Their smells are earthy and minerally, as they echo the earth and rocks from where they came. These natural finishes can be made and applied to absorb sound, thus creating

"The house should not keep us isolated from the outside world. It should select and filter, keeping out and expelling what is bad, and welcoming in and storing what is good. This is possible through the selection of the right location, appropriate materials and shape of construction, and the right technical installations.

Dr. Anton Schneider – *Bau Biologie*

charged ions. Healthy air is composed of predominantly small, negatively charged ions. This is the air that is found by the sea, mountains and forests, and contributes to us feeling so good in these environments. This is in contrast to industrial areas, which consist of mainly large, positive ions. This air lacks vitality, and does nothing to enhance our health. Research is currently being carried out in Germany to further explore this field.

Lime- and earth-based finishes can also be positive for psychological well-being. They are inherently sensuous, meaning that being around them can literally enliven our senses, and in an indirect way bring us back into contact with the natural world.

internal spaces that are quiet and gentle on the ears. They also lend themselves to creating soft, organically-shaped walls to echo nature's own asymmetrical forms. A rounded window reveal, for example, will create a soft shadow transition from dark to light. This is much gentler and more pleasing to the eye than the sudden, sharp changes that occur around window and door reveals composed of straight lines. Paints made out of natural earth pigments and lime contain tiny crystals that enables them to interact with light in special ways. For this reason they also change with the seasons and different times of the day. It can therefore be argued that, by using these natural finishes in our buildings, we can in both indirect and direct ways bring ourselves back into contact with nature, and benefit from the way it can nourish us on all levels of our being. By using these finishes we are forced to begin to encompass the whole, and not just focus on individual parts of this whole. Buildings incorporating these natural materials must always be viewed as a system. It is necessary to take into consideration the environment in which they are situated, the materials used to construct them, the way buildings are to be used, and so on. Lime and earth are not 'one size fits all' materials. They are softer than their cement counterparts, and must therefore be used responsibly and sensitively, and in relation to the distinct weather patterns and topography of the site. For this reason, the design of a new building utilising lime- and earth-based finishes must be carried out with their use in mind from the very beginning of the design process.

Chapter 1 outlines many of the building design details that must be put in place to ensure that the benefits of these materials can be fully realised. Through this design process we can begin to re-engage with learning about the place in which we live and the natural elements that we are shielded from when we spend less time outdoors and more time in controlled internal environments. This also allows our buildings to once again tell a story about the places we live, and enables them to rekindle their dialogue with the environment in which they are situated.

Building in this way can encourage the creation of structures that are designed not as a confrontation with nature, but that are driven by it, and work in harmony with it. This can link our contemporary housing stock with our vernacular building heritage, as vernacular buildings have always been built in this way. Using appropriate earth- and lime-based finishes to maintain and repair these historic buildings will keep them healthy, and ensure that they survive well into the future, and can continue to tell their stories.

Using lime and earth finishes in the modern world

There can be no doubt that there often seems to be a conflict between the ideals of the 'green' movement and the real situation that many people find themselves in. Not everyone has the means to build themselves a 'green' house from scratch that reflects the principles described above. Lime is also currently more expensive than cement, and so is hiring a professional who has knowledge of the skills and methods needed to apply it. Additionally, populations on the crowded British Isles are rising, and the government regularly announces the need for an astronomical amount of affordable homes that need to be built. The challenge here is therefore two-fold:

1. How to increase the use of lime- and earth-based materials for new housing.
2. How to create ways to incorporate these materials into existing conventional buildings.

Firstly, some argue that to meet the needs of point one, the centralised, large-scale production of certain types of lime is the key to bringing it firmly into the mainstream. There is evidence that the government is responding to this solution by creating a new British Standard for lime (BSEN 459-1). Indirectly, also, the new building regulation, 'Part L', has at its core the issue of the carbon emissions of a building and the materials that go into making it. New government audits, such as BREAM (eco homes assessment methods), are being more widely used, and if lime or earth is used in a building instead of cement, it gains more points. Additionally, there is new legislation to encourage the recycling of building materials. This includes taxes being placed on buildings that are built with hard cementitious materials that do not allow for material recycling (soft lime mortars can be easily chipped off without damaging the brick or stone). Lime and earth materials can now also be purchased ready made in sacks, needing only the addition of water or a further 'knocking up'.

All these points can serve as catalysts to make lime- and earth-based finishes more accessible, available and user-friendly. This can encourage the use of lime- and earth-based finishes in mainstream building. Additionally, by increasing the use of lime and earth in mainstream building, it will encourage economies of scale and hence drive the prices down.

The counter-argument to this, is that by centralising and standardising lime and earth production, an important element of using these materials will be lost – that of the diversity and regionality of traditional, small-scale, local lime production and use, and of locally sourced and selected earth for use in plasters, renders and paints. It is argued that mass production will further erode the varied character and identity of our countries' architecture, will create industries requiring large outputs of energy to maintain, and will further discourage people from rekindling their connection with local materials and their application in building.

We argue that there must be room for both approaches, running parallel to each other. To apply the principle of local, on-site production of materials for the mass housing market is too great a shift in the time scale within which we must make these changes. However, work must be continued to bring back traditional techniques of production so that diversity and local production is maintained. Maybe there will come a time when it can catch up, and surpass the large scale production plants. Right now, however, the potential for both approaches exists, and it is down to the individual's needs, means and desires as to which road they choose to tread.

The answer to our second challenge (how to create ways to incorporate these materials into existing conventional buildings) lies here in our book. We have included and encouraged methods of applying lime- and earth-based finishes to conventional materials – including plasterboard and cement blocks – as well as on traditional and 'green' materials. There are many people who live in conventional homes and who want to make any improvements that they can, to make their homes healthier for the inhabitants and kinder to the environment.

The German philosophy of *Bau-Biologie*, created in the 1970s by Dr Anton Schneider, encompasses a holistic approach to the science of building. It provides twenty-five principles, outlining points for creating socially and environmentally responsible and healthy buildings. Among these there are principles such as: 'Indoor air humidity shall be regulated naturally'; 'Walls, floors and ceilings shall be diffusible and hygroscopic'; 'Natural and unadulterated building materials shall be used'; 'Building activities shall not contribute to the exploitation of resources'; and so on. They uphold the idea that our homes must be safe places to be in, and that they should support and enhance all of life on earth. They should be designed either to shield us from the negative effects of our external environment, if we live in a polluted town or city, or to allow in the good things of the outdoor environment that make us healthy and happy. The philosophy of *Bau-Biologie* sees the building as our third skin, the first being our own skin, and the second being our clothes. A building covered with lime and earth finishes will breathe like our skin, serving as an extension of ourselves. It can also stimulate us physically and psychologically, making us feel and function better. By using the techniques and materials outlined in this book we can therefore help ourselves to become healthier and happier. For these reasons, we must not stop at using these materials only for our homes, but must work to bring them into schools and hospitals – places of learning and healing – to create strong, healthy and aware people: people who are better placed to be able to contribute what is needed to reinstate the balance of our ailing planet. ∎

These very finely applied earth plasters complement the timber of this Japanese-style home. By *Eastwind Construction*.

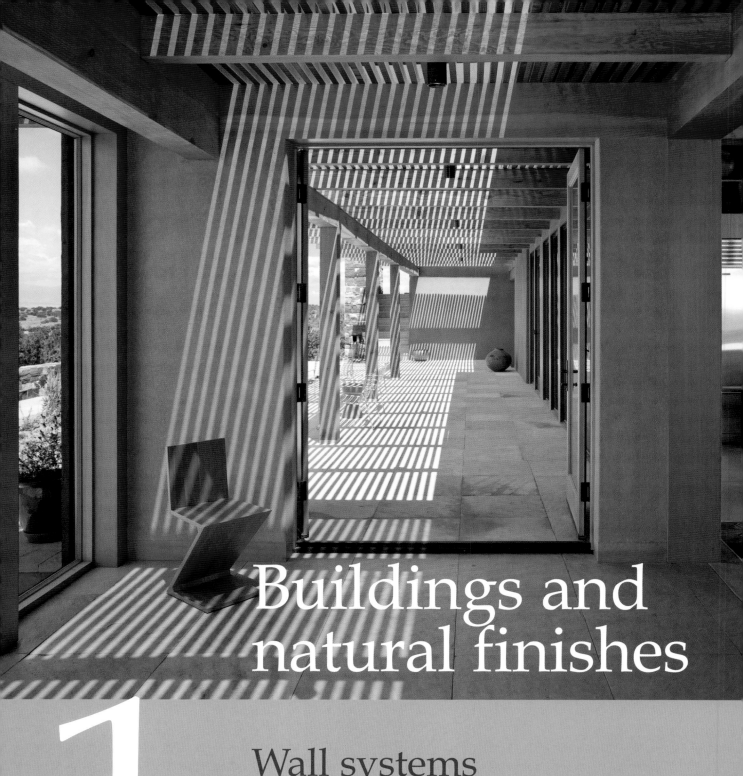

Buildings and natural finishes

1

Wall systems
Moisture issues
Building design

Lime- and earth-based plasters, renders and paints are highly suitable, if not essential, for use in conjunction with sustainable and traditional wall-building materials. Examples include earth (clay), timber, hemp, reed, straw-bale, low-energy bricks and stone. Many of these traditional walling materials have been used successfully for thousands of years and are now enjoying a renaissance, as the foundation for many of the contemporary 'eco-building' methods. A unifying characteristic between these walling materials is that they are all, to a degree, porous. They allow the free passage of moisture into and out of them, and therefore need to 'breathe' to remain healthy. Because of this, they are highly responsive to changes in relative humidity and temperature in the atmosphere. This means that structures made out of these materials will naturally move in response to these differences. All finishes applied to these materials must therefore match the hardness and porosity of the walling substrate below. They must be flexible enough to accommodate natural movements in the building without cracking, and need to have a high degree of vapour permeability to eliminate the potential for trapping moisture within the wall. A case can also be argued for the use of lime- and earth-based plasters, renders and paints (with certain preparatory measures in place) on some of the modern, conventional building materials, such as concrete block and plasterboard. Though their qualities of softness, breathability and flexibility are not essential when used with these conventional materials, lime- and earth-based finishes can bring benefits in the areas of decreased impact on the environment (their production, toxicity and ease of disposal), improved internal air quality, and by improving the look and general 'feel' of the building and the spaces inside.

Wall systems

This section introduces different walling systems that are compatible with lime and earth-based finishes. It also outlines the suitability of applying the various finishes to different substrates.

Earth walls

Earth walls can be constructed in many different ways. Building with earth (clay-rich subsoils) is the most ancient of all building methods. Many variations of earth building have been used throughout the world since man began building shelters. Most earth building methods consist of mixing together a clay-rich subsoil with other ingredients. These are most commonly some form of fibre (straw) to provide tensile strength, and aggregates to provide strength and stability to the mix. Most buildings made out of earth must be raised off the ground at least 450 mm (18"), and should have large roof overhangs to protect the walls from rain.

Many of the earth building methods are currently enjoying a revival because they provide a sustainable way of building. This is because most forms of building with earth have an incredibly low environmental impact, especially when locally resourced materials and simple techniques are used. Earth building materials can be indefinitely recycled, and biodegrade easily. They have tremendous health benefits, such as temperature and humidity regulation, high thermal mass (they can absorb and store large amounts of heat), good toxin and odour absorption, and excellent sound

Adobe block   Making compressed adobe blocks   Adobe with earth plaster   Cob

Modern adobe construction designed by Tony Atkins and built by Crocker Ltd.

insulation properties. Some of the earth building variations include:

Monolithic earth walls, such as cob, clob, wychert, clom, mud, clat, clay & clunch

A load-bearing walling system – an ancient building technique and material that is used throughout the world, with regional variations, such as 'cob' in the southwest of England. It is composed of clay subsoil, aggregate and straw. These ingredients are mixed together with water to produce a homogenous, malleable and sticky material, which is laid in 'lifts' of 300-600 mm (12-24") in one building session. Once the previous one has hardened, consecutive lifts are laid until full wall height has been reached. The cob is built up without forms or shuttering, but is compressed in place by foot or with a garden fork. It is then trimmed with a sharp spade to maintain a plumb line.

Unfired earth blocks, such as adobe, cob block, and clay lump

A load-bearing material used throughout the world for thousands of years. This is a system of creating building blocks out of raw clay-rich subsoil, aggregate and sometimes fibre. The material is either moulded in a plastic state into forms, or compressed by machine in a dry state. The blocks are laid in bonded courses, with either a mud or lime mortar, or simply wetted down and bonded through suction if the blocks are made with dry material.

Light clay   Fired clay bricks   Light clay

Rammed earth & 'pise de terre'

Monolithic earth walls built up between temporary shuttering. A load-bearing material, which is sometimes mixed (slightly moistened) with aggregate, or it can be used in its raw form if the right proportions naturally exist. It is tamped by hand or with a pneumatic tamper, between wood or steel shuttering. The shuttering is moved up until full wall height is reached.

Light clay & light straw clay
'Leichlem' (pronounced 'lie-klem')

A non-load-bearing walling material. Straw is coated with a clay-rich slip which is compacted between temporary shuttering, set within a timber structure.

Wattle & daub

A non-load-bearing walling system of tightly woven sticks (usually a green and flexible wood, such as hazel, willow or maple), set within a timber-framed panel. This lattice (the wattle) is then coated with a 'daub' mixture: a thick clay-rich subsoil mixed with chopped straw or hair, and sometimes animal dung for extra weather resistance and durability. This is squeezed into place between the sticks. The daub can either be finished with a limewash or coated in a lime plaster/render for extra protection. It can be used for exterior walls or interior partition walls.

All lime- and earth-based finishes are ideally suited for all types of raw earth construction. Cement and synthetic paints must not be used.

Straw-bale wall construction

Straw-bale wall construction originated in the USA around the end of the nineteenth century. It coincided with the development of baling machines. The straw bales are used like large building blocks, stacked on top of one another in staggered courses. They are usually speared onto pins – often sharp rods of hazel or steel. This ties them into the foundation and provides structural stability for the walls. There are many different methods of building with straw bales, but these can be broadly categorized into (a) load-bearing, where the bales take the full weight of the roof, and (b) non-load-bearing, where the bales are set within a timber structure and used as a wall infill between the posts. As with walls made out of earth, it is essential that the bales are built onto a raised plinth so that they do not come into contact with water. They also require large roof overhangs to direct moisture away from the wall face.

Straw-bale construction generally has a very low environmental impact, especially when materials are sourced locally. The use of large amounts of plant materials in buildings has the added advantage of being able to create 'carbon sinks'. This is due to the absorption of CO_2 from the atmosphere as the plant grows, and turns this CO_2 into oxygen. The more plant material that can be used in building construction, the more potential there is for decreasing the damaging levels of CO_2 currently present in the atmosphere. Straw-bale walls are

Rammed earth

Light clay

highly breathable and have excellent insulative properties. This gives straw-bale buildings the potential to provide a very healthy living environment. Straw bales are fully biodegradable and will last for hundreds of years if protected with breathable coatings and utilised within a well designed building.

Straw-bale walls must be protected from moisture, and need to be sealed to keep out draughts and protect them from hungry animals.

Straw is a breathable material, and hence must not be coated with any non-breathable renders, plasters and paints, such as cement and synthetic paints. These could lead to moisture getting trapped in the bales, which will eventually cause them to rot. Lime- and earth-based finishes are ideal. Straw-bale walls that are exposed to extreme conditions, such as on the weather-facing wall, may require additional protection from the elements such as timber cladding.

Lath & plaster

Lath and plaster is made up of thin, narrow strips of wood which are attached to wood battens, joists or studding and then plastered. This system can be used as an external and internal wall structure when set within a timber frame. It can also be used to create ceilings. Alternatively it can be used as a system on solid walls which are unable to receive plaster/render directly, such as impervious materials or damp substrates. The substrate is battened and then lathed with a suitable air gap for adequate air circulation. The wood laths can be split by hand (riven lath), or mechanically sawn. Straight-grained wood is necessary, and hand-split laths are considered to be stronger. Sweet chestnut, oak and Scots pine are the most suitable woods to use. The laths can vary in size, but the optimum size is 30mm (1¼") wide, and 5-6mm (¼") thick, at lengths up to 1500mm (4' 6"). They must be attached with non-ferrous or galvanized nails to prevent rusting.

The laths are fixed parallel to each other and spaced at regular intervals of approximately 10mm ($^3/_8$") apart. The vertical wood supports are spaced at 300mm (12") centres, and break joints are provided every 10-12 laths. The ends of the laths must be butted at a distance of approximately 3mm ($^1/_8$") to allow for potential swelling of the wood, as it absorbs moisture from the wet plaster. A well-haired lime mortar (not earth) is then applied onto the lath. The spacings between the laths allow the mortar to squeeze through the gaps, creating a 'hooking' action to attach the mortar solidly in place.

Lath and plaster can have a low environmental impact as long as sustainably harvested wood is used, and especially when hand-splitting (riven laths) methods of production are employed. They are non-toxic, breathable and fully biodegradable.

Straw bale

Reed mat

Reed mat

Reed mat consists of sturdy lengths of reed, bound together with a zinc-coated wire. Reed mat usually comes in rolled bundles of 10 metres (11 yards) in length, 2 metres (6' 6") high and 8 mm ($^5/_8$") thick. These mats are attached (similar to lath and plaster technique) horizontally onto wood uprights with sturdy staples. They can be used to create internal partition walls and ceilings, and are well suited for creating curved surfaces, due to their flexibility.

Reed mat can also be cut into smaller sections (with secateurs or a jigsaw) and used to prepare wall substrates for plastering or rendering. Examples include covering differential materials within a wall, such as lintels and timber uprights, or sections of repair. Reed mat provides a good alternative to lath and plaster as it is more economical, but it does not provide as solid a backing. Reed mats are perfectly suited to receiving lime and earth plaster/renders.

Reed mat has a low environmental impact during its production, and is easily biodegraded with the exception of the minimal amounts of zinc-plated wire that binds the reed together. It is also highly breathable.

Masonry

Masonry buildings are constructed out of individual building units which are laid in and bound together by mortar of varying types.

They must always be built up in staggered courses with no vertical joints, in order to tie the wall structure together.

Natural stone

There are many different types of stone used in building. This is a reflection of the varied geology across the world. Broadly speaking, stones can be categorized into the softer, more permeable stones, such as the sedimentary rocks of limestone and sandstone, and the harder, less permeable stones, such as the igneous rocks of granite, gabbro and basalt. Even within these categories, however, there are regional differences in strength, porosity and weathering between stones of the same type. For example, there are some varieties of hard limestone and sandstone, and some porous, soft granites.

Locally sourced, naturally occurring field stone has a low environmental impact, and can be eternally reused as long as suitably soft bedding mortars, such as lime, are used. Soft mortars can be easily chipped off without damaging the stone. The environmental impact of quarried stone depends on the methods of extraction employed, as well as the distance the quarried material is transported. Quarries can also disturb the natural environment.

On its own, stone is a poor insulator, but has high thermal mass. It is non-toxic and generally breathable, with the exception of very hard,

Lath and plaster   Cob block

impervious types. The determining factor for making a decision on which plaster/render is suitable is down to the hardness and porosity of the stone. Softer, more permeable stones will partner well with earth plasters and the weaker building limes, whereas a harder, less permeable stone will be better suited to the stronger, hydraulic building limes. Some less permeable stones will require a priming coat of some sort before they are suitably placed to receive a lime or earth plaster/render. However, the priming coat should not inhibit the vapour permeability of the stone.

Fired brick

Traditional bricks are made from clay, which is fired at high temperatures. The firing process drives off the water and creates an irreversible chemical reaction such that the clay will not be returned to a plastic state with the addition of water. These bricks remain relatively soft and very permeable. Many modern bricks are made from sand or flint mixed with lime. They are not fired, but are moulded under steam pressure. This method produces a much harder brick, with strength and permeability characteristics more in line with concrete (a reduced permeability).

As with stone, traditional porous bricks will work best with the softer, highly breathable finishes of earth and the weaker building limes, whereas modern bricks are more compatible with the stronger, hydraulic limes. They may require a

priming coat before receiving a first coat of lime plaster/render. Producing bricks is a very energy-intensive process (especially modern bricks), but they can be recycled many times over as long as a soft lime bedding material is used. Bricks will also last for a very long time if laid and finished with suitable mortars, such as lime or earth.

Fired clay honeycomb insulating blocks

These consist of a fired clay block with a honeycomb cross-section. They are suitable for use for both external and internal load-bearing walls, and have been widely used on the continent for many years. The honeycomb structure of the block means that it is only necessary to create a single skin, because the block itself provides excellent insulation properties. They can replace conventional cavity wall construction. Mortar is only necessary for the horizontal joint, due to a tongue-and-groove vertical edge which locks the abutting blocks firmly together. They are ideally suited for use with earth and lime mortars and finishes, and make highly breathable buildings.

Concrete block

In their most basic form, concrete blocks consists of cement, sand and aggregates. Concrete blocks are relatively cheap to produce, and are one of the most widely used construction materials for external walls in the UK and throughout most of the world. Other types of concrete block include lightweight concrete blocks, such as breeze block. There are also aerated concrete blocks, which

Honeycomb block   Natural stone   Stone and lime mortar   Clay board

are made from cement, sand and lime. They both have better insulating qualities than the standard blocks. Concrete can also be cast on site in shuttering. Cement finishes are most commonly used with concrete materials, but earth and lime finishes can be used, with suitable preparatory measures, to enhance the look, feel and internal air quality of a building.

Concrete blocks are not appropriate for use in any type of conservation or restoration work involving traditional buildings. This is because they are hard and impermeable, and will move differently from the traditional materials.

All concrete materials are very energy-intensive in their production, and are often transported long distances. Using concrete blocks made with secondary aggregates will go some way to reducing this impact. Concrete blocks can be recycled, or crushed up to be used as infill or road base. However, many of the additives used to make cement are potentially toxic and damaging to human health and the environment.

Hemp-lime construction

Hemp-lime involves hemp hurds being mixed with building lime, cement and water. It makes a lightweight, breathable construction material that can be applied in a number different forms. Hemp-lime can either be tamped between or sprayed against temporary shuttering. It is a non-load-bearing material, and must therefore be used as an infill, formed around a framing of timber and other structural materials. Hemp-lime can also be formed into air-dried, lightweight building blocks or panels, which are similarly built up between a frame structure. Hemp-lime is suitable for both earth- and lime-based finishes, and is ideally finished with a hemp-lime plaster/render.

Lime is fairly energy-intensive through its production, but goes a long way to offset this: as it carbonates (sets and cures), it reabsorbs some of the CO_2 it has released during its firing process. The cement element is highly energy-intensive in its production. Hemp, a natural plant fibre, has many excellent environmental benefits, such as its ease and rapid growth without needing chemical herbicides or insecticides. Its use similarly absorbs CO_2 from the atmosphere, creating a 'carbon sink' (as described earlier in the straw bale section). Hemp-lime as a walling material is highly insulative and breathable.

Building boards

All of the alternative building board options listed below have been developed and produced with the environment and human health in mind, and they all provide breathable walling systems. Bear in mind, however, that many of these products are currently produced on mainland Europe, and hence carry with them the implications of long-distance transport. Conventional gypsum plasterboard is energy-intensive in its production, although recycled industrial gypsum is often

Hemp lime

Clay board

used. However, this may potentially contain toxic elements, such as heavy metals and radioactive particles. Gypsum plasterboard also involves the use of toxic jointing compounds containing formaldehyde, although safer, more ecologically sound alternatives are available.

Reed board

Reed board is a rigid building board consisting of untreated reed, bound together with galvanized steel wire. It comes in varying thicknesses of 20mm and 50mm (¾" and 2"). It can be used as a rigid backing for lime and clay plasters, for ceilings and walls. It can also be used up against a solid substrate, such as concrete block, to provide a suitable backing for lime and earth plasters.

When used in this way it can be attached by pressing it into a bed of earth or lime mortar, and then mechanically attached with 15-20 mm (½ - ¾") zinc-plated washers, and large headed nails or screws (stainless steel, zinc-plated). Reed board can also be fixed to a timber frame with galvanized screws, with 15-20mm (½ - ¾") zinc-plated washers, or wood wool screws. This provides an excellent alternative to plasterboard from an environmental perspective, as well as the fact that it provides a fully breathable wall surface. It is also a very flexible material, making it ideal for creating curves in a wall.

Reed board is perfectly partnered with either lime- or earth-based finishes.

Wood wool board

Wood wool board consists of wood shavings or fibres bonded together with magnesite or a small amount of cement to create a solid building panel of varying sizes. It can create a highly breathable internal and external wall system, and is attached to timber supports. It also has good thermal insulation properties. If made without cement it contains no toxic products or synthetic chemicals. It is suitable for directly receiving an earth- or lime-based plaster or render.

Wood fibre boards

Wood fibre boards are made out of 100% waste wood from timber production. Softwood chippings are pulped and soaked in water, then pressed into boards by mechanical means. They are then dried and cut to shape.

The boards contain no glue or wood preservatives, but are bound together with the natural tree resin contained within the wood, which consists primarily of spruce or pine chippings. Wood fibre boards are highly breathable and provide an alternative to conventional board insulation. They can be used internally or externally on to masonry or a timber frame. They have excellent thermal performance and are vapour-permeable and hygroscopic (able to absorb and release moisture), making them efficient at regulating internal moisture levels. They are suitable to directly receive lime render or plaster.

Reed board   Wood wool board   Wood fibre board

Clay board

Clay board is a rigid building board for internal use. It is made out of clay, silt, sand, straw, hemp, reed and jute. It provides a perfect alternative to gypsum plasterboard for drywall construction, from both a health and environmental perspective.

Clay boards can introduce all the benefits of clay construction into a build, such as temperature and humidity regulation, odour absorption and sound insulation. They can be affixed to a solid substrate, such as masonry, or supported within a timber frame (not attached to structural timbers). They can also be used for ceilings and lining the interior of sloping roofs. Clay boards are suitable backgrounds for both earth- and lime-based finishes.

Conventional gypsum plasterboard – drywall, gypsum board, sheetrock, gib

Gypsum plasterboard is a rigid, internal dry lining board comprising of a gypsum plaster core encased with a heavy paper lining or fibreglass mat. It also contains fibreglass fibres, foaming agents and various additives that increase mould- and fire-resistance. Plasterboard is commonly used in the conventional construction industry on stud frames for creating internal walls, partition walls and ceilings. The use of gypsum plasterboard replaced the traditional technique of lath and plaster. Plasterboard can be primed to receive lime- and earth-based finishes to enhance them aesthetically, environmentally, and to contribute to creating a healthier internal environment (see Chapter 2).

The large roof overhangs on the buildings below protect the external earth finishes from the elements. (Buildings by *Econest*).

Moisture & buildings

Above left: External earth finishes are vulnerable to erosion if not designed into a building properly. *Right:* An excellent roof design to protect external earth finishes. This building is in a climate that allows for external earth finishes to be used (south-west USA).

Prolonged high levels of moisture, if allowed to build up within the fabric of a structure, are one of a building's worst enemies. All buildings, irrespective of what they are made of, will begin to disintegrate and eventually fail if moisture enters into their fabric and is then unable to safely exit. Buildings made of earth will eventually move from a state of stability and hardness into a liquid form, as the clay particles are forced apart and become unable to fulfil their binding role. Stone and soft brick walls will become susceptible to a build-up of harmful salts, leading to their decay. Any timber element within a building will rot and become susceptible to fungal attack – especially lintels and joist ends which are directly in contact with the damp walling material. Straw-bale walls are especially susceptible to damage from prolonged contact with moisture: it will cause them to mould and eventually rot.

Most building materials will not be damaged if in contact with moisture for only a short amount of time. Some, such as cob (earth) walls, even benefit from holding a certain amount of moisture within their structure, to maintain the integrity of the clay binder. The issue in moisture control is therefore not necessarily in striving for total exclusion, but more importantly to design a building so that moisture can always freely and easily escape. Breathing plasters (those that allow the free passage of moisture and air through them) are the most significant contribution towards achieving this. The use of such finishes will not only enhance the health and longevity of a structure, but will have the knock-on effect of enhancing indoor air quality and hence human health, as well as being less harmful to the environment.

How moisture gets into a building

Buildings receive moisture from many different sources. Externally, moisture can come from direct rain and snowfall on walls and roofs, and from humidity in the atmosphere. It can also rise up from the ground. Internally, moisture will be generated from human and animal respiration, and from human activities such as bathing, cooking and washing clothes. A new building will contain hundreds of gallons of water, held within new materials, such as in wood, mortars and paint finishes. Some of this moisture will be discharged into the internal spaces of the building as these materials dry out, and will cause the building to settle. It is therefore essential that measures are in place to allow this and any other sources of moisture to safely leave the structure. This is to avoid any of the associated problems which can occur when prolonged, high levels of moisture are able to build up within the fabric of a structure. The three most important strategies for ensuring that this build-up does not occur are:

1. Creating overall breathing, vapour-permeable constructions, so that water vapour can pass through elements of the building and not get trapped within its fabric. This includes using, for example, vapour-permeable (breathable) walling materials (listed at the beginning of this chapter).
2. Using hygroscopic (see definitions, p.34), breathable materials as wall plasters, renders and paints, such as clay and lime. These materials will absorb and store moisture in their pores when relative humidity levels are high, and then release this moisture when relative humidity levels are low. This will prevent moisture build-up and dampness in the walls.
3. Ensuring that some form of ventilation system is in place within the building, such as opening windows and using fans. This will allow moisture to be taken out of the building quickly and easily.

All buildings made out of breathable materials should also be designed with two things in mind:

1. Ways to minimise how much moisture enters a building.
2. Ways to maximise how it can get out.

What impact can a build-up of moisture have within a building?

If moisture becomes trapped within a building because it is unable to exit, it can have negative ramifications not only for the building fabric itself, but also for human health, and the health of the environment. Below is a discussion of each of these.

Building health

Many contemporary 'eco-builds' utilise materials and simple technologies that were used to construct historic buildings. The most important of these is the concept of the breathing wall, which can also be referred to as 'moisture-transfusive construction'. This worked on the main principle that walls were constructed out of porous materials that allowed a certain amount of moisture vapour into their pores at times of high relative humidity, or during rainstorms. They then released this moisture easily and freely when relative humidity levels dropped, or the rainstorm ceased. Historically, these breathing walls were constructed very thickly – up to 1m (3' 3") thick – and in monolithic mass. This meant that any moisture ingress into the external face of the wall would evaporate before it had time to reach the inside of the building. Examples of such traditional walling systems include thick cob earth walls, or those made out of permeable stone. These buildings, for extra protection, were always finished in materials that were equally (or more) permeable than those making up the walls. These finishes were made from either lime or earth, and acted as an extension of the breathing wall. They behaved like a sponge, holding moisture within its pores, and then allowing it to evaporate out again. This meant that moisture was generally prevented from ever reaching the wall at all. Thus, it is often said, that such coatings are also 'sacrificial', because they protect the fabric of the building at their own expense.

Historic buildings also relied on draughty windows and doors, and chimney stacks to provide excellent ventilation, albeit at the expense of losing valuable heat. This ensured that excessive levels of humidity were quickly

Lime finishes are used to create a healthy internal environment for the students and staff of this school in Japan.

wicked away, and levels of internal humidity were always maintained at safe levels.

Historic buildings were clearly designed and constructed to accept the ingress of a certain amount of moisture, but to then safely, quickly and effectively deal with it. Modern, conventional structures, on the other hand, are constructed to deal with moisture in a completely different way. In fact, one could say that they are not designed to 'deal' with moisture at all, but rather to be sealed off against it. This is achieved through a system of barriers, such as waterproof membranes, and

by being coated in impermeable finishes, such as those based on cement, modern gypsum plasters, and synthetic paints. Most modern construction also relies on the cavity wall system, which provides a break between the external and internal faces of the wall. In theory this prevents moisture from travelling from the external walls to the internal walls. In recent years there have also been efforts towards making these buildings more energy-efficient. This has included methods to make them more airtight, but this approach can create numerous problems. As well as failing to allow internally-generated moisture to escape quickly and easily, it will trap and intensify many of the toxic materials used to make the structure.

Contemporary 'eco-builds' tend to take methods from both traditional and modern, conventional builds. They are constructed with energy conservation in mind, but make full use of the breathing structure concept of old buildings. This allows for improvements to be made in the energy performance of buildings that borrow much of their (simple) technology from their historic predecessors. Such elements include making the building more airtight, better insulated and more efficiently heated, all with the aim of reducing heat loss. Using vapour-permeable, breathing finishes allows for these improvements to be realised, whilst maintaining the ability of the structure to deal efficiently with moisture.

Much insight into the effectiveness of breathing finishes has been learnt and witnessed first hand from the litany of disasters which has occurred over the last fifty years with regards the application of non-breathing cement and modern gypsum finishes to many old buildings. Cement and modern gypsum finishes, unlike those made out of lime and earth, are inherently impermeable, and therefore do not breathe. Cement consists of a microscopic structure made up of glass-like particles. Cement will readily absorb moisture through capillary action, but the moisture will remain suspended around these glass-like particles because they are non-absorbent. Furthermore, because these particles are so small and tightly packed together, this moisture becomes trapped in between the minute pore spaces and is unable to evaporate out.

There is only one way for this moisture to move: inwards into the building fabric. In theory this moisture could move, via capillary action, all the way through the full thickness of the wall, to be released via the internal face. However, two things

normally occur to prevent this from happening. Firstly, if a similarly impermeable coating has been applied to the internal face of the wall it will prevent moisture from escaping, essentially trapping it within the wall. Secondly, this trapped moisture will condense on the cooler surfaces present within the walls. This is due to the tendency for moisture vapour to turn into liquid moisture (condense) when it hits a cool surface. These two processes are instrumental in creating moisture build-up and damp within the fabric of a building along with a string of associated problems. These include structural damage, heat loss (most building materials lose their ability to insulate when they are damp), unhealthy internal air, and the development of mould.

Modern materials simply do not work alongside traditional materials. To reiterate, this is fundamentally because modern materials are generally hard, rigid and impermeable (not to mention highly toxic). Traditional materials are generally soft, flexible and permeable ('breathing'). Traditional materials are dynamic. They are able to respond to seasonal changes in humidity and temperature without compromising their structural integrity and without excessive cracking. Wood and earth, for example, will expand slightly when they are wet, and contract when dry. When rigid, brittle finishes, such as cement and synthetic paints, are applied onto these dynamic walling materials, they will tend to crack, craze and eventually fall off. This is a reaction to the inevitable movements in the walls. They are not able to respond and move in harmony with these movements. These cracks provide the perfect inlet for moisture to be drawn into the walls. This moisture is then trapped behind the impermeable coatings.

Furthermore, cement coatings tend to delaminate from the wall surface and detach in sheets. This can be dangerous and will also be detrimental to the wall face. The wall face is often weakened by the cement, and can therefore be pulled off with it, leaving voids and large holes. These problems can be further exacerbated when damp-proof courses are inserted into breathing buildings. Such a damp-proof course, placed at the base of the wall, will seal off yet another potential exit point for excess moisture to drain away into the ground. This means that if moisture has been trapped behind an impermeable finish, it can trickle to the base of the wall and accumulate. This can cause deterioration at the very point where the wall carries its maximum load.

It is a similar story with the use of waterproof membranes against straw-bale walls. Any moisture ingress reaching the space between the bales and the membrane is likely to condense, convert to liquid water, trickle downwards, and collect at the base of the wall. Consequent saturation, fungal growth, and rotting of the bales will ensue if liquid water accumulation is in excess of 20% for a prolonged period of time.

Personal health and indoor air climate

The achievement of a comfortable and healthy interior space is directly related to the amount of moisture vapour present in the atmosphere. It is clear that by using breathing finishes made out of earth and lime, in conjunction with breathing walling materials, such as straw bales and earth, there is a huge potential for creating the optimum conditions of comfort and health in an inside space. This is achieved because of their ability to directly balance levels of relative humidity. Natural fluctuations in relative humidity levels can therefore be buffered, such as at times of the year when the air holds more or less moisture, or in bathrooms or kitchens, when excess moisture is regularly loaded into the atmosphere.

A comfortable level of relative humidity for most people within an internal space is normally in the range of 40-50%. Some moisture vapour is necessary to prevent discomfort in the membranes of the eyes, nose and throat. Hence relative humidity levels of less than 30% may make the air feel too dry, and anything above 70% will generally make the air feel too moist. Additionally, air that is excessively laden with moisture is likely to condense on cool surfaces, such as window panes and other relatively cooler materials. This can cause localised damp and the ideal conditions for mould and fungus to thrive. Mould and fungus are instrumental in creating and exacerbating asthma and many forms of allergies.

The use of earth and lime plasters can also directly affect internal temperatures. This is related to their ability to hold excess moisture safely within their structure, thus preventing the moisture from penetrating deeply into the wall. A damp wall will not be as efficient an insulator, which will have implications on the amount of heat input needed to maintain a comfortable temperature (around 20°C/68°F). This is especially pertinent for cold climate periods. Suitably thick earth plasters also have the ability to regulate internal temperatures. They can absorb heat and re-release it when temperatures drop.

For an earth and lime plaster/render to fulfil its ability to buffer levels of internal relative humidity (to act as a 'moisture sink'), it is necessary that it is applied a minimum of 15 mm (½") thick. The thicker the total sum of the coats, the greater its ability to perform this regulatory function. This also means that, though preferable for the all-round healthy house, it is not essential to have walls made out of similarly vapour-permeable materials to be able to benefit from this regulatory function. A suitably thick (15 mm/½" minimum) lime or earth plaster on a conventional walling material, such as concrete block, will go a long way to improving the quality of the internal atmosphere.

Lime finishes have been used to protect the walls of this straw bale home in Wales. Self-build by Simon Dale and family.

Lastly, with increasing concerns over the need to build structures that demand less heat input to maintain comfortable interior temperatures in cooler climates, it is essential that the overall airtightness of a structure is integral to its design. This can, however, interfere with one of the three important strategies employed to keep the levels of relative humidity in check, that of ventilation. This was achieved historically though naturally leaky windows and doors, and open fireplaces. With this strategy no longer being suitable, it is even more important that breathing, hygroscopic finishes are used to manage moisture and therefore maintain comfortable levels of relative humidity on the inside. Some authorities also say that breathing walls and finishes are also beneficial to airtight structures in that they will provide a natural form of ventilation. This is achieved by allowing exchanges of air through their pores, without gaining or losing too much heat in the process. This is an especially useful tool in cooler temperatures, when windows are generally kept shut. It can provide a regular air exchange, removing stale air and replacing it with fresh air.

Environmental benefits relating to moisture control

It has already been mentioned above that damp walls do not insulate effectively. This naturally implies that if walls are damp, more heat input will be necessary to maintain comfortable interior temperatures when the weather is cooler. If more heat is required, it goes without saying that more CO_2 will be released into the atmosphere to create that heat. It therefore follows that any measures taken to maintain balanced levels of relative humidity in and around the structure will automatically benefit the environment.

How do lime- and earth-based finishes function differently from cement finishes?

Earth and lime materials work in a similar way to each other. They share the fundamental characteristic of being highly vapour-permeable ('breathing'/porous), thus allowing the unimpeded passage of water vapour through their pores. They are also both hygroscopic, (see definitions), but to different extents. They are therefore able to regulate moisture within a building, although there are some subtle differences in how they achieve this. Cement has low vapour-permeability. It is therefore unable to respond appropriately to moisture within a building.

Earth finishes

Plasters and renders which are made out of clay-rich earth are often referred to as being 'soft-skins'. This is because they are generally less durable and water-resistant than those made out of lime or cement. It is this very softness, however, that makes earth plasters exceptionally flexible and vapour-permeable.

Clay's most prized characteristic is its ability to readily attract and take up moisture from the atmosphere and retain this moisture within its pore structure. Earth plasters are therefore hydrophilic (water-loving) and hygroscopic (can safely hold onto this moisture – see definitions below). Furthermore, as it incorporates this moisture into its structure, it causes the clay molecules to expand, blocking the further passage of moisture through its structure. This forms a water-resistant barrier. This self-sealing ability can prevent moisture from wicking into the wall substrate beneath, whilst still allowing moisture to move back out. This function will, however, be overridden if a constant stream of liquid water, such as direct rainfall, hits its surface. In this situation it may fail and be washed away. For this reason earth plasters must be carefully designed into a building, and only used in suitable areas. An earth plaster's ability to attract and hold water makes it highly suitable for use on straw-bale walls and against wood. Because earth plasters are more hydrophilic than straw and wood, they will readily take up any excess moisture in both materials and then release them into the air (as long as the air is drier than the earth plaster). Compare this to cement, which is less hydrophilic than most 'soft' building materials. In this case the reverse action would take place, with the cement loading moisture into the wood or wall substrate. This is why it is conventional practice to insert a waterproof membrane or capillary break between wood that is in direct contact with cement, in order to prevent moisture accumulation in the wood and potential rotting.

Lime

Plasters/renders made out of lime are often referred to as 'semi-soft skins'. They fall somewhere in between those made out of earth ('soft-skin'), and those made out of cement ('hard-skin'). This is in regard to their strength, durability and vapour permeability. The type of lime used will determine the levels of these characteristics, with the non-hydraulic and weaker hydraulic limes being more vapour-permeable and hence breathable, and the stronger hydraulic limes and pozzolans being denser and less permeable (see Chapter 3).

Like an earth plaster, a well prepared lime plaster/render can be made fairly water-resistant, but not waterproof. Lime plasters/renders are more resistant to water erosion than earth. This is why they are often used externally as a top-coat on earth plaster base coats. Lime, too, is hygroscopic, and will readily absorb excess moisture and hold it in its pore structure like a sponge. This moisture will then be easily transferred back into the atmosphere when humidity levels drop. Unlike earth plasters high in clay, however, lime does not have the ability to self-seal. Its structure will remain unchanged as it receives moisture, and even though lime can store moisture within its open pore structure, it can also wick moisture via capillary action into the walling substrate during prolonged precipitation.

However, it could be argued that the potential for this to happen to the detriment of the walling system is slim. Its high vapour-permeability will ensure that the moisture is released out again before allowing it to penetrate into the wall substrate. For this reason it is generally not necessary to insert a capillary break when lime is used against wood.

Lime is generally considered to be fairly flexible, and the addition of fibrous materials will allow it to move in harmony with a building's natural cycle of expansion and contraction without cracking. However, some micro-cracking in any plaster/render must be expected, especially in new-builds, and lime possesses a characteristic that can often counter this. It has a unique ability to 'self-heal', due to the presence of free lime (lime that has not carbonated) within its structure. This free lime can be re-deposited within the cracked surface and then carbonate once exposed to the air, thus closing up the crack (see Chapter 3). Breathing finishes should, wherever possible, be used on both internal and external faces of the wall. However, where this is not possible, application onto one side of the building will go some way to helping the structure balance its levels of moisture.

Conclusion: on rain gear technology and buildings

Our changing attitudes towards how to manage the relationship between moisture and buildings can be compared to the changing technology of rain-gear for humans. The prevailing thought used to be that 'waterproofs' should act as a shield to completely prevent any penetration of moisture through to our underneath clothing and skin. This failed to take into account that moisture was generated internally from our bodies, and that it was impossible to prevent rain from entering through wrist cuffs and around the neck. This internally accumulating moisture was unable to escape, and would leave the wearer

Lime finishes and natural paints work well in all areas of a house, to regulate the internal atmosphere and beautify the space.

Above and below right: Lime finishes have been used to protect the external and internal walls of this eco-housing development in Shropshire. (*Living Villages, The Wintles*). *Below left*: A beautiful lime finish used in a kitchen in France. (By *D'Ocres*)

sweaty and wet inside. *Gore-tex*, the most recent wet weather gear technology, provides a more intelligent approach to moisture management. Consisting of a fabric with very fine holes, it prevents liquid moisture (rain) from entering, but allows the smaller molecules of moisture vapour (perspiration), generated from the body, to escape. This leaves the wearer much more comfortable.

So too with buildings: there is a change of approach from that of exclusion of moisture (using impermeable cement coatings and paints) to one of management (breathing clay and lime finishes). Similarly there is a change from reacting (dealing with the consequences of excess moisture build-up) to responding (executing measures which allow the building to maintain its own equilibrium, and to be able to be sensitive and responsive to seasonal differences in temperature and humidity). The bottom line is that moisture will find its way into a building, and is indeed

Breathing finishes and the building regulations

Part C of the UK building regulations deals with the issues of moisture and buildings: namely, protecting the building and its inhabitants from the damaging effects of excessive moisture build-up within its fabric. The approved document guidelines refer to the 'resistance' of moisture and "the ability of a building to resist the passage of moisture from the outside to the inside of a building". Technically speaking, the language of this guidance document refers to the impermeable cementitious renders of modern buildings and ignores the fact that excessive moisture build-up can also be internally generated. The building regulation guidance documents are, however, not 'prescriptive'. This means that as long as the requirement is ultimately fulfilled, for example by creating a structure that is not subject to dampness, you can get there how you choose. There is much more awareness these days amongst building inspectors about how structures

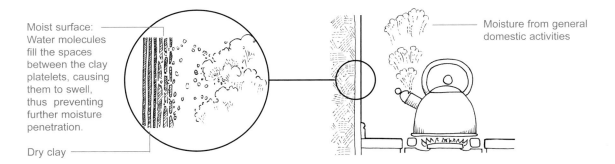

Moist surface: Water molecules fill the spaces between the clay platelets, causing them to swell, thus preventing further moisture penetration.

Dry clay

Moisture from general domestic activities

created from within the building itself. Building design should therefore be aimed at providing strategies which allow this excess moisture to safely escape, as well as minimising how much gets in. It is an added bonus that these same strategies will also enhance the internal climate of the building, improve our health and well-being, and will go some way to relieving our excessive burden on the planet.

made out of breathing, porous materials function. Hence the use of lime and clay finishes should be well supported for meeting Part C of the Building Regulations. These should obviously be used in conjunction with other moisture prevention strategies, such as effective drainage, suitable foundations, good window detailing and others. (See 'Design details' later in this chapter for more information on these strategies).

Impermeable
Material lacking pores or interstitial spaces (open spaces between individual particles) that would allow moisture to transpire through the material.

Permeable
A material that has pores or openings that permit liquids or gases to pass through them, such as air and water vapour, without damaging or altering the material as it does so. They are therefore 'breathing' materials.

Porous
Having pores or spaces permeable to liquids and gases.

Impervious
Forming a barrier to water in its liquid state.

Capillary action
Pertaining to a material that draws moisture through its body, without holding onto it.

Moisture vapour
Small molecules of moisture held suspended in the air.

Relative humidity
The relative humidity of air at a given temperature is the measure of how much water vapour it is holding, compared to how much it could potentially hold. For example, a relative

humidity of 80% means that the air is holding 80% of the water that it could potentially hold at that temperature.

Dew point
The temperature at which condensation occurs, i.e. when water vapour turns into a liquid state.

Condensation
Droplets of water formed when water vapour in the air cools and becomes liquid. In buildings this often occurs when moisture-laden air comes into contact with a relatively cooler material, such as a pane of glass.

Hydrophilic
'Water-loving' - a substance that attracts moisture, such as clay.

Hygroscopic
A substance that will readily take up and retain moisture from the air, such as lime, clay or timber.

Waterproof versus water-resistant
An earth plaster is often said to be water-resistant because it can resist the passage of moisture through it unless subject to a steady flow of water, which will cause it to erode. Something that is waterproof, such as an impermeable paint, will repel water completely.

The basic principles of how moisture and buildings interact

This is a complex science, but the points below set out the basic principles of the subject.

1. Warm air has the capacity to hold more moisture than cool air.
2. Moisture moves from areas of warm air to cool air, and water vapour moves from areas of high concentration to low concentration ('diffusion').
3. Water vapour moves in response to pressure gradients. Air pressure is generally higher inside than out. Air therefore has a tendency to move outward, and also take water vapour suspended in the air out with it, down the pressure gradient.

How moisture movement can create damp buildings

During times of cool weather, when internal spaces are generally warmer than external temperatures, the warm, moist internal air will move towards the external, drier, cooler air. When this moisture-laden air reaches a cold surface, such as a window or wall (generally the inside surface of the external face), it will cool. If it cools enough (such that the dew point is reached), the water vapour in the air will condense and turn into liquid moisture.

If a non-breathing finish is used, this moisture will remain trapped in walls, causing damp and decay, and reducing the ability of the walls to insulate. This process can happen in reverse when the external temperatures are warmer than the internal ones, especially when air conditioning is used.

This straw-bale building has been designed effectively to protect it from the British climate. (National Trust 'Footprint Project', Lake District NP, UK)

Building design

Designing buildings for earth and lime finishes

If embarking on a complete new-build and using a breathable walling system, similarly breathable finishes should be utilized to protect and beautify the walls. This is necessary to ensure that the structure functions to its maximum potential, and that the fabric of the building is not damaged by the build-up of moisture.

Finishes made out of lime and earth are inherently softer than cement. For this reason, it must be accepted that these finishes will always be, to a certain extent, sacrificial. They may therefore require more regular maintenance so that their protective function be upheld. To minimise these cycles of maintenance, a building that employs the benefits of earth and lime finishes must be designed to minimise direct exposure of the walls to the elements: wind, snow and most importantly, rain. These elements of building design are not radically different from good general building design practice, but include some more specialized measures. This is especially the case when the walling substrate of the structure requires maximum protection from moisture, such as straw-bale walls.

A building structure acts as a protective barrier for its inhabitants, and consists of many lines of defence to fulfil this role. The first line of defence should be careful siting and positioning of the building to protect it from the worst of the elements. The second line of defence should include details that are incorporated into the structure itself to direct water away from the building. These include, for example, large roof overhangs, and measures to encourage good

This National Trust straw-bale building in the Lake District has been finished internally and externally with lime and clay plasters/renders, and natural paints. It was built using locally sourced materials. The construction team included Lambert-Gill contractors, Amazon Nails, and many volunteers who participated through organised workshops. It was designed by Paul Crosby Architects. The building has been designed with generous roof overhangs and good window and door detailing, to prevent moisture ingress into the walls. The bales have been suitably lifted off the ground to keep them dry and healthy. The lime and clay finishes will allow the straw-bale walls to breathe.

surface drainage. The third line of defence is the wall finish itself, which serves to protect the wall beneath. The fourth line of defence includes measures taken to seal around openings, such as window and door frames, to prevent moisture from entering into the wall at these points. The fifth line of defence is the wall itself. A thick, monolithic walling material, such as stone or cob, will be resistant to the elements and will take some time to deteriorate. Straw-bale walls, on the other hand, are more vulnerable to the decaying influence of the elements. A building incorporating such walls should therefore be designed even more carefully than other building substrates.

Even with the most intelligently sited, designed and executed building operation, it must be accepted that moisture will find its way into a building in some way, at some time. To reiterate the philosophy surrounding this, the focus should be on ensuring that this moisture is never able to accumulate to a point that it can cause damage to the building. Bruce King, structural engineer and straw-bale specialist, sums this approach up in two very concise points:

1. Minimise what gets in, through design and siting.
2. Create safe exit points by using vapour permeable finishes.

Or, said another way, "Make it as hard as possible for water to get in, and as easy as possible for water to get out."

Siting a building

Wherever possible a building should be sited to minimise its exposure to the elements of rain, wind, snow and sometimes, strong UV light. This involves getting to know and understanding the weather patterns of the region and of the specific site at all times of the year. This includes gathering information, such as where the prevailing winds and driving rains come from, which can be used to work out which walls receive the most direct onslaught of weather. The building can be designed specifically in accordance with this information, such as selecting particular finishes and making extra long roof overhangs on walls where exposure is severe or very severe. A study of traditional farmhouses throughout the UK shows that most are sited so that they are nestled into berms or built low into sheltered areas, to protect them from the prevailing weather.

Exposure

Extreme
Severe
Moderate
Sheltered

Weather exposure map for the UK

Measures can be taken to protect extremely exposed walls by creating a buffer, such as by plantings, and by placing the building within the context of other buildings close by. Plantings could include tightly planted bushes or trees. However, these should be placed far enough away from the building so as not to create moisture build-up within the foundations, and to avoid leaf drip directly onto the walls.

The British Standards map inset is a useful tool to help with siting a building within the UK. It provides guidelines for the levels of exposure for all parts of the country. It can help to assist in making an assessment of the general severity of exposure for a building on both a micro and

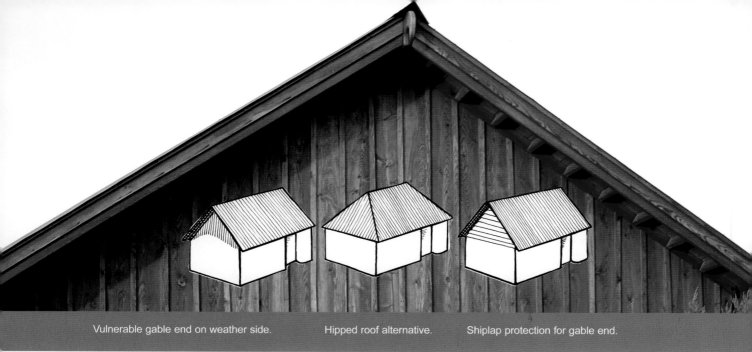

Vulnerable gable end on weather side.   Hipped roof alternative.   Shiplap protection for gable end.

macro level. It should be remembered, however, that each site is unique and a building should be designed with this in mind.

Building shape and roof design

A tall, cube-shaped building will provide large expanses of wall space. These walls will be vulnerable to direct exposure to wind and rain. This is especially the case if built onto an exposed site. A building designed to prevent large amounts of direct, wind-driven rain or snow will therefore be low-rise, and will incorporate large roof overhangs and a carefully considered roof design. Roof overhangs should be at least 600mm (24") or more for severely exposed sites. This will ensure that most rain falling off the roof will be shed away from the wall. The taller the walls, the greater the amount of wall exposure, and hence the larger the roof overhang should be. Roof overhangs can be varied on different walls, depending on their levels of exposure. For walls that face the direction of the prevailing storms, a roofed gallery (open or closed in) can be built to protect the walls. Glass can be incorporated into the roof of such an addition, to maintain passive solar gains from the south/south-west (in the northern hemisphere). The design of the roof is also important. A peaked roof (as opposed to a flat or single-pitched roof) will provide the most protection for the walls, and will also evenly distribute the water runoff to the ground. A standard peaked roof, can however, leave the gable ends of a building exposed, especially in the top triangle. Providing hipped roofs on these elevations will therefore diminish the exposed areas of wall. Another alternative to protecting these exposed areas includes using timber cladding on the top triangle. Ideally, this should be laid horizontally in overlapping courses, with the bottom course protruding away from the wall at the junction where it meets the render below. This will effectively shed water away from the wall.

Gutters and downpipes will assist the roof in redirecting water away from a building, but should not be relied on to effectively perform this function without a good roof design. All gutters and downpipes must be regularly cleaned and well-maintained.

Wherever different buildings abut each other at below the main roof level, care should be taken that properly executed flashing details are incorporated. The roofing materials will also influence the speed of the water run-off. For example, a turf roof will absorb much of the rain that hits it. A thatch roof will slow down water runoff, whereas a slate roof will shed water quickly.

Surface drainage and foundations

The first line of defence of any building in redirecting water away from it must start at the level of surface drainage. Good surface drainage will ensure that any water that has been shed from the roof will quickly and safely be taken away from the building. It will also prevent surface water run-off from pooling around the perimeter of the building, which can be wicked up into the walls, causing problems with the walls and finishes. A well-executed drainage system, designed to efficiently carry water away from a building, can vary; however, it should generally incorporate some or all of the following points:

- The site should be graded so that water runs away from the building and does not accumulate around it.
- All earth and straw-bale walls should be raised off the ground by means of a plinth, constructed out of a material such as stone, brick or block. The walling material should protrude slightly where it meets the stem wall so that water is directed clear from the wall and does not find its way into the wall at this seam.
- The perimeter around the building, especially the area under the roof eaves, should not consist of a hard, impermeable material, such as cement or tarmac; this would encourage splashback from the water running off the roof, hitting the ground, and then bouncing back onto the base of the walls. Ideally, the perimeter should consist of a layer of stone, gravel or mulch. The gravel can be set within a trench 450mm (18") wide and 450mm (18") deep, with appropriate grading and drainage to take the water away from the building.

Sources of moisture ingress

This is an example of a well designed building that has inbuilt measures to cope with external and internal sources of moisture.

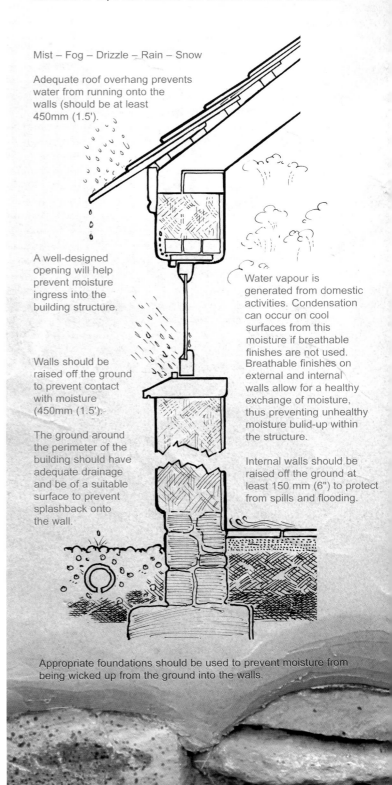

Mist – Fog – Drizzle – Rain – Snow

Adequate roof overhang prevents water from running onto the walls (should be at least 450mm (1.5').

A well-designed opening will help prevent moisture ingress into the building structure.

Walls should be raised off the ground to prevent contact with moisture (450mm (1.5').

The ground around the perimeter of the building should have adequate drainage and be of a suitable surface to prevent splashback onto the wall.

Water vapour is generated from domestic activities. Condensation can occur on cool surfaces from this moisture if breathable finishes are not used. Breathable finishes on external and internal walls allow for a healthy exchange of moisture, thus preventing unhealthy moisture build-up within the structure.

Internal walls should be raised off the ground at least 150 mm (6") to protect from spills and flooding.

Appropriate foundations should be used to prevent moisture from being wicked up from the ground into the walls.

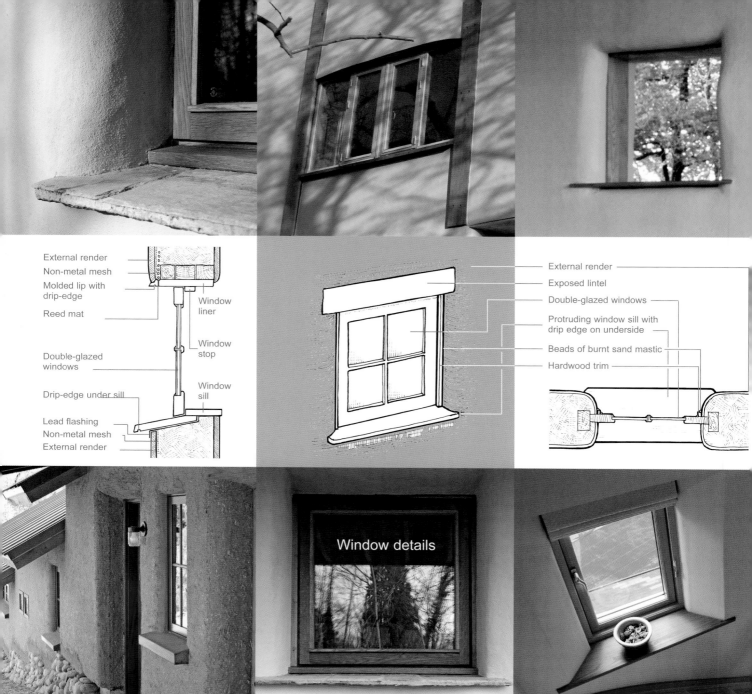

External render
Non-metal mesh
Molded lip with drip-edge
Reed mat

Window liner

Window stop

Double-glazed windows

Window sill

Drip-edge under sill

Lead flashing
Non-metal mesh
External render

External render
Exposed lintel
Double-glazed windows
Protruding window sill with drip edge on underside
Beads of burnt sand mastic
Hardwood trim

Window details

How to prepare traditional burnt sand mastic:

1. Mix together special kiln-dried, burnt sand with enough boiled linseed oil to make a thick paste.
2. Prime surfaces with a little linseed oil.
3. Apply mastic with a palette knife. Ensure a tight seal is achieved.
4. Protect the area for at least 24 hours after application to allow it to set. **Use the mixed material in one day, as it will set quickly.**

- On very exposed wall surfaces, window jambs may require additional overlapping flashing.
- Avoid the use of waterproof membranes around openings in conjunction with breathing building materials as they can create condensation and trap unwanted moisture.

Above diagrams adapted from designs by Kelly Lerner and Barbara Jones.

- The exterior render should always finish well above the final grade, and should never come into contact with the ground.

- Walling materials should never be in direct contact with concrete foundations, as water can be wicked from the ground into the wall. To avoid using a plastic damp proof membrane (if using concrete foundations), provide a capillary break by using stone, such as slate.

Window placement

Window and door openings provide huge potential for the ingress of moisture into a building. Specific design details to deal with this will be presented in the next section, 'Design details'. Where the window sits within the thickness of the wall will be dependent on many things, such as personal preference and levels of exposure. A window that is set towards the inside face of a wall will afford more protection to the vertical seams of the casement, but may provide potential problems around the horizontal sill area. Here, water can pool and find its way in. For this reason, a sloping sill detail must be incorporated to deflect water off this surface (see sill details below). A window that is set towards the exterior face of the wall will not be as protected along its vertical seams, but will minimise moisture accumulation on the horizontal sill area. In all situations, the window should never be set so that it is flush with the outside face of the wall. This would create potential ingress of moisture at the top and bottom of the window frame. The roof overhang should be large enough to protect the top of the window.

Protective coatings for severely exposed wall surfaces

Earth plasters, and the softer limes, simply will not stand up to repeated, severe weather conditions, such as wind-driven rain. For this reason, it may be necessary to consider using other materials to protect the walls.

A hydraulic lime is one option, though the vapour permeability and strength must always be matched with the walling material. Other options include lapped timber cladding or specialised metal lathing coated with a strong hydraulic lime. Any cladding material should incorporate a suitable air gap between it and the walling material to provide ample circulation of air. If used in conjunction with a straw-bale wall, the bales should be coated with at least one coat of a lime or earth render before the cladding is attached, to seal them against air infiltration.

In Scotland, and other areas of Britain on the west coast, where weather conditions are often severe, a harled finish is traditionally used. This provides an open textured surface, which slows the water run off and provides a large surface area for rapid drying of the wall surface.

Design details for plastering / rendering

Design details include all the elements that need to be incorporated into the building on a micro-level. These are put in place to complement the protective functions being carried out by the plasters and renders. These include measures that will further minimise the ingress of moisture at vulnerable points, such as around openings. It also includes plastering/rendering details and practices, which minimise the potential for cracking at vulnerable points in the wall.

Around windows and doors

To reiterate, the area around windows and doors, the sill, the head of the opening and the side jambs, are the most vulnerable points for water entry. The following provides some suggestions to minimise this potential ingress.

Sill details

- The sill should be downward-sloping, and should protrude at least 37mm (1½") from the face of the wall.
- A notch or curf should be present on its

underside. The notch should be at least 40mm (1.6") away from the face of the wall, to prevent water from running back onto the wall below.

• Some form of flashing (lead etc.) should run underneath the sill and window frame, and extend out beyond the wall, with a drip edge (see diagram on p.40).

• The sill should consist of a material of low water-permeability, such as slate or a tight grained hardwood. If it is to be bedded into a mortar, a natural hydraulic lime should be used.

Details at the head of the opening

• Window heads that are high up the wall will generally be protected from the roof overhang, especially if the window is set toward the middle of the wall.

• On windows that are more exposed, a bevelled drip edge or mould should be attached to the lower edge of the face of the lintel. This will effectively shed water away from the window head. The render should run over the lintel face to meet the top of the drip mould (see diagram). Reed mat should be attached to the lintel and up the wall about 200 mm (8"), to provide an attachment point for the render over the wood.

Window jambs

The point at which the render meets the window jamb is a highly vulnerable spot. This is because lime and earth renders will tend to shrink away from the wood once dry. Below are some suggestions to improve this interface:

• Aim to get as tight a join as is possible between the render and the wood, using a small sculpting trowel (see Chapter 2).

• Use a hardwood trim detail between the render and the window frame, to cover and seal the vulnerable join. Either side of this trim should be filled with a traditional burnt sand mastic. This provides a flexible and safe alternative to the synthetic, modern caulking agents that are environmentally destructive, toxic and will degrade rapidly from UV sunlight. They are also rigid and therefore prone to cracking when used in conjunction with traditional and natural materials.

Special reinforcement around openings for straw-bale walls

The window and door openings of straw-bale walls require reinforcement to prevent cracking in the plaster or render. This is because straw bales, though becoming quite rigid under plaster/render coatings, are still relatively flexible. Cracking can occur due to the impact of the vibrations created from windows and doors, and from differential movement created from the temperature differences between windows and walls. Reed matting can be used for this purpose. It should be attached with 150mm (6") stainless steel staples into the straw bales, and attached to the window jamb (buck) with heavy duty 50mm (2") stainless steel staples, with a chisel point. Care should be taken not to damage the reed mat while attaching. Other vulnerable areas for moisture ingress into a building include any exposed joins between the render skin and a different material, such as wood uprights. It therefore makes sense to design these details out of a building wherever possible, especially on very exposed wall surfaces. A continuous render coating with few or no seams will provide the most effective protection for a wall.

Plastering/rendering over differential materials embedded within the wall

Some surfaces, such as wood, metal or concrete will not bond well to an earth or lime plaster/render. Additionally, any differential materials within a wall that provide a fault line where they meet can produce cracking and even failure in the plaster/render coating at this point. The following provides guidelines as to how to successfully plaster/render in such circumstances:

Covering wood or concrete lintels and uprights

Using reed mat

To cover wood or concrete lintels with a lime or earth plaster/render, reed mat should be attached to the lintel lengthways. The reed mat should overlap the lintel going up the wall at least 100mm (4") (see diagram p.45). The reed mat should be securely attached with appropriate fixings depending on the substrate, and it should be coated with a fibre-rich base coat of plaster/render. Immediately following the application of this coat (whilst it is still wet), a glass fibre or hessian meshing (glass fibre is best for lime) should be well pressed and worked into the plaster/render by hand, and then floated in using a standard laying-on trowel. The meshing must overlap the reed mat join by at least 150mm (6") on all sides. The purpose of this meshing is to prevent cracking where the reed mat meets the wall substrate. To cover a timber upright, it should be covered with reed matting laid horizontally to the wood. The reed mat should overlap the wood by roughly 100mm (4"). Ideally, the reed mat should be attached only to the wall substrate, and not the wood. This is to minimise surface tension in the plaster/render created by differential movement between the wood and the wall substrate. The reed mat should subsequently be covered with a well-fibred base coat mix. Whilst this coat is still wet, hessian or glass fibre meshing should be pressed into the base coat, covering and overlapping the reed mat by at least 150mm (6") on all sides (see diagram).

Using burlap dipped into clay slip

This is a European tradition for covering wood uprights within a wall. It involves dipping strips of burlap into clay slip, and immediately applying these wet strips onto the wood. The burlap strips need to overlap on the wall surface by at least 100 mm (4") either side of the wood.

Traditional methods of covering wood

Julie Haddow, an excellent lime plasterer, provides three traditional methods for covering wood with lime. These methods all involve providing some form of mechanical key (as the reed mat method above also provides) to the wood. It is also essential that a well-haired mix be used in conjunction with these methods to accommodate any differential movement between materials, and to help strengthen the plaster/render.

Creating grooves in the timber

Most likely the earliest method for successful adhesion of plaster/render onto wood was to create grooves by hacking into the timber with an axe or adze. The grooves should be created using a downward or diagonal motion, leaving small wooden flaps for the plaster/render to key into. The timber should be well dampened before applying a well-haired mix.

'Spragging'

'Sprags', or nails with large heads, are hammered into the face of the timber. The 'sprag' or nail should be 30mm (1 1/4") long, and 20mm (3/4") wide. 10mm (3/8") of the nail and nail head should be left protruding. The nail head provides a key for the plaster. These 'sprags' should cover the timber face at approximately 20mm (3/4") centres. The timber should be dampened before applying a well-haired mix.

Timber lathing

Sawn or riven timber lath is nailed into the timber horizontally. There should be a spacing of approximately 8mm (5/8") between each lath. This method should provide enough key for the plaster/render to attach to, although counter-lathing will improve the attachment by raising the horizontal laths off the surface of the timber to provide a better key. To do this, fix counter-lath (the same strips of lath wood cut down to the appropriate size) vertically at approximately

Above: Using reed mat to reinforce around straw-bale window openings. The earth plaster base coat is squeezed between the openings in the reed mat to help create a solid key.

Above: Reedmat around internal window. Glass-fibre mesh is embedded into the lime at the junction of the reed mat and the wall, to prevent cracking in the plaster.

Below: Using reed mat to cover timber in the straw-bale wall. Glass-fibre mesh is embedded into the earth base coat to prevent cracking at the junction of reed mat and wall.

200mm (8") centres along the length of the wood. Apply the lath horizontally onto this frame, with an 8mm (⁵/₈") gap between each lath. Thoroughly dampen the lath before applying a well-haired plaster mix. For more information on plastering lime onto lath, refer to Chapter 3.

Prepping wood with a sanded adhesion coat

A method used by many North American natural builders to cover small expanses of wood is to apply a sanded adhesion coat or primer.

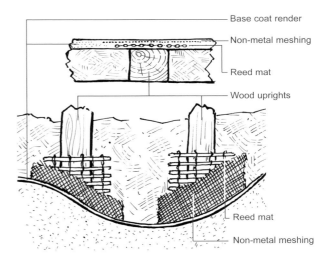

- Base coat render
- Non-metal meshing
- Reed mat
- Wood uprights
- Reed mat
- Non-metal meshing

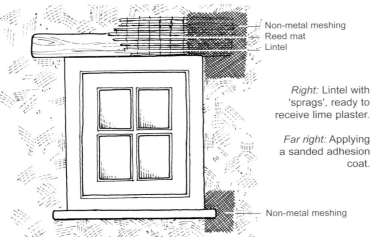

- Non-metal meshing
- Reed mat
- Lintel
- Non-metal meshing

Right: Lintel with 'sprags', ready to receive lime plaster.

Far right: Applying a sanded adhesion coat.

It is suitable for use on expanses of wall under 600mm (2'). It should not be used on exposed, external walls, or on internal walls in moist areas. This sanded adhesion coat provides a suitable 'tooth' for the plaster/render to key into, thus improving the bond. It will also prevent the wood from drawing moisture too quickly out of the wet plaster/render, which can create excessive cracking. It has mainly been used in conjunction with earth plasters, but success has been achieved with this method using lime plasters/renders as well. For the recipe and information on this, refer to Chapter 4.

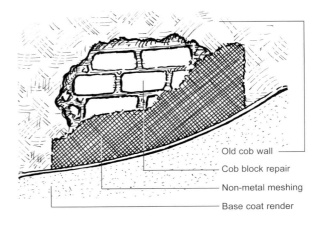

- Old cob wall
- Cob block repair
- Non-metal meshing
- Base coat render

It is also recommended that a glass fibre or hessian meshing be incorporated into the plaster/render over the area where the two different materials meet, in order to avoid cracking at this junction, as described above. This is also a good method for covering other materials such as cement, concrete and metal.

Covering repairs in the wall surface

Old masonry and mass earth walls often require repairs and the filling-in of large voids, using stone, brick, and earth blocks. These repairs can often create stress cracks in the plaster/render coating. Incorporating a mesh into the base coat of the plaster/render will minimise the potential for this cracking to occur. The mesh should overlap the repaired area at least 250mm (10") on all sides (see diagram on the previous page).

Reinforcing the corners of openings

The corners of openings are highly vulnerable to diagonal stress cracks, which are created by differential movement between the window and door, lintels and the wall. To minimise the potential for this to happen, strips of glass fibre, hessian or burlap meshing can be embedded into the base coat of the plaster/render at these points.

Corner detailing

It is not recommended that corners be reinforced with metal beading when using earth and lime plasters/renders, as is the case with conventional building. This is because it may lead to differential wear between the softer plaster/render material and the hard metal. Also, it will be prone to rusting due to the vapour permeability of the breathing lime and earth plasters/renders.

This is especially the case on exterior faces that are subject to constant wetting. The strongest corners for these kinds of materials is slightly rounded – approximately 4mm ($^5/_{32}$") radius or greater. This will reduce the risk of chipping and general damage. This also applies to metal stops along the bottom edge of the exterior render.

Plastering over electrical wiring

In conjunction with building regulations, all electrical wiring must be encased in plastic conduit. Ideally, this conduit should be chased into the wall, to avoid creating a protruding bump in the finished plaster. This conduit can then be plastered over as normal, using a well-fibred mix. Glass fibre or hessian meshing should be embedded into the plaster, covering the area. This will prevent cracking (see above).

If it is not possible to chase the conduit into the wall, it should be firmly attached to the surface of the wall using long stainless steel u-nails, and then plastered over with numerous coats. Some form of meshing is essential.

Protection for internal plasters at ground level

Earth plasters and the softer lime plasters are best raised a few inches off the ground. This is to protect them from damage, from minor flooding – if for example, a pipe bursts or leaks – as well as for household chores such as mopping, sweeping and hoovering. This will also protect against heavy usage and energetic children. A timber skirting board will ensure good protection and will provide a good plaster stop at the base of the wall. ∎

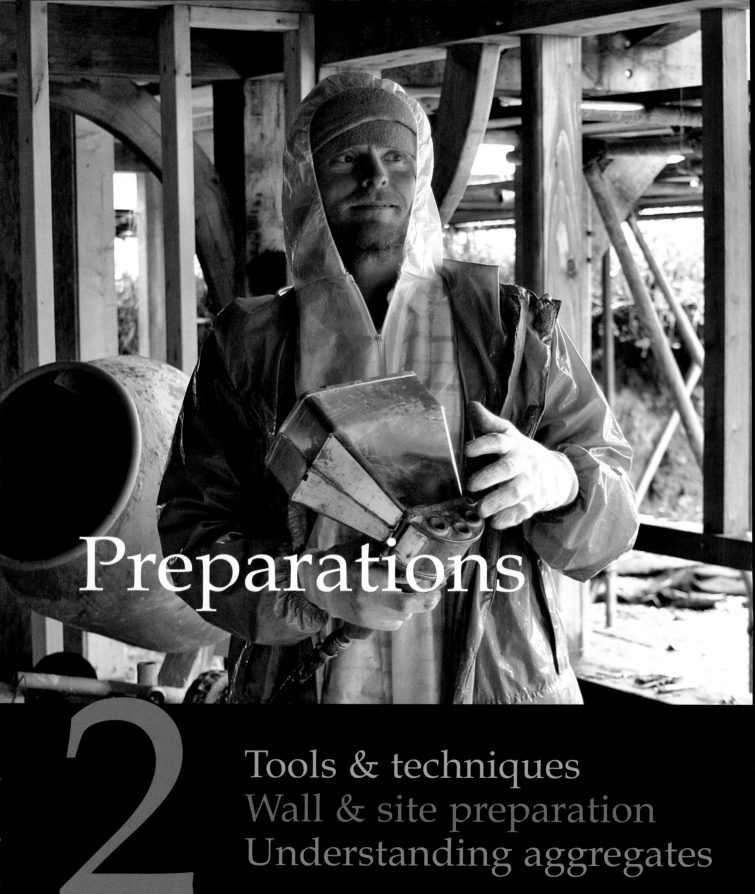

Preparations

2

Tools & techniques
Wall & site preparation
Understanding aggregates

The aim of this chapter is to prepare you for plastering, rendering or painting with materials made out of earth and lime. Topics that will be covered include a thorough discussion of the most common tools and techniques used when working with these materials, how to prepare walls and the site before work commences, and a review of the best types of aggregates that should be used to produce successful plasters and renders.

Having a basic understanding of the above topics will help to maximise the potential for successful finishes to be achieved. Much of the work involved in any type of construction happens before the actual execution is carried out. With regards to finishing work, this involves an awareness of the materials used, properly preparing the walls, having all the tools needed to hand, and familiarising yourself with the basic techniques.

The importance of organising the site before work commences cannot be emphasised enough. This is necessary from both a health and safety point of view, and so that maximum efficiency can be achieved with regards to mixing materials and delivering them to the areas of application. Overall, a project will run much more smoothly if it has been well thought out and planned ahead of time.

Below left: A range of wood floats, used for applying and scouring lime and earth finishes.
Below right: A hawk and trowel with a coloured finishing coat clay plaster.

Tools

... as precisely as the tree is known by its fruit, so is the workman known by his tools ...

W Millar

Top: Render gun with hose and different spray attachments.

Right: (clockwise from top) European style hawk, standard hawk, plastic finishing trowel, plastic detail trowel, rigid Japanese trowel, standard laying-on trowel, large rounded pool trowel, harling trowel.

Bottom left: Laying-on trowel.

Bottom middle: Rounded pool trowels.

Bottom right: A selection of Japanese plastering trowels.

Mortar application tools

The laying-on trowel

The grandfather of traditional lime plastering, William Millar, says: "Most good craftsmen include at least two laying-on trowels in their kit of tools. First with a stiffish blade, is kept for applying the rendering and floating coats (base coats). The second being a springier, thinner blade and is reserved for the finishing coat."
The laying-on trowel is the standard tool used for applying and spreading mortar onto the wall. The standard size used for general plastering/rendering is 280x115mm (11"x 4"), with a wood or plastic handle, and a high quality, well-tempered steel plate. Laying-on trowels also come larger or smaller, depending on preference. It is important to find a handle that fits your hand comfortably, and to use a size that is compatible with your strength.

Gauging trowel

This is traditionally used for 'gauging' – adding small amounts of additives to the main lime or earth mortar. It is a handy trowel to have for getting into awkward spaces, such as around window and door openings. Gauging trowels can also be good for beginners and for application onto undulating walls.

Specialist Japanese trowels

These are beautifully hand-crafted trowels, which come in a variety of sizes, in plastic or steel, and range from rigid to flexible. Rigid ones are best used for application onto straight walls, whereas the more flexible ones are best for application onto undulating walls and for finishing work (smoothing or polishing) on internal finishing coats. Japanese trowels tend to have smaller handles, which fit nicely into the hand.

Rounded pool trowel

These are generally used for applying earth plasters. The rounded edges make them easier for beginners, as they eliminate the tendency for the square-edged laying-on trowels to cut into the wall, especially if the walls are undulating and the user is inexperienced. They come in a variety of sizes, with wood or plastic handles and a well-tempered steel plate.

Harling trowel

The harling trowel is used specifically for the harling technique. The trowel consists of a square, slightly curved blade with no sides. The curve allows for the mortar to be scooped up and held on the blade momentarily, before being flicked onto the wall. A coal shovel with a sawn-off end can also be used.

Render gun

A render gun can be used for applying earth and lime mortars onto a wall as an alternative to application with a trowel. It consists of a steel hopper, into which the mortar is fed. The hopper is attached to a hose. The hose is attached to a compressed supply of air. The air is fed through the hose, which causes the mortar to be forced onto the wall at high speed, once the trigger at the front of the hopper is opened. This releases air from the nozzles inside the hopper, and pushes the mix out through the holes in the front plate of the gun. Different plate attachments, with a variety of hole sizes and shapes, are used for different materials and finish textures. The plates with larger holes produce a coarser finish texture, and allow for more rapid application. A diesel or electric air compressor can be used, with varying lengths of hose, enabling all areas of the wall to be accessed. The air compressor should generally be at a setting of 35Cfm @ 50PSI. This may need to be adjusted slightly depending on the consistency of the mortar, and hence the pressure needed to force it out of the hopper onto the wall. For example, for liquid clay slips, less pressure will be needed than for a stiffer lime mortar mix.

Render guns are good for speedy coverage onto large expanses of wall, and provide excellent bonding between the mortar and the wall substrate. This is because of the force at which it is being thrown from the gun.

Render guns are not ideal for applying fibre-rich mortars, as these are prone to getting caught in the exit holes. Maximum aggregate size suitable for use with a render gun is 5mm (0.2"). Occasionally, a small stone or piece of debris can block the holes during use, and prevent the mortar from being fired out smoothly. This can be remedied by emptying the hopper and removing the blockage. The render gun must be cleaned thoroughly after each use, especially when using lime. As well as scrubbing all parts of the hopper, it should be submerged underwater while still attached to the air supply, and activated to clear the nozzles. The trigger should be kept well greased, and the hopper kept lightly oiled.

Hawk

A hawk consists of a flat piece of wood, metal or plastic, which is attached to a round handle that fits comfortably into the hand. It is used for holding the mortar before it is applied to the wall, so that it can be easily worked and scooped up by the trowel. Traditionally, wood was used, but the modern plastic or aluminium ones are lighter and easier to hold for longer periods of time. A cushioned foam pad at the top of the handle makes it more comfortable to hold for any long period of time. It is also possible to purchase smaller hawks, which are easier for smaller people to hold. There is also a European style of hawk, which consists of a cross-bar that lays across the forearm instead of being held by a handle.

Detail trowels

There are a variety of smaller trowels that can be used for detail work. These include sculpting tools, leaf trowels, corner trowels (rounded and straight), angle trowels, and small Japanese trowels, to name but a few. These are invaluable for getting into tight spaces and where a tight edge is needed, such as when plastering up to window or door frames. They can also be used for creating relief work in the plaster or render. Angle trowels and corner trowels can be either rounded or straight. These are useful for creating rounded or angular external and internal corners.

Wood floats

Wood floats are used for scouring earth and lime mortars, and for producing open-grained, textured finishes. Cross-grained floats are generally best used for straight walls, and straight-grained floats for undulating walls. A variety of shapes and sizes can be used for different situations, with custom-made, smaller ones being useful for getting into tight spaces. Most wood floats are made from a softwood, such as a fine-grained pine.

Skim floats

Fashioned out of wood as above, but generally with a thinner blade than the standard wood float used for scouring. Skim floats are sometimes used for laying on the first finishing coat if it is being laid on in two thin coats. This creates a rougher surface for the second finishing coat to key into.

Scratching tools

Scratching tools are used for scratching up base coats to provide a key for the subsequent coats to attach to. There are a variety of styles used for different purposes:

- Comb scratcher – has a plastic handle with metal prongs. This is used for scratching up the scratch coat of both earth and lime-based plasters/renders.
- Lath scratcher – consists of three pieces of wood lath brought to a point at one end. They are attached together at one end at approximately 100mm (4") spacing between each point, to create a fanned scratcher.

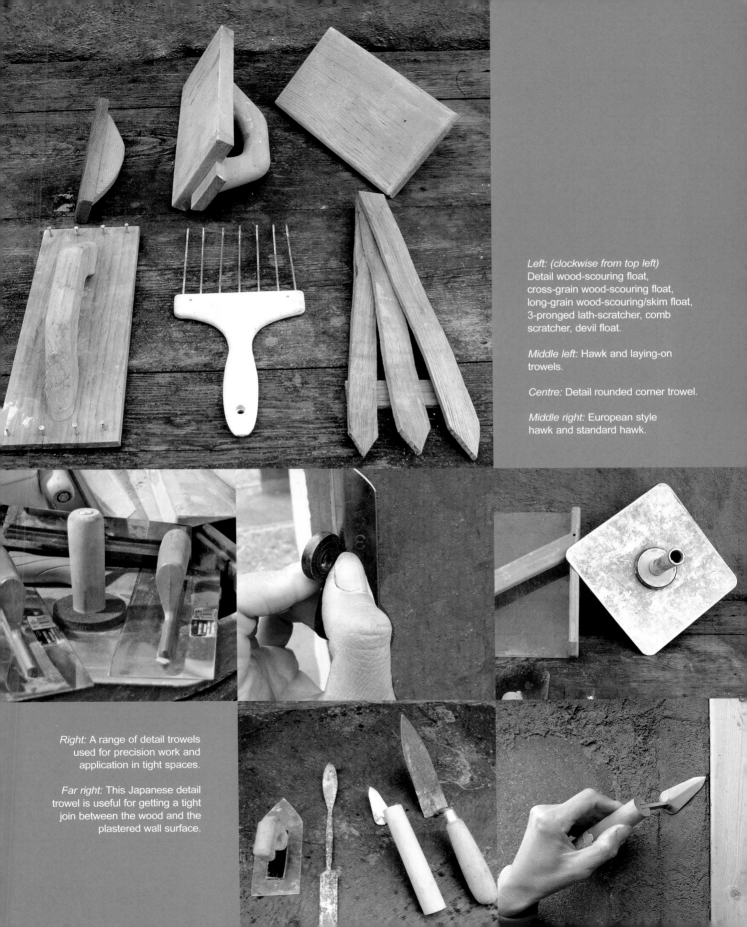

Left: (clockwise from top left)
Detail wood-scouring float,
cross-grain wood-scouring float,
long-grain wood-scouring/skim float,
3-pronged lath-scratcher, comb
scratcher, devil float.

Middle left: Hawk and laying-on
trowels.

Centre: Detail rounded corner trowel.

Middle right: European style
hawk and standard hawk.

Right: A range of detail trowels
used for precision work and
application in tight spaces.

Far right: This Japanese detail
trowel is useful for getting a tight
join between the wood and the
plastered wall surface.

Top right: (clockwise from top left) Detail sponge float, standard sponge float, sponge, 'tadelakt' polishing stones, plastic utensil, plastic finishing trowel.

Middle left: Fine-mist water sprayer. Middle right: Spot board.

Bottom: Traditional grass-fibre limewashing brush (far left), a range of standard and detail paint brushes

Care and maintenance of tools and machinery

Tools that come into contact with lime should always be thoroughly cleaned and dried after each use. Steel tools will benefit from being oiled regularly to prevent rust, as well as the wooden handles, to keep them from drying out and splitting. Wood floats must be dried with the blades flat and out of the sun, to prevent the wood from drying out too quickly and warping. Fine-mist sprayers will not last long if handled with lime/earth covered hands. Small particles of grit will clog the spray hole and pumping mechanisms. Wash gloved hands or bare hands in clean water (keep a bucket nearby whilst working), before handling, and wash the sprayer well at the end of each session. Paint brushes should be thoroughly washed clean with water after each use, and allowed to dry. No chemicals are needed for cleaning off any of the natural paints described in Chapter 5.

They are used for scratching up the scratch coat in mortar applied onto wood laths.

- Devil float – this consists of a skim float with small lath nails implanted into each corner of the blade, protruding 3mm ($^1/_8$") from the surface of the float. The nails provide a key that is maintained at the correct depth. They are used for scratching up the penultimate coat, so as to prevent deep indentations from showing through into the thinly applied finishing coat, and to prevent cracking along the line of the indentation.

Sponge float and sponges
These are used once the finishing coat has been applied. By rubbing a damp sponge over the plaster/render it serves to eliminate trowel marks, even out the material on the wall, and provide a uniform finish. It also serves to further compress the material after scouring. Sponges can also be used to close up small cracks that may appear as the mortar dries out.

- Sponge floats – a thin strip of sponge attached onto a rectangular, plastic base with a handle. Different colours denote different densities of sponge. An orange sponge is generally used for most general plastering/rendering work.
- Sponges (as opposed to a sponge float) are easier to use on undulating walls, and to access tight spaces. A nylon tile sponge or small car washing sponge works well. The pores of the sponge should not be too large, as they will tend to drag the material while it is being worked.

Finishing trowels
Finishing trowels are predominantly used for creating smooth, polished finishes on internal walls. Plastic finishing trowels are often used because they do not leave oxidation marks (dark staining), as can happen with steel trowels. If a steel trowel is used, it should be slightly flexible, and of a high grade stainless steel, to prevent oxidation and staining. Specialist

Japanese and Italian (Venetian or Marmorino) finishing trowels are well suited for this purpose.

Plastic utensils
- Yoghurt lid – with the lid edges cut off, and the dimple removed. For applying and smoothing out mortar in tight, rounded spaces, such as niches and arched openings. It can also be used to create rounded internal and external corners, and for buffing and polishing earth plasters.
- Rigid plastic tool – this is used for smoothing out material in specialist plaster work, such as 'Tadelakt' (a specialist Moroccan plaster, see Chapter 6).

Darby (or straight-edge)
A darby is used to create a flat, even surface in the plaster/render over a large area of wall. It consists of a flat piece of aluminium, or traditionally wood, approximately 1-2m long (3'3"-6'6"), or smaller. It has two handles to help guide it along the wall (see p.68).

Spot board
This consists of a solid, thick piece of plywood, or other non-warping, rigid piece of timber or steel, set up onto trestles. It is placed close to the wall being plastered/rendered as a stage to deposit freshly mixed mortar. This system enables easy access to the material while working (p.54).

Paint brushes
Paint brushes are useful in plastering/rendering work for a number of jobs, besides painting. For example, old paint brushes can be used for damping down the walls in preparation for plastering/rendering and painting, rather than using a fine mist sprayer. A paint brush can also be used to flick water onto the wall whilst scouring and fine polishing.

Paint brushes are needed in a variety of sizes for applying paints and washes. The standard size for applying limewash and other paints is approximately 100-125mm (4-5"). Smaller brushes are useful for detail work and for painting areas of trim. Natural fibre brushes work well with the water-based paints and washes, such as limewash, as they tend to absorb and hold more material when dipped in the bucket. This helps to prevent excess dripping and allows for more material to get onto the wall in a shorter time. Synthetic brushes work OK, as long as the bristles are not excessively shiny, as the watery paints/washes will tend not to absorb into the bristles. This can make application slow and frustrating. The bristles should be fairly stiff. Short, stubby brushes are good for fairly flat walls, whereas longer bristled brushes work well on old, 'knobbly' cob walls. Really long bristles are hard to use, because they tend to create sloppy work.

A traditional limewash brush is made out of plant fibres. Because of their large size they are good for covering large expanses of walls – especially uneven, exterior surfaces. The bristles should be soaked in water before use, to make them soft and flexible. They do a good job of transferring the material onto the wall, and produce even coverage, but can be messy for first-time limewashers (see p.54).

Mixing tools & machinery

Standard drum cement mixer
A standard drum cement mixer can be used effectively for mixing earth and lime mortars, although modifications are needed in some circumstances (see Chapters 3 and 4).

Mortar Mill (also known as roller pan mixer)
The mechanical mortar mill is the crème-de-la-crème of mortar-mixing machines. Most specialist lime suppliers make their non-hydraulic lime putty mixes with these machines. They provide the double function of thoroughly mixing and squeezing the lime mortar ingredients together, and of crushing aggregates to the desired size, as well as bricks and clay tiles, to be used as

pozzolanic additives. The mill consists of a large pan with two revolving rollers and bottom and side scrapers. The revolving rollers are the mechanism which crush the aggregates. They are adjustable in height so that the wheels can roll over the mix with or without the crushing function. They also act to crush and squeeze the ingredients together, ensuring that intimate contact between the sand and lime is made, and all lumps are eliminated. The scrapers help to push the material into the line of the rollers.

A lime putty aggregate mix can be worked to perfection, without the addition of any water, in roughly four minutes. Earth plasters can also be mixed successfully in these machines. They are twice the size of a standard drum cement mixer, and hence are most suitable for mixing large volumes, the smallest amount being 200 litres (20 gallons).

An advantage of using a mortar mill is that old lime mortars can be crushed and utilised as part of the aggregate.

Pan mixer (also known as a paddle mixer)
A pan mixer falls somewhere between a drum mixer and a mortar mill. It is similar in style and action to a large bakery dough mixer, with central rotating blades and sometimes side and bottom scrapers. They are typically less expensive than mortar mills. A pan mixer will thoroughly and efficiently mix ingredients together into a good workable mix within approximately 10 minutes. They do not have the capacity to crush aggregates, or squeeze the mortar ingredients together like roller pan mixers.

Plasterers' bath
Traditionally, plasterers' baths were wooden. The modern ones are available in plastic. They are excellent for mixing and storing material and for pre-soaking clay.

Top left: Industrial-sized pan mixer (paddle mixer) mixing up a lime mortar with animal hair.

Top middle: Whisk attachment onto a 'SDS' drill with a standard 15 litre (3 gallons) bucket.

Top right: Standard pan (paddle) mixer.

Middle left: Standard drum mixer.

Middle middle: Adding hair to a mortar mill (roller pan mixer).

Middle right: A range of sieves with different mesh apperture sizes, for sieving aggregate and clay.

Bottom: Plasterers' bath with home-made sieve for sieving large amounts of clay.

Having a range of bucket sizes is useful for lime and earth finishing work.
From left to right: 25 litre (5 gallon), 20 litre (4 galllon), 15 litre (3 gallon), 10 litre (2 gallon).

Paddle whisk or whisk attached to a drill

A paddle whisk is a purpose-made electric mixing tool, which is held by hand. Alternatively, a paddle whisk can be attached onto a standard, high-powered drill, such as an SDS drill. These tools are indispensable for mixing paints and washes, clay slips, earth mortars, and for beating lime putty prior to mixing in a machine or by hand.

A range of sturdy buckets, including a gauging bucket

A range of sturdy buckets: 15 litres (3 gallons) – a standard builder's bucket; and 25 litres (5 gallons). Select one bucket and reserve it for accurate batching of mix ratios (a gauging bucket). It should be of a size that can be lifted easily into a mixer when full of material.

Plaster/render reinforcement tools

- Knife or blade for cutting meshing materials.
- Different types of meshing: glass fibre, hessian, jute and burlap.
- Scrim for taping joints between building boards.
- Reed mat.
- Secateurs, metal pliers or jigsaw for cutting reed mat.

General tools and utensils

- A range of spades and shovels and hoes is needed for hand mixing, and for handling and moving materials, such as sands.
- Wheelbarrows.
- Waterproof gloves – up to the elbow for lime work.
- Safety glasses.
- Dust masks.
- Overalls.
- Protective plastic and masking tape.
- Tarpaulins.
- Hessian cloth/protective sheeting (old sheets) for protecting walls from sun/cold/rain, post-application.
- Large dustbins for soaking and storing clay slip.
- Water source/hoses.
- Fine mist sprayer.
- Sieves of a variety of mesh sizes 3, 6 and 12mm ($1/8$, $1/4$, $1/2$"). British Standard testing sieves for aggregates, kitchen sieves.
- Stiff and soft-bristled brushes for cleaning tools, brushing down walls and finalising earth plasters.
- Scaffolding, ladders, step-ladders, trestles and sturdy scaffolding boards.

Application techniques

Japanese Master plasterer
Naito Yoshizo applying a
traditional Japanese earth plaster.

59

Outlined below are diagrams and explanations for the most common plastering/rendering application techniques. These are relevant for both lime and earth plastering/rendering, unless otherwise stated. This section should be used in conjunction with the specific application sections in the earth and lime chapters, to provide details and visual references for all the techniques described.

Techniques for applying earth and lime plasters/renders, and the tools used, are a very personal thing. Obviously, there are some standard tried and tested techniques, many of which have been used for hundreds if not thousands of years. There are also some golden rules which must be observed if good quality work is to be achieved. These are described in the relevant chapters. As long as these rules are observed and upheld, however, it is extremely important that each individual discover and use tools that fit their own hand and body type, and that techniques are developed that can be sustained for long sessions of work without creating undue strain on the body.

It is no use sticking rigidly to a particular system if it does not resonate with your body type and way of working. This can only be achieved through experience and practice, and through a process of literally finding your own rhythm.

The techniques are shown roughly in order, from the beginning of the application process through to the final steps carried out for the finishing processes.

Turning and working the earth/lime mortar on a hawk with a trowel

This is to further plasticise the mortar to create a workable, consolidated material that will spread easily onto the wall. Two or three scraping and dropping motions are adequate. For detailed description, see the diagram opposite.

Applying mortar with a laying-on trowel with or without hawk (see pp.62 & 63)

There are two slightly different methods dependent on experience and situation:

The first method utilises a hawk and is the easier option for beginners because it catches any scraps of mortar that don't make it onto the wall.
1. Work the mortar on your hawk, standing square onto the wall.
2. Hold the hawk up against the wall.
3. Scoop the mortar onto the trowel and press it into wall into an upward arc.

In the second, more efficient method, you use the trowel only, and do not hold the hawk against the wall. This is for the more adept and experienced practitioner, and is, generally speaking, the faster method of application.
1. Scoop the worked mortar onto your trowel.
2. Position the trowel up against the wall with the leading edge open.
3. Spread the mortar onto the wall in a wide upward arc.

Using the body to enhance technique

It is very important that adequate pressure is applied with the trowel, to achieve a good bond between the plaster/render, and the wall. Knowing how to use the body correctly will greatly improve the ability to carry this out successfully. It will also assist in helping to sustain long stretches of plastering/rendering without tiring prematurely.
1. Use the shoulder muscles and arms, and keep the wrist firm but not rigid.
2. Use the body weight to lean into the wall, and give more power to the stroke.
3. Use the power of the legs and buttocks to help the upper body achieve the necessary forceful pressure.
4. Aim to maintain a relaxed body to encourage fluidity, and be aware of not holding unnecessary tension throughout the body.

Turning & working using a hawk & trowel

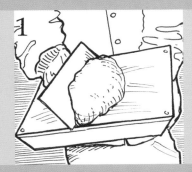

Ready to go. The mortar is on the hawk and the trowel ready for action.

Scoop up the mortar onto the trowel with a swift movement.

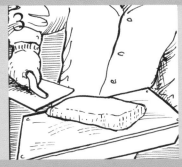

Drop fairly forcefully onto the hawk. Then repeat.

Note: It is always very important to wear safety glasses and gloves when working with lime.

Applying mortar with hawk & trowel 1

Working mortar on hawk standing square onto the wall.

Hold hawk up against the wall and push mortar onto wall.

Mortar scooped onto trowel and pressed into wall into an upward arc.

Additional tips for using a laying-on trowel:

1. Apply with vigour and confidence, in steady upward strokes.
2. Create a sweeping arc of the arm, applying pressure into the trowel as it makes contact with the wall.
3. Keep an open trowel (keep the leading edge of the trowel raised slightly off the wall, and the trailing edge tight against the wall).
4. Each trowelful of mortar should slightly overlap the previous one, ensuring that the joint between them is worked smooth (blended together).
5. Compress the mortar well into the wall to drive out air and to achieve solid contact with the wall.
6. Avoid overworking or smoothing the mortar with the steel trowel immediately after it has been placed on the wall. This will draw the binder (earth or lime) to the surface, creating a binder-rich layer on top of a binder-depleted layer. This will create a weak plaster/render, and may lead to failure. Use one to three strokes with lots of pressure.
7. Start from the top and work down, so as not to damage work done below.
8. Apply the mortar in manageable sections of the wall, working out strategic stop points if

Applying mortar with hawk & trowel 2

Worked mortar on hawk. Scoop up mortar onto trowel.

Position trowel up against wall with the leading edge open.

Spread mortar upwards in a wide arc.

the total area to be covered is not achievable in one session.

9. Keep the trowel as clean as possible: the handle needs to be clean for a good grip, and the trowel face for smooth application. Dip in water or wipe with a rag or on clothing regularly.

Application without a hawk

This method involves forcefully throwing handfuls of mortar onto the wall, smearing them together, and pressing them into the wall with a trowel. This is a good technique for beginners who are not confident or familiar with using a hawk, or for those who find it hard to hold a hawk for sustained periods of time.

Applying material with the hands

This method is more suited for use with earth mortars, but can be used with lime mortar base coats, or more rough work, with success.

1. Scoop up a handful of mortar
2. Using a cupped hand, hold hand against wall
3. Spread mortar onto wall maintaining a cupped hand, using an upward motion, whilst applying pressure.

Once applied onto the wall with the hands, the mortar can be left rough or further pressed in and smoothed out with a trowel (this is advisable when using lime).

Throwing mortar onto the wall by hand

Scoop up a handful of mortar and mould into a flat pancake.

Stand close to the wall and forcefully throw ball of mortar.

Once a few balls have been thrown, blend together and compress well into wall.

Application with a render gun

This is perfect for applications onto large expanses of wall, especially for base coats. It is especially useful for application onto substrates that are lacking in mechanical key or are not very porous (the gun method enhances suction between the mortar and the wall, for good bonding). It is also the preferred method for applying slip coats onto straw-bale walls. The force at which the mortar is fired onto the wall enables it to penetrate into and around the straw fibres, producing a superior bond to hand application.

1. Scoop up the slip material into hopper.
2. Stand about 300mm (approximately 12") from the wall. Aim the render gun at the wall and pull trigger to spray. Move along the wall until complete. The finish can be left rough to provide a good key for subsequent coats.
3. Go back over missed bits of wall (where substrate is visible), as well as details such as window edges and doors. Can leave rough for key, or press back with a trowel for a smooth finish.

Applying clay/lime slip onto straw-bale walls with a render gun

1. Make a fibreless 'slip' (refer to Chapter 4). If using lime it should be made wetter than a normal mix, but not as liquid as a clay slip.

2. Make a scoop (a cut-off clothes-washing detergent bottle works well) to scoop the liquid slip from a bucket into the hopper of the render gun. Work with a partner – one person scooping material into the hopper, the other spraying it onto the wall.

   The sprayer will have to block off the exit holes with the hand whilst material is being placed into the hopper, to prevent it from spilling out. The stiffer lime mix will not be as runny, and will hold its form in the hopper.

3. Stand roughly 300mm (12") away from the wall (closer than when applying a normal plaster).

Additional tips:
- Ensure that all windows, floors and wood are adequately protected, as a lot of mess can be created.
- Take care on scaffolding, especially when working with clay slip, as spillage can lead to a slippery surface.
- Recycle spilled material (as long as it is from a clean surface) back through the render gun.

Applying clay/lime slip with a render gun onto a straw-bale wall

Stuff the crevices between the straw bales with straw coated in clay slip.

Spray the wall with clay or lime slip standing back approximately 300mm (12") from the wall.

Work the mortar into the bales with the hands to coat the straw and fill holes and crevices.

Harled application

This is a technique that takes some time to master. It is essential that full safety gear is worn (as for render-gunning), and all areas, i.e. floors, wood, windows, etc. that need to be protected are covered accordingly, as it can be messy until the technique is well mastered. A special harling trowel should be used. A harled coat does not need 'scratching up' unless it has been pressed back with a trowel.

1. Stand at a right angle to the wall (about 450mm (1.5') away from wall), holding a bucket of mortar under the arms. This avoids the need to have to continuously bend down to get material.
2. Scoop a handful of material onto the harling trowel.
3. Use a flicking action of the wrist – backhand or forehand – to forcefully project the mortar onto the wall. Move along the wall in an even, rhythmical and relaxed pace so as to create a uniform, even texture on the wall.

Scratching up

Scratching should be carried out between applications of base-coat render/plaster to ensure proper adhesion of subsequent coats. There are three principal methods, each for specific applications.

1. With a comb scratcher:

This is carried out after the scratch coat has been applied, to provide adequate key for the next coat. It should be carried out once the plaster/render has slightly set up. Do not scratch through the full depth of the mortar: scratching too deep may create cracks in the subsequent coats along the scratch line, and may show through to the next coat (if only applying two coats). Draw the comb scratcher along the wall in a horizontal wave motion.

2. With a lath scratcher:

This is specifically for use when scratching up the first coat ('pricking-up coat') onto laths. The plaster/render should be scratched first in

The harling technique

Thoroughly wet substrate to provide adequate suction.

Stand at right angle and forcefully flick the mortar onto the wall evenly.

Apply further trowled or harled coat(s) as needed. Harled material can be pressed back or left rough.

Scratching techniques

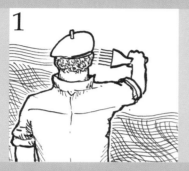

Comb scratcher used to create horizontal wavy scratch marks.

The lath scratcher is used to achieve a diamond lattice pattern.

Use the devil float in a circular motion to achieve circular squiggles.

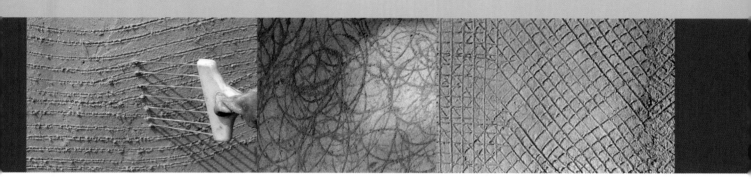

a 45 degree angle in one direction, and then repeated in the other direction, to create a diamond pattern. Do not scratch through the full depth of mortar.

3. With a devil float:
Used for scratching up the straightening coat (the penultimate coat), to create a controlled scratch depth. Move the float in a tight, circular motion, to create an even coverage of circular indentations. On undulating walls it is easier to focus pressure on the toe of the float.

Scraping off raised protrusions created by scratching up
Sometimes the scratching-up process can create raised protrusions of mortar along the line of the indentation. These should be removed when the mortar is dry, before applying each new coat. Scrape a trowel downward with leading edge in contact with the wall (see p.68).

Using a darby to level the wall
A darby is used if walls require straightening up (i.e. made flat). Apply mortar onto the wall. When still wet, drag the straight edge in a downward or sideways motion to knock off high spots and expose low points (see picture on next page).

Scouring with a wood float
This process is carried out for five main reasons:
- To consolidate and harden the surface of the newly applied mortar.
- To prevent cracks in the immediate surface of the plaster/render (and hence in subsequent coats) through the act of consolidating the

Scraping Scouring

Scrape edge of trowel downward to knock off protusions created by scratching process, when dry.

Use a wooden float to scour damp mortar in a tight circular motion to prepare for finishing coats, and as a finishing technique.

Below: Using a darby in wet mortar will help to achieve a flat surface.

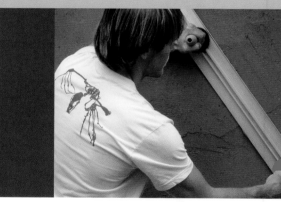

plaster/render, and by closing up any cracks that may have developed as it dries.
- To press the new coat into the coat below, thus ensuring a really good bond.
- To encourage the formation of an open-grain texture, which allows humid carbon-dioxide-carrying air into the body of the plaster/render. This will aid in the carbonation process, when using a non-hydraulic lime putty mortar mix.
- To illuminate high and low spots in the wall. This will indicate where it is necessary to fill with extra mortar, if straight walls are the aim.

Scouring flat walls is an easy and satisfying experience. For mildly undulating walls, it is more challenging but equally advantageous. Using a straight-grained wood float makes it slightly easier to follow the lumps and bumps in the wall, as opposed to using a cross-grained float for straight walls. It is not possible to scour walls that are heavily undulating, because the flat trowel is not able to ride smoothly over the surface of the wall. In this case, the final sponging will go some way to carrying out the scouring functions.

General points for successful scouring include:

1. Scour when the surface is firm but not dry. If the surface is too moist, the plaster/render will simply be displaced from its position and

lose its unified form on the wall. If the surface is too dry, it will be impossible to work – compressing and closing up any cracks will be hard, and there is a potential that the plaster/render will be damaged in the process.

2. The wood float should be held with the hand at the bottom of the handle, with most of the weight pressing into the heel (bottom) of the float.

3. Avoid pressing into the top of the float (unless scouring undulating walls), or applying pressure over the entire surface of the float (so the float is flat on the wall), as this will make it difficult to ride the float smoothly over the wall.

4. The top section of the wall is usually ready to scour first because water has a tendency to drain down the wall.

5. The wood float should be applied onto the wall in a tight, rapid, circular motion, with a lot of pressure.

6. If the plaster/render feels a little on the dry side (i.e. there is no give) the surface can be lightly dampened with a fine mister or through the flicking of a wet paint brush onto the wall.

7. The wall should be scoured twice, with an interval of at least four hours in between (depending on drying conditions), when scouring very fine work.

8. Ensure that the wall is thoroughly and evenly scoured, and avoid scouring some bits more than others.

Finishing techniques

Sponge float and sponge finish

This technique can be used to produce a sanded, slightly grainy or textured finish. It is suitable as a final surface finish for both external and internal walls. The grainy texture provides excellent key for a limewash or natural paint to adhere to. The final texture and graininess will be determined by the length of time the plaster has had to dry out. The drier it is, the less grainy and textured it will

be. Also, the wetter the sponge, the more grainy the texture.

A nylon tile sponge or small car-washing sponge can be used, or a sponge float. The first two are good for tight spaces and undulating walls, whereas the last works well for flatter areas. Its rigid base helps to consolidate the material as it smooths.

1. The sponge should be worked in overlapping, circular patterns, with light pressure. More pressure may be needed if the plaster resists being worked. The aim is to homogenize the surface: remove any remaining trowel marks, close up any small holes or cracks, and move material from high spots to low spots.

2. Only the top fraction of the plaster coat should yield to being worked. If it is moving the full thickness of the coat, and the base coat starts to show through, it is too wet. If the plaster does not yield even to firm pressure, dampen the surface and work again.

3. Clean the sponge in clean water regularly, especially when the sponge pores fill with material.

4. Once the entire surface has been sponged, wait a few minutes before dusting over the plaster with a clean, well wrung-out sponge, to remove loose sand particles.

5. To improve the finish, scour the material with a wooden float first, then follow with a sponge float or sponge.

Wood float finish (scouring)

This technique will produce an open-grained, textured, but very well compressed finish. It is an excellent finish for external walls. The open grained texture works well to provide a large surface area for increased water runoff, and for encouraging quick drying of the render after a rain-storm. It will also provide a good key for all kinds of paints and washes.

The process for producing a scoured finish is

the same as that described above for the general scouring technique (p.68). Work the wood float in small, overlapping circular motions over the whole area of the wall.

Hard trowel finish – burnishing and polishing

This will produce a very smooth surface finish. It should be used for internal wall surfaces only, as the smooth surface will not shed water efficiently, and hence will not weather well. There are two techniques for this:

1. Polishing motion – using tight, circular movements to buff the wall.
2. Smoothing the trowel in quick sideways arcs across the surface of the plaster.

The best tool for this job is a flexible, plastic trowel (Japanese or Italian Venetian trowels work well) with a 1mm ($^3/_{64}$") thick blade. Alternatively, for earth plasters only, a flexible disk of plastic (made from a yoghurt lid) can be used. Plastic trowels are often used instead of steel, because the steel trowels can leave oxidation stains or burnishing marks on the plaster. When using steel trowels for this purpose, they should be specialist trowels made from high grade steel.

Before carrying out either of the techniques, the plaster should be sponged or scoured. Once the shine of the water on the sponged surface has diminished, the chosen finishing method can be commenced.

Polishing: This involves working the trowel in a tight, circular motion to literally polish the surface. Flicking (with a paint brush) or spraying a small amount of water onto the surface of the wall as you polish, will create an even smoother, glassy effect.

Finishing techniques

Use a sponge float in a tight, circular motion, to compress the material and create a uniform finish.

Below left: Sponge floating a finishing coat.
Middle: Hard trowelling with plastic trowel in sideways arcs.
Below right: Rounded corners can be achieved with a wet piece of plastic run along the edge, or by working a trowel across the corner in a horizontal direction (for vertical corners).

Top left – opposite page: Scouring with a wood float.
Bottom left – opposite page: Using a sponge float.
Right – opposite page: Using a sponge onto an alis.

Quick sideways arcs: Work the trowel in broad, quick, overlapping arc strokes, with the trowel held at a low angle. A fair amount of pressure should be used against the wall whilst carrying out this motion. Again, applying a small amount of water onto the surface of the wall as this is being carried out will further close the grain of the plaster and enhance the smoothness of the finish.

Optional finishing step

This is an optional step for earth plasters, which can be carried out if a really fine quality finish is desired. It is most often used on earth plaster finishes that are not to be painted. It involves brushing the surface with a stiff, horse-hair or coconut fibre brush, after the plaster has been either sponged or hard-trowelled. The purpose is to further compact, strengthen and harden the plaster, and also to remove any loose particles of sand that may be sitting on the surface of the plaster. It will also create a surface that can be wiped, as long as enough pressure is exerted with the brushing. The improved durability and strength is largely due to the brushing action encouraging the plate-shaped clay particles to lie flat on the surface of the wall.

1. The surface should first be wiped over gently with a damp sponge, and then brushed firmly. The timing is crucial. The plaster should be almost fully dry, so that it is quite firm and will resist indentation from the bristles. If the wall is too dry however, too much material will be brushed off. If this is the case, the wall should be misted before brushing.

2. After brushing, the wall should be allowed to dry further, and then a final brushing carried out with a soft brush, to remove remaining loose material.

Do not carry out on plasters that are applied less than 2.5mm ($^3/_{32}$") thick as the process removes some of the plaster.

Wall preparation

Earth plaster test samples onto a cob wall being prepared for plastering

Any form of plastering or rendering work begins at the stage of preparing the walls to be covered. The overall performance of the materials, once applied to the wall, is dependent on this stage. The extent and type of wall preparation needed will depend on the type and condition of wall to be covered. Below provides a breakdown of the necessary steps needed to be taken for most types and conditions of wall substrates.

Preparing building boards: filling the joints (scrimming)

When building boards are fitted together, a joint is created. This joint must be filled in and/or covered with meshing. It is also necessary to cover screws and screw holes to prevent cracking developing at these points. There are a variety of ways to do this, depending on the type of board being used. The type of reinforcing mesh (scrim) used will depend on whether it is for external or internal walls, as well as the finish being applied. Glass fibre mesh is best used externally, in areas where there is lots of moisture, and when using lime. The natural fibre meshes (jute/hessian), can be used in drier areas and with earth finishes.

General methods

Option One

Apply a thin layer of a fine finishing coat mortar (lime or earth, depending on the material being used) between the joint. This should overlap approximately 50mm (2") on either side of the joint. Whilst still wet, sink in a strip of meshing. The mesh should cover the joint and the 50mm (2") overlap on either side of the joint. Rub it in well with the hands, and then smooth over with a trowel so that it is well embedded.

Option Two

To create a well-reinforced wall surface, such as when using more flexible building boards like reed board, instead of filling only the joint, the full surface of the wall is covered with mesh. A thin layer of basecoat mortar is first applied onto the full wall surface, and then the mesh embedded into this whilst it is still wet.

For both options, allow the material to dry before commencing with plastering/rendering.

Plasterboard

Option one provides a suitable alternative to using a conventional joint compound. The conventional method can, however, be used, although these joint compounds are best avoided. They mostly contain formaldehyde and other undesirable chemicals. Alternative, less toxic products can be sourced (see naturalbuildingresources.com).

Reed mat

Reed mat can be prepared in the same ways as the above. For extra reinforcement, the reed mat can be overlapped at the point where the two mats meet, by 100mm (4"), and then attached together with a non-corroding strip of wire. This point should be reinforced with a strip of mesh once the base coat has been applied.

Getting walls into shape before work begins

Ensuring the material and the wall forge a good bond

The success of all lime and earth plasters/renders is dependent on there being a good bond between the material and the wall surface. This bonding is dependent on:

1. Having a clean surface

The surface should be free of loose material, such as dust, organic matter (vegetation), loose stones or earth. The wall must therefore be brushed with a stiff brush or broom prior to application. Take care on friable surfaces such as old cob, soft stone, or soft brick. This also includes ensuring that surfaces are free of rust stains, mould and soot, which will eventually show through the finishing coat. Smoke and soot should be completely scraped off walls. If the soot will not scrape off completely, the traditional method of applying a cow dung poultice onto the wall to absorb the soot or smoke can be tried. This entails applying fresh cow dung onto the wall and allowing it to dry. It is then removed for the base coat of plastering to proceed.

2. Assessing the absorption capacity of the substrate

This should be assessed before work begins, to ascertain how much moistening of the wall, if at all, is necessary. Walls made out of materials that have a low- or zero-absorption capacity should not be moistened before application: when wetted down, the water will not be absorbed. This includes impermeable stone and engineering bricks. For porous walls that have a high absorption capacity it is necessary that adequate pre-moistening takes place. When wetted down, they will quickly soak up the moisture. If the mortar is applied to a dry wall, the moisture present in the mortar will be rapidly stolen by the wall, causing the mortar to dry too quickly. This may cause excessive shrinkage and hence cracking, poor carbonation (if using a non-hydraulic lime), a poor hydraulic set (if using a natural hydraulic lime), and potentially delamination of the mortar from the wall. It is therefore **absolutely vital** that the wall substrate (and also subsequent coats) are sufficiently dampened, preferably using a fine misting sprayer, or by flicking on water with a brush.

Do not use a forceful hose onto soft, friable substrates (some old walls), as it will over-saturate the wall and may damage it. On very thirsty backings, this moistening should be carried out the previous day, and then again immediately before work commences. In all cases it should be done shortly prior to work begins, allowing the water to absorb into the backing before application commences. Avoid having water run down the surface of the wall, as this could provide a slip plane for the mortar to slide off. For lime work, lime water or a weak limewash can be used to dampen down the wall as an alternative to plain water. This will have the added advantage of helping to consolidate a friable surface, and it will have a slightly hardening effect when it dries. It can also help to improve the bond between the scratch and the stipple coat. Lime water is the clear liquid which can be found on top of mature lime putty, and sometimes in tubs of pre-made lime mortars. It should be drained off the top of the material and then diluted with clean water to make it go further.

3. Having adequate key

If the wall substrate is very flat, without any indentations that would provide a good key for the scratch coat to hook into, it will be necessary to create a mechanical key by either:

- Harling or spraying on a stipple coat.
- Hacking into the substrate with a sharp, pointed tool to create indentations at regular intervals over the wall surface. Flat, soft, wood-felt panels should be scratched up with a devil float to create a good key.
- On smooth substrates, such as plasterboard, where it is not possible to create indentations, it is necessary to coat the surface with a home-made sanded primer, or pre-manufactured primer (see below).

Examples of substrates where this may be necessary include smooth rammed-earth walls, adobe, smooth earth blocks, modern engineered brick and concrete blocks. If the wall substrate consists of mortared units (masonry or earth blocks), avoid deeply raking out the joints to provide a key, as this will create differential thicknesses of mortar when the scratch coat is applied. These areas of different thickness will dry at different rates and may cause excessive cracking to occur, and hence an unstable scratch coat. On any walls that are made from masonry units that have been mortared into place, such as stone, brick or block, it is necessary to ensure that the joints are appropriately prepared to take a lime mortar. This will involve one of two processes, depending on the size of the hole or joint:

- Pinning the joints with small stones and mortar if the joints are wide and deep. For smooth adobe or earth blocks, these pinning stones can function as a good key also. In adobe construction these are known as 'rajuelas'.
- Pointing the joints with a suitable lime mortar. Most likely it will be the same lime mix used as for the scratch coat. This is appropriate if the joints are small and shallow (less than 12mm (½").

How to pin the joints:
For large joints between masonry units.
1. Clean out the joint or hole of any loose debris.
2. Thoroughly dampen the area with water or lime water.
3. Partially fill the hole or joint with a suitable mortar. For porous, soft substrates, when using lime mortars, a non-hydraulic lime can be used, as successful carbonation (curing and hardening) can occur. This is due to the

availability of carbon dioxide, which can gain access through the open pore structure of the substrate (see Chapter 3). For impervious substrates, a non-hydraulic lime with a pozzolan or a natural hydraulic lime should be used, as no carbon dioxide will be available for carbonation (curing and hardening) inside the joints.
4. The mortar should be thoroughly packed to the back of the hole or joint, and should not be filled more than 15mm (½") thick in one go. For deep holes that are difficult to access, and for improved adhesion, throwing the mortar with force into the desired area will help.
5. Tamp the small pinning stones into the mortared joint recess (using porous pinning stones will help a non-hydraulic lime mortar to carbonate), so that their faces are relatively flush to the rest of the wall. Using pinning stones that do not have flat faces will provide a good key for the scratch coat to hook into.

Pinning out for adobe blocks or smooth earth blocks
Known in adobe construction as the 'rajuela' system, this involves the use of small, sharp stones which are embedded into the vertical and horizontal joints, at intervals of 300mm (12").

Left: Brushing the wall to remove dust and loose particles. *Right:* Misting the wall down to create adequate suction.

Left: Trimming straw bales with a hedge trimmer. *Middle:* Trimming bales with a strimmer (weed whacker). *Right:* Protecting timbers with plastic before plastering. The timber above the bales has been covered with an adhesion coat ready for plastering.

They should be embedded into a wet lime or earth mortar in the joint. It is therefore easiest to carry out when the mortar joints are still wet. If dry, the joint will need to be raked out to a depth of 18mm (¾") and refilled with a fresh lime or earth mortar. Every vertical joint should receive one embedded stone. Each stone should protrude very slightly at approximately 10mm (³/₈") beyond the surface of the adobe/earth block. Allow at least 4-6 days for the mortar to dry out and begin curing in the joints before applying the scratch coat.

Applying an adhesion coat or sanded primer

Some substrates, such as plasterboard, have very smooth surfaces, and therefore do not provide the necessary mechanical key for the long term adherence of earth and lime finishes. To provide this key, a sanded primer can be applied. Surfaces such as plasterboard are also highly absorbent, meaning that they will quickly suck the moisture out of a wet plaster/render, causing it to dry prematurely, crack and

potentially delaminate from the wall surface. Applying a sanded primer will also serve to slow this absorption rate down. A sanded primer includes a binder of varying sources, which acts as a glue, and grains of well-graded, sharp sand. The glue binder enables the sand to stick to the smooth surface, which then dries to provide a hard, toothed surface. Sanded primers can be home-made with wheat flour paste and manure, acting as the glue binders, and sand to provide the tooth (see Chapter 4). Alternatively, pre-made sanded primers can be purchased from specialist suppliers. The latter are made from a variety of safe ingredients and are generally suitable for chemically sensitive individuals. They are also breathable and humidity regulating.

The application of an adhesion coat or sanded primer requires little more than a large paint brush or a paint roller. The surface of the wall should be clean, dry and dust-free. Apply the

Left: Spiking reed mat into the bales using u-nails. *Right:* The reed mat has been used to cover timber in a straw-bale wall. An earth plaster is being squeezed through the gaps to key it into the wall beneath.

primer in an even coat over the full surface of the wall, ensuring that all corners are fully coated. The sanded primer must be fully dry and hardened before applying the first coat of plaster/render. One coat should be sufficient, but a second one may be necessary if even coverage has not been obtained in the first coat. Do not moisten the sanded primer before applying the first coat of plaster/render.

Covering wood and other materials embedded into the wall

Any wood or other materials that will not take a lime or clay finish directly, must also be suitably prepared with a suitable sanded primer. This is covered in detail in Chapter 1.

4. Ensuring that walls are tidy and to the desired profile (level of plumbness)

For straw-bale walls this entails trimming the bales with a weed whacker and or garden shears. This will remove all loose ends of straw to create a compact surface on which to plaster/render. All crevices within the bale walls must also be filled so that there are no deep pockets. This should be carried out by stuffing the crevice first with dry straw (if it is a deep hole), and then with straw dipped into clay slip. This should be allowed to dry before applying the slip coat. For other substrates, any deep recesses in the wall (more than 18mm (¾") must be dubbed out with a stiff scratch coat mortar mix in layers of no more than 12mm (½") in one go. Each layer should be allowed to dry in between, and each layer should be scratched up to provide adequate key for the next to successfully adhere to it.

Protecting timber and other elements while plastering/rendering

Before beginning work, it is essential that all elements within a building that are not being plastered/rendered are suitably protected with tape and/or plastic. Lime will stain wood and leave markings on most materials.

A non-marking tape can be used around trim where it is important that a crisp line is to be achieved. Taping guns are a useful tool for this.

When to plaster/render a newly constructed building

Newly constructed buildings contain large amounts of moisture, which will cause movement and settling of the building as it is released and dries out. Load-bearing straw bales will also undergo some settling as the roof bears down on the bales, causing them to compress and settle. For these reasons it is always best to wait as long as possible (6 months to a year ideally) before applying finishes. This is often hard when

there is a pressure to protect the walls from the elements, and occupants need to move in. Certain compromises can be made to accommodate these needs. Straw-bale walls can be coated in both the slip coat and scratch coat, to give initial protection to the bales. Any settling cracks can be absorbed by the straightening coat once the walls have fully settled. For buildings made out of other materials, one side – either the external or internal surfaces – can be covered with a scratch coat, allowing the moisture to be released through the uncovered side. The uncovered side and the remaining coats of the covered face can then be carried out when drying out has been completed, and most of the settling has occurred.

Site preparation

Scaffolding needs to be erected to allow for easy and safe access to all parts of the wall. Scaffolding needs must be well thought out before work commences. All scaffolding (including scaffolding boards), whether fixed or free standing, should be set clear from the wall so as to avoid 'lift' lines in the plaster/render. Additionally, the scaffolding poles should not butt into the wall, as the areas behind the poles will be inaccessible, creating holes of unrendered wall. These will be hard to fill and successfully blend in at a later date.

If using fixed scaffolding, it should be erected high enough so that the top platform projects past the highest point of the wall being rendered. This will enable sufficient protection for the walls during application, and for a few weeks after (during the crucial drying-out and curing process), from direct rainfall, sun and wind. It will also provide purchase for hanging protective sheeting if needed. A good method to protect freshly applied renders is to attach a tarpaulin behind the guttering

system that can be rolled quickly up and down as needed. For direct sun onto freshly rendered walls, dampened hessian, dust sheets or old bed linen can be hung in front of the walls. This will help maintain humidity levels and allow the plaster to dry slowly. It is essential that all sheeting has an air gap of at least 600mm (24") to prevent the build-up of condensation. This could prevent the plaster/render from drying out, and could lead to mould in earth renders and improper curing in lime renders. Prior to working, always ensure that the ground beneath the wall is either free of debris, or that clean boards are laid down. This is so that any mortar that falls onto the ground during application can be scooped from the ground and reused.

It is essential to ensure that all rainwater goods such as gutters, downpipes and drainage systems are in place as soon as possible and fully working. This will guarantee that all rainwater is quickly and efficiently moved away from the wall.

Aggregates

It is essential that the correct type and amount of aggregate is used, when producing a lime or earth plaster/render. Getting this part of the process right is key to producing a successful wall finish, especially considering that the aggregate can comprise of up to 85% of the mix. The quality, size, shape and distribution of the particles are of the utmost importance.

Aggregates are formed from the weathering and erosion of rocks into smaller particles of different sizes, shapes and colours. They are composed of different minerals, depending on the parent material. In this context, the term 'aggregate' refers to the collective group of these different particles of rock, which can be categorized by their particle size. The classification system which exists to define these sizes is determined by the passing of the aggregate through a particular mesh aperture size, as can be seen in the diagram (page 84). An aggregate used in a plaster or render is classified as 'sand' or 'fine' if it is 2.36mm ($^3/_{32}$") or less, and 'grit' or 'coarse' sand if it is 2.36 - 5mm ($^3/_{32}$ - $^3/_{16}$"). Within these parameters, is an optimum range that should be used to make an earth or lime plaster/render. This is discussed below. Throughout this book we have used the term 'aggregate' to cover the full range of particle sizes.

The optimum particle size range for mixes will be different depending on whether the aggregate is being used as an internal or external plaster/render, or used for base coats or finishing coats.

Functions of the aggregate

1. Providing structure and strength

The aggregate component within an earth or lime plaster/render provides the body or structure. The lime or earth binds this structure together by filling the remaining voids within the aggregate, and then dries and hardens to produce a solid material. Seen another way, the aggregate is like a skeleton, on which the flesh – the binder – is hung. This structure plays an important role in providing the overall strength and hence the performance of the plaster/render. This also includes compressive strength. The aggregate component of a plaster/render is largely responsible for enabling it to stand up against weathering.

2. Providing stability

Most aggregates used in plasters and renders are chemically inert and non-reactive, such as those composed of the quartz minerals, including silica. These are very hard, and are good for providing strength and bulk to a mortar and for filling out the voids within the binder. Their chemical inertness also imparts stability to the plaster/render. This is especially important for earth plasters, which do not set chemically: they remain volatile even when fully dried. This can be seen through their tendency to expand and contract when they take on and lose moisture.

3. As a filler to diminish cracking

As mentioned above, aggregates are incorporated into a lime or earth binder in order to fill most of the void spaces within the binder. For this reason, aggregates play an important role in diminishing the potential for cracking as the mortar dries out. As the mortar dries out, it releases water molecules which have been held in suspension within the material. As these molecules escape, the binder is drawn tightly together. Without the aggregate to fill most of the spaces, the dried mortar would shrink, crack excessively and fail to adhere to the substrate.

4. Provides the colour of the mortar

The aggregate is also largely responsible for the final colour of a lime mortar (or pale clay).

5. Encouraging a speedier set (optional)

Traditionally, a proportion of the aggregates used in lime mortars were often made up of reactive aggregates, derived from calcium carbonate. These included crushed limestone, shells, calcareous sands and old lime mortar. They were used for their air-entraining properties to improve and speed up the process of carbonation (the process by which non-hydraulic lime mortars harden and cure – see Chapter 3). This improved the internal bonding of the mortar, and also frost-resistance. Most specialist lime suppliers can supply calcareous aggregates, such as crushed limestone and lime chippings. It is important to have an understanding of how these aggregates work, and is therefore essential that advice be sought from a specialist supplier or practitioner familiar with working with these aggregates.

Traditional lime mortars sometimes also incorporated pozzolanic aggregates (these materials react with water to produce a chemical set) to encourage an earlier set to a non-hydraulic lime mortar, and improve its durability. Traditionally, these included materials such as brick dust and coal and wood ashes. The most suitable and commonly used modern pozzolanic aggregate is fine brick dust (under 50 microns). Again, a specialist lime supplier will be able to give details on the use of this material, and more information on this subject can be found in Chapter 3.

6. Can be sourced to improve insulation
Another type of aggregate currently being used in plasters and renders is expanded vermiculite. This is a lightweight material consisting of a honeycomb structure. It can be useful in situations where there is a need to improve thermal insulation and frost-resistance in the render.

General rules for aggregates used with lime and earth mortars
Not all aggregates are equal when it comes to making earth or lime plasters/renders. It is a very important element of the process to get right, in order to produce an attractive, durable, well-functioning and long-lasting finish. The following

provides a breakdown of the most important of these basic rules. All aggregates must be:

1. Well washed and clean
By this, it is meant that it should be free from all organic matter, salts and other impurities. The presence of salts in a lime or earth finish will encourage the retention of excess moisture within the plaster or render, hence affecting its setting properties, and ultimately its strength and ability to protect the walls. Salts will manifest as unsightly efflorescence – white blotches – on the surface of the plaster/render, which are hard to get rid of. The presence of salts could be brought about by the use of improperly washed beach and sea sands. Aggregates should also be virtually free of clay and silt – never more than 6%. This is especially important for lime plasters/renders. The presence of clays and silts will increase the water demand of the mortar mix, making it more likely to shrink and crack, thus diminishing its strength and durability. A clean aggregate will allow for maximum adhesion between the aggregate and the binder material. If sourcing aggregate for use within an earth plaster, it is less of a problem if clay is present. Carrying out appropriate test samples in this case should reveal how the overall mix needs to be modified, e.g. adding more aggregate to provide the ideal mix ratio.

2. Well-graded
A well-graded aggregate will consist of a wide range of different particle sizes, from very fine to coarse. These different particle sizes should ideally be distributed so that the highest proportion of the aggregate consists of the medium-sized particles. There should then be decreasing proportions towards either end of the size range (the smallest and largest) – this is known as the 'grading curve'. The reason for this is because, if only a couple of sizes are present, and if they are not properly distributed, the grains will not pack tightly together to produce a cohesive mortar. The finer particles serve to fill the spaces between the larger

- Place the aggregate sample into the container, half full.
- Fill the second container with water, half full also (it must be the same as the amount of aggregate), and gently pour the water into the container of aggregate, until the water has saturated the sand and the air bubbles have stopped rising. No water should sit on top of the aggregate.

The following formula will calculate the void percentage, and hence the optimum percentage of lime to be added to that aggregate in order to produce a good mix:

Volume of water added, divided by volume of sand, multiplied by 100.

For a well-graded aggregate, the resulting figure should be in the range of 33-35%. 1 part lime to 3 parts aggregate should be used. This is the ideal ratio for most mixes, with the exception of internal finishing coats. These can afford to be more lime-rich, because they are laid on more thinly, thus minimising the potential for shrinkage and cracking as the mix dries.

If the sand void ratio test produces a result that reads wildly out of the ideal range, it indicates that the aggregate is not suitably well-graded. It will be necessary either to amend it by adding a more varied selection of aggregate particles, or to consider sourcing a different aggregate.

Sourcing the correct aggregate for the job in hand should set you up well for producing good quality work. ∎

Left: Fine silica sand used for clay alis paint finishes. *Right:* Adding fine silica sand to a clay alis.

3 Lime-based plasters & renders

Chapter 3

L ime, which is derived from the raw materials limestone, chalk or coral (all rich in calcium carbonate), has proven itself throughout history and into the present day to be one of the most versatile, durable and adaptable binding materials. It can be used for a wide variety of construction purposes. It is mixed with sands and aggregates to form both a bedding and pointing mortar for masonry, and as a breathable, flexible internal and external protective finish for many building substrates. The latter is the focus of this chapter.

The utilisation of lime today as an increasingly popular material within the ever-growing 'eco-build' and conservation/restoration sectors, is supported by thousands of years of successful, traditional building works throughout the world.

The oldest known examples of lime being used in a wall plaster have been found in Jericho in the Jordan Valley and Tel-Ramad in Syria, dating from around 7000 BC. The Greeks and Romans, at the beginning of the first century AD, used lime as their main building binder to construct their vast empires, and as a finish for both their temples and private houses. During the medieval period in England, after a fire destroyed London Bridge in 1212, King John passed a law that all shops along the River Thames were to be plastered and whitewashed with lime both inside and out (from A. D. Cowper – see Bibliography). The lime finish was used because of its fire-resistant properties. During the Renaissance, the Italians created their famous stuccos out of lime plaster. These were later emulated in other parts of Europe as a finish of the highest order. Lime, throughout history has always been used simultaneously for both the formal,

Left: Applying internal lime plaster. *Middle:* Mediaeval craftsmen applying external lime render. *Right:* Applying lime onto straw bales.

Left and middle: Traditional harled lime finishes in Scotland. *Right:* Herringbone brick infill laid in a lime mortar.

'high' architecture of the elite, and for the more simple dwellings of the rural populations.

Until the coming of the railways at the time of the Industrial Revolution, the production of lime was principally a local industry. Each town or village, wherever there were suitable limestone deposits, would have had its own lime-burning kilns. Many of these still remain today, scattered across the country, buried under ivy or engulfed by the contemporary townscape. Small clues remain if you look closely: road names such as *Lime Kiln Lane* or *Kiln Avenue*. Each region produced distinct lime mortars which encapsulated the unique properties of the geological compositions of both the local limestone and the sands and aggregates added. In addition to this, many regions developed their own unique application procedures and styles that reflected the climate. An example of this is the rough, open-grained harled finish used in Scotland on a stone substrate, developed to withstand the harsh climatic conditions of the North. The rough, textured surface improves durability as it enables water to be shed more effectively from the render surface. This can be compared with the flat-trowelled finishes onto wattle and daub panels of the south of England, where the climate was less harsh. Similarly, there have always been distinct differences between the exterior building finishes of the more formal townhouses across the country, where work would have been of a very

high quality, multiple coat system. This produced a very straight, regular finish, often referred to as a 'polite' finish.

In contrast to this was the less formal, less time-consuming finishing work of rural buildings. This would often comprise fewer coats and would therefore follow the natural undulations of the stone or mud wall beneath.

In 1824, Ordinary Portland Cement (OPC) was developed and patented in England. Despite this, lime still remained in common use throughout England, Scotland, Wales and Ireland up to the end of World War II. At this time there was a need for the rapid construction of new housing, to rehouse those whose homes had been bombed. For this, cement's characteristic speedy setting, strength and all-weather building capacity meant that lime, with its more weather-dependent setting processes and softer, more flexible nature, virtually fell out of use. From the 1950s onwards, Portland Cement rapidly became the primary building binder both for new-build structures and for repairing historic structures made out of the traditional, softer materials, such as stone, brick, mud, wattle and daub and lath and plaster. This transition was set within an era where there was a dramatic move away from small-scale, local production, and towards greater economies of scale through the mass manufacturing of most

Flat-trowelled lime renders applied onto traditional timber-frame structures.

goods and services. The use of cement was aggressively marketed as a quick, all-weather, and hence economically superior solution to building, through powerful cement lobbies across the world. The use of cement rather than lime on these traditional buildings had, and continues to have, a disastrous effect on the health and overall structural integrity of the building fabric. There are two basic reasons why cement does not work well with historic buildings: firstly, due to its unforgiving strength, it is unable to accommodate the natural movements of the structure, and hence can crack and allow the ingress of moisture. Secondly, cement has a low permeability (it is unable to allow the free passage of liquid moisture or moisture vapour). Because of this it does not allow the building fabric to breathe, and to relinquish any moisture that gets trapped behind the render/plaster façade.

In the 1970s, certain groups of people began to identify the damage that was manifesting through the use of cement on these old buildings. This instigated the beginnings of a lime revival, primarily concerned with conservation work on historic structures. One key group of people in the UK who identified the benefits of the use of traditional lime finishes, was a team working on the restoration of the west front of Wells Cathedral, Somerset. This was known as the 'Great West Front Project'. Simultaneously, other European countries,

from the late 1960s onward, were coming to the same conclusion, as they witnessed their historic building stock begin to suffer the same ill health.

In the late 1960s, Dr. E. F. Schumacher founded the *Intermediate Technology Development Group* (now known as *Practical Action*), which further researched and educated worldwide about the use of lime. Out of this organisation came the ground-breaking book *Building with Lime: A Practical Introduction* by Stafford Holmes and Michael Wingate (1997). This book has fuelled the way forward for making accessible the techniques and methods for the use of lime in building. From this revived interest in lime, also burgeoned a dedicated group of UK and Irish suppliers of high quality lime products, to provide materials, education and training to the growing number of practitioners utilising this material once more.

The lime revival within the conservation building sector has brought us to where we are today, with the increasing use of lime not only in traditional buildings but also within the emerging 'eco-building' sector. Lime performs better than cement in many areas. It produces structurally healthy buildings, and healthier internal living environments. It also enables the use of low energy construction materials, such as cob, straw bale and hemp, and is an all round more environmentally friendly material than cement.

91

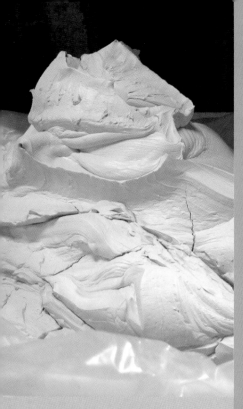

Non-hydraulic lime putty maturing after it has been fired in a kiln and slaked with water.

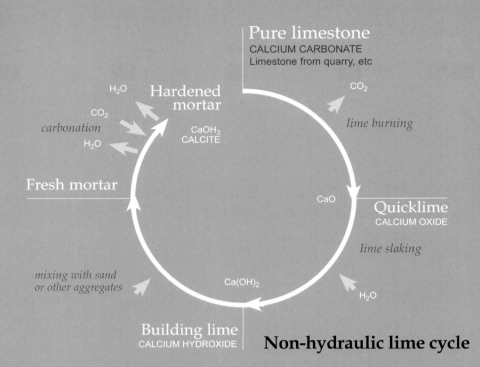

Pure limestone
CALCIUM CARBONATE
Limestone from quarry, etc

CO_2

H_2O
CO_2
carbonation
H_2O

Hardened mortar

CaOH₃
CALCITE

lime burning

Fresh mortar

CaO

Quicklime
CALCIUM OXIDE

lime slaking

mixing with sand or other aggregates

$Ca(OH)_2$

H_2O

Building lime
CALCIUM HYDROXIDE

Non-hydraulic lime cycle

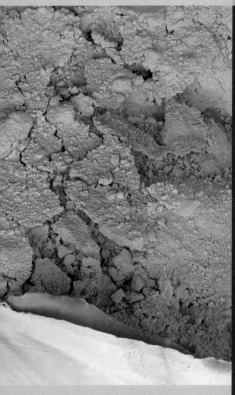

Natural hydraulic lime powder after it has been fired in a kiln and slaked with small amounts of water or steam.

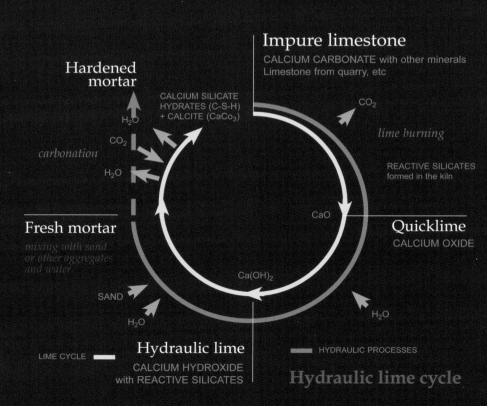

Impure limestone
CALCIUM CARBONATE with other minerals
Limestone from quarry, etc

Hardened mortar

CALCIUM SILICATE
HYDRATES (C-S-H)
+ CALCITE ($CaCo_3$)

H_2O
CO_2
carbonation
H_2O

CO_2

lime burning

REACTIVE SILICATES
formed in the kiln

Fresh mortar

mixing with sand or other aggregates and water

CaO

Quicklime
CALCIUM OXIDE

SAND

$Ca(OH)_2$

H_2O

H_2O

Hydraulic lime
CALCIUM HYDROXIDE
with REACTIVE SILICATES

LIME CYCLE ▬▬▬   HYDRAULIC PROCESSES ▬▬▬

Hydraulic lime cycle

How lime-based plasters work

Lime, in the context of building, is a binding material processed from materials made up of calcium carbonate. This includes different types of limestone, chalk or coral. To make a lime mortar it is mixed with well-graded aggregates. The lime serves to fill the voids between the different-sized particles of aggregate, and to bind it all together into a tight matrix. During the mixing process, the lime binder is prepared as a fluid, sticky paste. This enables the bond to be made between itself and the particles of aggregate. Once applied to the wall, or used as a mortar between masonry, it chemically cures and hardens, allowing the aggregate to be held in place. This provides a cohesive structure and a durable wall finish.

Cement is also a binding material which is mixed with aggregate and dries and hardens to form a similarly cohesive structure and durable wall finish. The nature of how these two materials perform this binding function is, however, chemically very different. The lime binder maintains an open pore structure when dry, whereas a cement binder dries with a denser pore structure, making it less porous. Lime also maintains a degree of flexibility, thus accommodating slight structural movements in a building, whereas cement dries rigid and hard and is unable to move with the building.

The production of lime and the lime cycles

The raw material used to make lime must always be processed (by hand or machinery) if it is to be used in building, and hence as a plaster or render. As has already been established, it is produced from calcareous materials such as chalk, coral, shells, or limestone deposits. Chalk, corals and shells are composed of relatively pure calcium carbonate (approximately 95%+). Limestone deposits, however, vary in their purity. Some consist of pure calcium carbonate, whereas others are made up of calcium carbonate plus different amounts of impurities (by 'impurities' we are not implying something that is negative, but which makes up an essential element in the production of hydraulic limes). These impurities consist of clay, primarily in the form of silica, but also secondary components including aluminium, iron, potassium and other minerals. As will be covered later in the chapter, the chemical composition of the parent material, combined with the method of production, will produce varying types of building limes, with different properties, for use in a wide variety of situations.

Lime is manufactured through a two-step process. First, the burning of the raw material in a kiln to produce quicklime, and secondly, the addition of quicklime to water, known as the slaking process. Both of these procedures, as well as its final curing once applied to the wall, produce a number of chemical reactions.

This set of procedures is often referred to as the 'lime cycle'. This is because, the lime mortar (depending on its purity) literally returns back to its original chemical composition of calcium carbonate, although the material produced is different from that of the original parent material. The lime cycle can be simplified to illustrate the chemical reactions taking place at each step of the process (see diagram). There are, however, distinct differences between the reactions taking place between impure limes (known as natural hydraulic lime) and relatively pure limes (known as non-hydraulic lime), which will be described below (see diagram opposite).

Step one: lime burning

The burning of the raw material (chalk, limestone, etc.), takes place in a lime kiln. The kiln is heated to specific temperatures, depending on the raw material being utilised and the type of lime to be produced.

Relatively pure (non-hydraulic) limes

Raw materials containing minimal amounts of impurities produce a simpler chain of chemical reactions during their production, as compared to those containing impurities. Their production process is therefore more straightforward. The raw material must be exposed to temperatures within the kiln of 800°C (1470°F), before free water is driven off in the form of steam and the carbonates present in the material begin to decompose and relinquish their carbon dioxide. As the carbon dioxide escapes, small holes are formed in the raw material, leaving a sponge-like texture. These holes are crucial for the eventual setting and curing process (carbonation), whereby the carbon dioxide in the atmosphere is reabsorbed back into these spaces.

Traditional kilns were fuelled by wood, coal or peat and came in many sizes and regional variations. They were generally constructed out of stone and later brick, so that the fabric could withstand the heat produced in the inner chamber of the kiln. The ashes of the fuels used were incorporated into the resulting lime, because of the way the lime was stacked in alternate layers with the fuel in the burning chamber. This created further chemical reactions within the material. Modern kilns are fuelled by gas or oil. Many people claim that the cleaner burning kilns of modern day produce a much blander, less interesting and sometimes less effective final product, because they do not contain the ashes of the traditionally fired kilns.

Impure limes (natural hydraulic limes)

Limestones containing impurities have a much more complex burning process. As established above, this is because they contain clay minerals, which become reactive towards the calcium carbonate in the raw material when heated in the kiln. These reactions occur in addition to the basic chemical processes, which take place with the calcium carbonate as described above. For these reactions to take place, slightly higher and more controlled temperatures are required within the kiln. The clays present in

the raw material begin to change and will start to decompose at between 400 and 600°C (between 750 and 1110°F). They then combine with some of the lime, forming calcium silicates and calcium aluminates (specifically di-calcium silicate (belite) and calcium aluminates, at between 725 and 1250°C. These are the main reactive constituents in hydraulic (impure) limes. Once made into a mortar, they will react with water and set (this is known as the hydration process). For this reason, hydraulic (impure) limes do not create an entirely closed cycle (see diagram p.92). If temperatures in the kiln go above 1250°C, tri-calcium silicate (alite) will be produced. It is the presence of this compound (alite), which distinguishes hydraulic lime from Ordinary Portland Cement.

The resulting material that is produced from both burning processes is called quicklime (also known as lump lime or live lime). Quicklime is essentially calcium oxide, which has a chemical composition of one part calcium to one part oxygen. The original raw material (calcium carbonate, $CaCO_3$) loses its carbon atom and two of its oxygen elements via the process of the addition of heat, which drives off carbon dioxide into the atmosphere. Quicklime earned its name because of its quick reactivity with water. This leads to the next stage of production, the slaking process.

Step two: the slaking process

The quicklime (calcium oxide, CaO) produced in the kiln comes in the form of lumps of hard material of different sizes. For the best quality lime, these are taken straight from the kiln to be used immediately for slaking to minimise exposure to the air and moisture. If this were to occur, the quicklime would start to carbonate. The slaking process involves the addition of water to the quicklime. This initiates a chemical reaction, whereby the quicklime (CaO) combines with the water (H_2O) to form calcium hydroxide ($CaOH_2$). This generates heat. Calcium hydroxide is the end-product of the manufacturing process. It is this

material which is added to aggregates to be used as a building binder.

The slaking process varies depending on the purity of the lime. For the purer calcium limes (non-hydraulic), the quicklime can be slaked in its lump form, because it is extremely reactive with water. The less pure limes are less reactive with water. The quicklime is therefore sometimes ground to a fine powder before slaking to increase its reactivity. There are also differences in the quantity of water added to the quicklime, depending on the type of lime being slaked. To produce a non-hydraulic lime putty, a greater amount of water is added in order to produce a wet paste. Non-hydraulic limes can also be slaked with minimum amounts of water or steam, to produce a powder (known as a dry hydrate). This produces a building lime that is less reactive than those described above, and should therefore be avoided when making lime plasters, renders or washes. When a natural hydraulic lime is slaked, a more controlled amount of water is added, and sometimes steam. This also produces a dry powder (dry hydrate). If an excess amount of water were to be used, a chemical reaction would take place between the water and the reactive clay impurities, instigating the chemical setting process also known as hydration.

When slaking non-hydraulic lime putties, once the water has been gradually added to the quicklime, it must be stirred regularly to produce a thick, creamy consistency. The liquid putty is then run into a tank or pit to mature and settle out.

This involves the water draining out of the mix to produce a stiff putty. For fine, top-coat lime plastering (internal work), sieving is sometimes required to achieve a fine putty for a smooth finish.

Lime slaking is a skilled procedure. Because of the high reactivity and alkalinity of the lime it is highly caustic, and is therefore a potentially dangerous operation. It is possible to purchase quicklime direct from some suppliers and to slake your own lime putty at home (this is not possible for the more impure limes due to their more complex slaking procedures). There are, however, so many excellent suppliers across the breadth of the UK and Ireland, that it is more time- and cost-effective to purchase it already slaked. If you are interested in learning more about home slaking, contact one of the listed lime suppliers or lime resource training centres listed in the online resources and suppliers list (naturalbuildingresources.com).

Defining the different types of lime

There is a whole spectrum of different building limes, each with a different quality, which can be used in a wide variety of conditions and circumstances. The two main types of lime suitable for plastering and finishing work are non-hydraulic lime, known as lime putty, 'fat lime' or 'air lime'. This is produced from the purer limes as described above, and comes in a wet paste form. Secondly, natural hydraulic limes (NHL 2, 3.5 & 5). These are produced from the impure limes. They come in a powder form in a range of strengths. Both kinds are available from specialist lime suppliers. You can also find in some builders merchants a type of lime called 'hydrated' or 'bagged' lime. This also comes in a powder form and is a non-hydraulic lime. It is thought by many to be an inferior product and is therefore not suitable for use as a plaster, render or limewash because it has inferior setting and workability

Left: Throwing water onto Moroccan quicklime to illustrate its reactivity during the slaking process.

Middle: Quicklime beginning to break down after its contact with water.

Right: Small-scale slaking of non-hydraulic quicklime with water.

properties. It has principally been used in the conventional building industry as a plasticiser, added to cement to make it more workable.

Non-hydraulic lime putty

Lime putty, which is a non-hydraulic lime (i.e. it will not set in the presence of water, but sets solely by reacting with atmospheric CO_2 through a process known as carbonation), is made from a relatively pure limestone deposit containing no more than 6% impurities. This form of chalk and limestone is made up from predominantly sedimentary rocks, which are formed from the calcium-rich skeletons and shells of marine animals, and from weathered rocks. These are deposited on the sea bed and compressed under the weight of the sea for millions of years.

As established above, lime putty is slaked with an excess amount of water so that a thick paste of lime is created. This lime putty is matured in open pits for a minimum of three months before it can be mixed with other materials to be used as a plaster, render or limewash. This is necessary to allow all particles of quicklime in the mix to fully slake. Failure to do so could lead to any unslaked particles to continue slaking on the wall, creating 'pitting and popping' on the surface, and a weakened wall finish. All reputable lime suppliers will stick rigorously to this three-month rule.

One of the benefits of working with lime putty, is that, like a good red wine or cheese, it will improve with age, leading to improved workability and performance. For prestigious conservation work, lime putty that has been matured for a very long time will be used to ensure that work of the highest quality is achieved.

A plaster or render made out of lime putty will result in an extremely sticky, 'fatty', and hence

Right: Non-hydraulic lime putty must be stored for maturation for at least three months, from the time that it was slaked.

Bottom right: Non-hydraulic lime putty *(left)*, and natural hydraulic lime powder *(right)*.

Below: Non-hydraulic lime putty-aggregate mix with fibre, ready for application.

workable mix. They have a slow setting time and are therefore more forgiving to work with than hydraulic lime mortars, which set faster. Lime putty mixes produce a soft, porous, permeable and flexible finish. This makes it excellent to use on old or new buildings constructed out of soft materials such as soft stone and brick, or earth materials such as cob, clay lump, wattle and daub, as well as straw bales etc. These substrates depend on a healthy moisture exchange to remain structurally intact, and finishes that can accommodate slight structural movements without cracking. Lime putty finishes can provide both of these. They act, in effect, as a sacrificial weathering layer. A lime putty-aggregate finish is more breathable than one made out of a natural hydraulic lime. This is because it develops a less dense structure and because the sand and lime putty particles do not fuse together as tightly, thus making available a more open pore structure. When used in the right circumstance, this is a very positive attribute.

Where and when to use non-hydraulic lime putty
Due to its soft nature and unique slow setting properties, a pure lime putty aggregate mix should not be used on external areas that are in an exposed environment. It also must not be applied in temperatures of 5°C or below, and where these temperatures will not be in danger of occurring for at least two to three months after application. This is because lime putty-based plasters are slower to carbonate (cure) in cold temperatures or excessively wet conditions. Temperatures above 30°C will also hamper effective carbonation.

They are most suitable for sheltered external areas, and make an excellent internal plaster. Please refer to the charts on page 136 for additional information on this.

Natural hydraulic lime (NHL)
Whereas a non-hydraulic lime putty is produced from raw materials containing mostly pure calcium carbonate, natural hydraulic limes are produced

from limestones containing different percentages of impurities. These impurities originate from clayey alluvial deposits. They occur where material containing calcium carbonate has been mixed with silt brought into the sea from rivers.

Natural hydraulic limes come in three strengths. The strength of the lime is dependent on a few different factors. These include the percentage of clay-rich compounds present in the limestone (although some NHLs of differing strengths are produced from one source of uniform rock), the temperature at which the rock is fired, how long the rock is in the kiln for, and the rate at which the fired material is cooled. Generally it is considered that the more clay impurities present within the limestone, coupled with high firing temperatures, produces a lime with a higher degree of hydraulicity. The current classifications are NHL2, which has 6-12% reactive clay, NHL 3.5, which has 12-18% reactive clay, and NHL 5, which has 18-25% reactive clay. This specification, through the European and British Standard EN 459, defines the material's performance relating to the level of minimum compressive strength after 28 days once mixed with aggregates and used as a mortar. This test is based on the curing time of cement, which fully hardens and cures within 28 days. In reality, natural hydraulic lime mortars take much longer to fully cure (especially the weaker ones) and hence this test would be more accurate if taken at 90 days.

These classifications came into being around 1930, where they were changed from those defined by the French civil engineer, Louis Vicat (1786-1861). This original classification was based on the ability of the lime to set under water and therefore in damp places – hence the term 'hydraulic'. These were known as feebly hydraulic, moderately hydraulic, and eminently hydraulic. These relate loosely to NHL2, NHL3.5 and NHL5 respectively.

Natural hydraulic limes set primarily through a process of chemically reacting with water, known

Left: Steaming non-hydraulic lime putty stored in 1-tonne sacks after it has been slaked. *Right:* 1-tonne ready-mixes being delivered to site.

as hydration. This occurs through the hydration of the di-calcium silicate compounds present in the lime, as well as a secondary process of slow carbonation (the absorption of CO_2 in the atmosphere) over a longer period. This means that natural hydraulic limes are suited to a wide variety of external situations, where there is more exposure to harsh weather conditions. Historically, they have a successful performance record. They were commonly used in damp and wet places well before Ordinary Portland Cement was invented. They were used for many great engineering works, such as London Bridge, and to construct harbours and dams. Smeaton's Tower, the famous lighthouse now situated on Plymouth Hoe, was built using natural hydraulic lime by John Smeaton, commencing in 1756.

Natural hydraulic limes come as a dry powder in plastic-lined paper sacks. Natural hydraulic limes cannot be stored as a wet putty, because the chemical setting processes between the clay impurities and the water would begin to take place almost immediately. The one exception to this rule is feebly hydraulic lime (NHL2) which, due to its low hydraulic set, can be obtained in a putty form, although it is not currently commercially available in the UK in this form.

Ideally, bagged natural hydraulic lime powders should not be used in excess of 6 months from the time of manufacturing, and most types should be used within 24 hours of being opened. This is because exposure to moisture in the air will instigate the chemical reactions implied in the curing process. For these reasons, bagged hydraulic lime powders must be stored off the ground, in a dry, well covered area. If you do not end up using a full bag of natural hydraulic lime powder in a day's work, the remaining contents of the bag can be decanted into a plastic tub and stored with a tightly fitting lid until it is next needed.

Unfortunately, from the UK perspective, the majority of natural hydraulic limes are currently being produced and imported from continental Europe – predominantly France – although there is a company producing a hydraulic lime in North Lincolnshire. The UK does, however, have other suitable limestones which produce good quality natural hydraulic limes. There have been numerous other quarries in the past producing home-grown hydraulic limes, such as the blue lias limestones of Somerset. It is hoped that with the burgeoning interest in lime, this industry will once again become active.

Jeff Orton

Master plasterer

Jeff Orton is a master lime plasterer and one of the most well-respected and experienced authorities on lime work in the UK.

He has worked on some of the most prestigious historic buildings for the National Trust and English Heritage, as well as for private clients.

He also lectures and gives demonstrations on lime plastering throughout the country.

1. What sort of training did you undertake that enabled you to work with lime?

When I left school at age 14, I went straight into a full plastering apprenticeship with a traditional family firm. This apprenticeship was for five years, with some time spent doing day-release at the Leicester College of Art and Design, Department of Building. At college we were taught a mix of traditional plastering techniques and modern gypsum and cement work. Although I was given a very thorough knowledge of traditional skills, they were at this time (mid-1960s) very much in decline. Luckily, the firm that I was apprenticed with were still doing some lime work, which was beginning to be an unusual thing. Very few contractors were using lime even by this time. I was able to glean information about lime from the men that I was an apprentice under. Most of them had begun work in the 1920s and 1930s, when traditional methods of preparing and using lime were very much the norm for most plastering work.

2. When did you start working with lime?

I first began working with lime in 1972. At this time I was self-employed, working on old buildings. However, at this point I was making my own lime putty from a dry hydrate (considered an inferior type of lime) and using plaster of paris in my top coats. I could defiantly say, therefore, that my work with lime putty (a higher quality form of lime) started in the year 1988 with the plaster repairs on the Jephson Memorial in Leamington Spa, Warwickshire. I was then working with 'Trumpers', a building conservation group in Birmingham. For this project we slaked our own lime. This was a first for me. I immediately noticed how much more workable it was than the

previous (lower grade) lime that I had been using. This really was a time when things were changing within the building conservation/restoration world in the UK. Many more projects were beginning to be specified with high quality, traditionally prepared and applied limes for their repair. From here on until the present day, my lime plastering career has allowed me the privilege of having an involvement in many great restoration/conservation projects throughout the UK.

3. Please could you provide five tips for a novice in plain lime plastering?

- *Make sure that you are physically very fit and are fairly strong.*
- *Have a good kit of tools, the right ones for the job in hand.*
- *Understand the materials for the specific undertaking, and for the various coats.*
- *Be patient! Working with lime plasters is a slow process.*
- *But most important of all, work alongside a craftsman who really knows the subject, and is very experienced in what is being done. Just follow him and copy him, and the rest will come.*

3. What are your favourite trowels?

Well, one of the best to use is a floating trowel for the backing coats; this has a thicker blade which must be perfectly flat and straight. Also, the finishing trowel, used for the setting coats in lime plastering. The blade need not be as springy as the modern trowels that were developed for gypsum plaster. Both these laying trowels should be approximately 275 x 112.5 mm (11 x 4½"). But I do get a lot of pleasure from using a gauging trowel in various sizes for various jobs. Unfortunately today it seems only possible to obtain the 175 mm (7") ones.

When and where to use natural hydraulic limes

Because natural hydraulic limes achieve a quicker set than lime putty, it is sometimes said that there is less risk of failure from frost or water damage when work must be carried out in the winter months. However, they can still take up to a couple of months to fully cure and achieve their full strength. This is especially true for the weaker ones (NHL2 & 3.5). This has meant that natural hydraulic limes have sometimes been specified and used solely because of the need to carry out work in the colder, wetter months. It is, however, more important that the deciding factor of which lime is to be used should be based on the needs of the walling substrate, and the long term exposure of the area to be plastered or rendered. For best practice, it is also best not to carry out work in temperatures of less than 5ºC (41ºF) or higher than 30ºC (86ºF).

When deciding in what circumstances it would be beneficial to use natural hydraulic limes, it is essential to keep in mind that the three grades have very different properties and will therefore be used in different circumstances. In general terms, some practitioners prefer to use them in situations where reduced permeability is not an issue and an increase in strength is an advantage. They are also useful (on the right walling substrate) where continued dampness is an issue. Such a situation would be on harder masonry, and where there is a continuous occurrence of aggressive weather conditions. These include driving rain, harsh winds and long spells of freezing temperatures. They may also be suitable in internal areas where high levels of moisture are continuously present, such as in bathrooms and laundry rooms, especially when these rooms would need to be put to use soon after plastering.

NHLs are not as sticky or as fatty as non-hydraulic limes, and are therefore generally less workable and less adhesive. However, they have a lower shrinkage than lime putty and therefore tend to crack less if well mixed and applied.

The rule for deciding which grade of hydraulic lime to use should, however, largely be based on the premise that the plaster/render should never be stronger than the substrate. This should always form the basis of your decision as to what material to use. For example, a wall made out of soft materials, such as earth, should never be coated with anything stronger than an NHL2, even if in an exposed weather area. Please refer to the charts at the end of the chapter for more information on this.

In all circumstances, the choice of materials cannot be substituted for good workmanship. All lime materials need due respect and understanding with regards their individual characteristics, when it comes to their selection, mixing, application and aftercare.

The setting/curing processes for non-hydraulic and natural hydraulic limes

All lime mortars begin their setting process through the loss of moisture. This is via suction from the backing onto which they are placed, and through evaporation into the air. This causes the mortar to lose its plasticity and to begin to stiffen. Non-hydraulic limes complete their set via the process of carbonation alone (see below), whereas natural hydraulic limes will set via a combination of a reaction with water (hydration) and carbonation.

Carbonation (primarily non-hydraulic limes)

The carbonation process is one of nature's marvellous phenomena. It is the part of the lime process that brings it back to the beginning of the cycle. The material eventually reverts back to the exact chemical composition from whence it started as calcium carbonate.

The carbonation process involves a chemical reaction, which converts the calcium hydroxide ($CaOH_2$, the slaked lime which has been made into a mortar with aggregates) back into calcium carbonate ($CaCO_3$). It relinquishes its water molecules and reabsorbs the carbon elements from the carbon dioxide present in the air. This is achieved via a chemical reaction between the lime and carbon dioxide (CO_2), and involves the carbon dioxide dissolving in the water present in the mortar. This CO_2 then reacts with the calcium element of the lime to form calcium carbonate ($CaCO_3$) again. The carbonated calcium hydroxide becomes calcite, which consists of a network of fairly loosely interlocking crystalline structures. The spaces between the crystals, as well as between the calcite and the aggregate, give non-hydraulic limes their characteristic porosity and permeable nature. This material is chemically identical but generally physically softer than the original material.

If full carbonation has not occurred within the lime, subsequent carbonation can occur at a later date. This has positive implications for non-hydraulic limes, and is the reason that they can sometimes have an ability to 'self-heal' (known as 'autogenous healing'). This can be beneficial for any micro-cracking that may develop in the dried plaster or render. Any uncarbonated calcium hydroxide i.e 'free lime' that is still present within the region of the crack will subsequently carbonate as it is exposed to CO_2 and moisture in the atmosphere, thus contributing to healing the crack. This process can also occur as an external render face weathers and erodes. For this reason, the process of carbonation can continue for the full life of the finish.

Optimum conditions for carbonation to occur

The most important factor for carbonation to successfully occur is that there is enough moisture present in the plaster/render to allow for the above chemical exchange to take place. The purpose for the extensive aftercare necessary for lime plasters/renders (see below) is to encourage and maintain the ambient conditions necessary for optimum levels of carbonation to take place. This is because it is rare to be blessed with naturally perfect weather conditions for lime work. These ambient conditions must exist to encourage the render/plaster to stay gently moist for as long as possible. A lime render/plaster will not carbonate effectively if saturated with water, because the excessive moisture will prevent absorption of carbon dioxide into the body of mortar. Carbonation will also be inhibited if the lime mortar dries out very rapidly and there is no moisture present for the essential chemical reactions to take place. This can occur if there is rapid evaporation of moisture from the surface due to aggressive winds, draughts, or direct sunlight. For these reasons, work must be properly protected for at least two weeks, or more in bad weather conditions. and sprayed with water if rapid drying is taking place. It can also dry out too quickly if there is rapid suction from the wall substrate behind the finish. This can be minimised by ensuring that the surface is adequately dampened and prepared before work proceeds (see Wall Preparation, Chapter 2).

There is no standard timescale in which carbonation will occur. Each project will be unique. Factors affecting rates of carbonation include:

1. Temperature and humidity of the atmosphere.
2. Moisture content of the lime mix.
3. Air movement over the surface of the plaster/render.
4. The reactivity of the lime – how pure the lime is and its quality.
5. The texture of the lime surface – the more open the texture of the finish, the more open the pore structure will be and the easier it will be for carbon dioxide to enter into the lime mortar.

Rates of carbonation increase when atmospheric conditions are warm and moist, and the more

Before and after restoration of old cob barn, with lime render and pigmented limewash. The lime render will allow the cob to breathe, ensuring that the structure will remain healthy well into the future. Finishes by Mike Wye & Co.

permeable and porous the lime is. As temperatures decrease, so too will the rate of carbonation. This is why work must not take place when temperatures are at 5°C (41°F) and below, and when these temperatures are liable to occur within two to three months of application. If work does take place in such temperatures, the lime will be susceptible to frost damage, as the water present in the pores of the lime mortar freezes and expands. Internal lime mortars can take longer to carbonate as there is often less air circulation to carry away water molecules.

Lime mortars cure from the outside in, and after four weeks of average weather conditions carbonation should have occurred at depths of at least 3mm ($^1/_8$"). There is a simple alkalinity test that can be carried out to test levels of carbonation within the lime mortar by using liquid phenolphthaleine (available from most lime suppliers). As lime mortars carbonate, they become less alkaline. A small fractured section of plaster/render should be sprayed with the liquid phenolphthaleine. It turns bright pink if the lime is not carbonated, and will remain clear if it has.

Douglas Kent

Society for the Protection of Ancient Buildings (SPAB)

Douglas Kent is the technical secretary of SPAB. He is a chartered building surveyor with an MSC in the conservation of buildings. He is responsible for the Society's technical activities, including enquiries, publications, and courses of a technical nature. He manages the SPAB technical helpline.

*Several years ago the SPAB received far more queries asking why it was necessary to use lime. The reasons are now more widely appreciated, and it is the type of lime mortar that should be used that we are more frequently asked about.

What are the most frequent queries that you receive over the SPAB helpline regarding the use of lime?

1. Which lime should I use?* The SPAB generally advocates the use of repair materials that match those used originally (taking care, though, not to copy any inappropriate later work). In most cases, existing mortar can be adequately assessed from visual inspection coupled with local knowledge. Where it is not possible or desirable to closely match what exists, a newly designed mortar will be needed. Our forefathers appreciated that the more hydraulic a lime, the greater its strength, but the lower its permeability and flexibility; so the right balance needed to be struck for the particular job in hand. The slow set and workability of non-hydraulic lime, for example, is ideal for internal plasterwork. Where, however, extra durability in early life is required – say with a moderately exposed external wall – a weak hydraulic lime (or, if unavailable, a non-hydraulic one with a pozzolanic additive such as tile dust) might be appropriate for pointing or rendering.

2. What are the proportions for lime-based mixes? This depends on what you are matching, and the type of sand used. A sharp, well-graded sand is often suitable with lime. Typical mix proportions (by volume) are 1:3 or 1:2.5 lime to aggregate for newly designed pointing mortar, general render and plaster (with hair added to the latter).

3. What is the best method of removing inappropriate cement renders? Cement renders can sometimes be removed by working over the surface with a hammer, aided where necessary with a chisel. Great care must be exercised. If large sheets

are levered off, soft underlying materials can be seriously damaged. Various power tools can be suitable, but only in highly experienced hands.

4. Is it possible to skim over old lime plaster? It may be possible where the finishing coat is detaching rather than the plaster generally disintegrating, but is often inadvisable. There can be problems from shrinkage unless the wall is very carefully dampened down first, and because the old plaster is usually hacked to provide a key, this method is destructive. It is usually best to patch repair rather than to attempt to skim an old plaster wall.

5. Why is my limewash dusting off – is this normal? Good quality limewash applied properly to a suitable substrate should not rub off readily onto clothing. Reasons for poor adhesion can be preparation with ordinary bagged lime, coats being applied excessively thickly, inadequate dampening down before limewashing, or too rapid drying-out.

6. Why do you think my new lime mortar has failed? A high proportion of failures occur because adverse weather is ignored. Where possible, avoid using lime outside in winter. Whatever the time of year, ensure new work is adequately protected from frost, rapid drying (by the wind or sun) and rain. Poor preparation also causes failure.

7. Where can I learn more about the construction of limecrete floors? You could attend one of the technical courses that the SPAB runs from time to time. You could also contact one of the specialist lime suppliers listed in the online resources and suppliers section of this book (see pages 252-253).

The setting/curing processes for natural hydraulic limes

Natural hydraulic limes set and cure primarily via a chemical reaction that takes place between the calcium silicate and calcium aluminate compounds in the lime (which were formed in the kiln), and the water that is added to the lime during the mixing process. It is known as the hydraulic reaction or hydration process. These compounds remain non-reactive in the bag until they come into contact with water.

The reactive silicates and aluminates are hydrated, (through a process of complex chemical reactions) to become calcium silicate hydrates (C-S-H) and calcium aluminate hydrates (C-A-H). Calcium silicate hydrates (C-S-H) are the main hardening and strengthening compounds in hydraulic limes. The hydrates that are formed are essentially salts, which is why this reaction creates a solid crystalline structure within the mortar as it dries.

The above hydration process is dependent on the solubility of the silica present, so that it can dissolve in the water to facilitate the chemical reactions. The silica is transformed from a state of insolubility into one of solubility only once it has been heated in the kiln. Once the hydrates (C-A-H, C-S-H and others) have been formed, they are then rendered relatively insoluble. Hence the cured render should not be affected by external influences, such as rain.

The micro-crystalline structures created between the calcium and the silica are formed because of an affinity between these two compounds. Over time, they partner up and create thousands of crystalline structures, creating a dense network. Hydraulic limes form much denser networks of crystals than non-hydraulic limes, hence creating a less open pore structure. This is why hydraulic limes are less porous and permeable in nature. This porosity decreases with the strength of the hydraulic lime (i.e. NHL 2, 3.5 & 5).

At the same time as the hydration process is taking place in hydraulic limes, there is a simultaneous carbonation process that occurs. This contributes to the curing and ultimate strengthening of the lime. This process is identical to that which takes place in non-hydraulic lime. This carbonation manifests due to the calcium hydroxide that is also present in the lime. The rate of carbonation that takes place is dependent on the hydraulicity of the lime. For example, an NHL5 will have less calcium hydroxide present than an NHL2. At the same time, a more hydraulic lime will develop a denser crystalline matrix, thus making it more difficult for CO_2 to enter, leading to lower levels of carbonation.

The hydraulic set that is achieved with a natural hydraulic lime means that they tend to reach a quicker initial set than non-hydraulic limes. They are therefore less fragile in the first few days after application. However, for successful hydration to occur, it is essential that there is adequate water present in the mortar for a long enough period after it has been laid, to allow for the reactions to take place. It is therefore necessary to prevent rapid evaporation of moisture from the material. For this reason they are still affected by extremes of weather, such as continuous heavy rain (which will wash the material off the wall whilst still wet), strong drying winds and direct sunlight. They also are susceptible to frost damage before becoming fully set. This means that fresh work should be protected in the first few days after application. The rate of hydration generally increases the warmer the temperature, and decreases as it gets cold. At 5°C (41°F) and below, the hydration process virtually stops.

Pozzolanic additives

A pozzolan is a material which can be added to a lime mortar mix to increase the speed at which it sets and to improve its durability. They are generally added to non-hydraulic limes to impart a weak hydraulic set. When added to a non-hydraulic lime, it creates what is known as an 'artificial hydraulic lime'. The traditional non-

Left: Well-graded fine aggregate for internal finishing coats (left hand), and well-graded coarse aggregate for base coats and external finishing coats (right hand). *Right:* Home-sieving aggregate to create a well-graded mix.

hydraulic limes produced from kilns that were fired with wood or coal would have contained remnants of the ashes of the fuels used. These ashes often added a slightly hydraulic set to the lime. The non-hydraulic limes that are commercially produced today are generally fired in kilns with cleaner burning fuels, such as gas or oil. These limes are therefore much purer than the traditional non-hydraulic limes. They may therefore require the addition of a pozzolan, when being used externally in exposed or continuously damp conditions, instead of using a natural hydraulic lime. There is a range of pozzolans, from both natural and artificial sources, that are suitable for use with lime. The word pozzolan is derived from a specific volcanic mineral that has been mined for centuries from a particular town called Pozzuoli near Naples in southern Italy. The term 'pozzolana' is retained for this specific material, whereas the generic term for any material with a pozzolanic effect is called a pozzolan.

Other pozzolanic materials from natural sources include 'trass', which is a volcanic ash imported from Germany and Holland. Pozzolanic materials from artificial sources include ground brick dust from clay bricks fired at low temperatures. (Note: most modern bricks are fired at temperatures too high to produce

a pozzolan). Another artificially produced pozzolan, is 'metakaolin', sourced from kaolin clay. This is commercially available as 'Metastar 501' and is a popular pozzolan in the UK. It can be sourced from most specialist lime suppliers. A greener, cheaper, but less reactive alternative is granulated ground blast furnace slag. This is made from a waste product from power stations (see www.naturalbuildingresources.com).

Pozzolans imitate the setting actions of natural hydraulic limes by providing a supply of clay minerals, namely the compounds of silica and alumina. They do not harden in themselves when mixed with water, but will react with the calcium hydroxide (present in the lime) in the presence of water to form the same hydrated calcium silicate and aluminate compounds found in natural hydraulic limes. As with natural hydraulic limes, this reaction will provide the primary setting/curing process within the lime mortar, depending on the amount added and the type used. It will be supported by the carbonation process with the remaining calcium hydroxide present.

Fine pozzolans, such as finely crushed brick dust or fired kaolin clay, must be considered as part of the binder (the lime). Coarse pozzolanic material should be considered as part of the

106

Left: Different aggregates used for making lime plasters and renders. *Right:* A range of synthetic and natural animal fibres used to give tensile strength in lime renders and plasters (yak, goat and horse hair, and polypropylene fibres).

aggregate proportion. They are normally added in a quantity that accounts for no more than 10% by volume to the mixed mortar (see below). It is essential to recognise that pozzolans will have an effect on the structure of the mortar. If too much is added, it will densify the mortar paste, making it less permeable and more brittle. Research done by the *Foresight Project* has shown that if more than 20% pozzolan is added to a non-hydraulic mortar, the resultant mortar will be less permeable and more brittle than mortars made with cement.

Pozzolans should be made into a slurry with a minimum amount of water before being added to the lime/aggregate mortar mix. They must be added immediately before use, because the mix will begin to set as soon as it has been added. Like natural hydraulic limes, the pozzolan-gauged mortar must be used within 12 hours and should not be remixed at a later date. It is best used as soon as possible.

Preparing plasters & renders

Materials for making lime plasters & renders

A good lime plaster or render is made up of two or three basic materials: a non-hydraulic or natural hydraulic lime binder; well-graded, clean aggregates; and for all but the finishing coat, a fibrous additive. This is traditionally some form of animal hair. Each provides a unique function

within the plaster/render. If well selected and appropriately added, each contributes equally to the overall performance of the finish.

Aggregates

The importance of the specific selection of aggregates to be used with the lime binder cannot be emphasised enough. They are responsible for providing the structure for the mortar, which in turn will determine its overall strength, durability and performance. A good lime can be ruined by an inappropriately selected aggregate.

In Chapter 2 we have covered in more depth many aspects of the functions and selection of aggregates for use in plaster/render mixes, and we strongly advise you to read this before embarking on any lime work. To sum up briefly, however, the most important elements for a suitable aggregate are: that it must be clean, well-graded (a variety of particle sizes at specific ratios), they should be within a range of particle sizes that are suitable for the desired finish, and the particles should be present in a range of angular shapes, so that they can lock together to provide a cohesive structure.

Fibre reinforcement

Animal hairs are usually added to lime mortar undercoat mixes. The primary function is to provide flexural strength to the mortar. This is achieved by producing tensile reinforcement. The hairs form a cross-matting effect as they interweave, holding the plaster together. This enables the mortar to accommodate minor movements within the building structure. Its second function is that it can help reduce shrinkage in the dry mortar, and hence decrease the potential for cracking to occur.

When plastering/rendering onto wooden lath, the addition of the hair is absolutely essential. Not adding enough hair to the plaster/render mix is one of the principle causes of failure of a lath and plaster finish.

Many different types of animal hair can be used in lime mortars. These range from goat, cow, horse, yak, donkey and even reindeer hair. Some people believe that cattle and goat hairs are superior because they have barbed edges, enabling them to grip better into the plaster. However, horse body hair is used very regularly by many suppliers and practitioners with very good results. Horse tail and mane should not be used, because they are too smooth and wiry. If providing your own horse hair, the longer body hairs from post-winter grooming are best. Vegetable fibres such as hemp, straw, flax and jute can also be used to good effect.

The fundamentals for a useful hair for plastering/rendering include:

1. The fibre should be between 25mm (1") and 75mm (3") long. If the hair is too short it can cause lumps in the plaster/render which can cause weak spots. If using a render gun to spray the mortar on, the hair will need to be at the shorter end of the spectrum to minimise clogging of the sprayholes.
2. The hair should be strong.
3. The hair should be free of grease and impurities. If providing your own animal fibres, washing them in lime water (a weak mix of lime and water, or the liquid found on top of lime putty) will help to remove the lanolin naturally present.

4. The hair should not be wiry.

Modern synthetic fibres can be used with success in lime plaster/render undercoats. Most notably, polypropylene fibres. These are a by-product of the rope industry.

A range of suitable animal hairs and fibres can also be purchased from most specialist lime suppliers. They usually come in bundles. It is also possible to obtain haired, pre-mixed, non-hydraulic lime mixes. These should be stored for no longer than four weeks from the hair being added, because the alkalinity of uncarbonated lime can attack the protein in the hair and cause them to decompose. If they are stored for longer than this period, it is recommended that fresh hair is added to the mix when 'knocking up' immediately prior to use (see below).

As mentioned above, hair should be added to the mix as close to the time of use as possible. For non-hydraulic lime-aggregate mixes, which have been stored and matured, hair should be added during the knocking up phase. For natural hydraulic lime mixes, they should be added during the mixing stage. Before being added to the mix, it is helpful to tease the hair out to break up any clumps. The strands should be added to the mix slowly and carefully. Any clumps of hair will tend to develop as weak spots in the plaster/render, which could lead to failure. The hairs should therefore be evenly distributed throughout the mix.

It is hard to provide exact specifications for the amount of hair to be added to a mix in terms of volume, because this will vary greatly depending on what species of hair is being used. Below we have laid out a few different guideline specifications:

1. The best gauge of whether or not enough hair has been added to the mix is to carry

out the traditional 'beard' test. This involves scooping up a trowelful of the haired mix, and assessing how many hairs can be seen protruding from the edge of the trowel. The hairs should be very closely spaced at roughly 1mm intervals.

2. As a guideline, use 0.5kg (1 lb) hair to 100 litres (3 cubic feet). This is the full capacity of a standard drum mixer, and roughly a standard sized wheelbarrowful.

3. Two large handfuls of teased hair (bear in mind that hand sizes can differ), or one tied bundle of 4cm (1^1/$_2$") hair to one mix – i.e. one barrowful/one standard drum mixer.

Ultimately, the best gauge will come with experience.

Water

The quality of water used to mix up a lime mortar is important and can have implications for the final strength and setting processes. It must be clean and free from impurities, such as organic matter. Especially important to avoid is water that contains dissolved salts, which will negatively effect the durability of the plaster/render. Potable drinking water is the most suitable for use.

Health and safety issues when working with lime

Lime, in the form of calcium hydroxide, is extremely alkaline and therefore highly caustic. It will dehydrate and even burn the skin if there is prolonged exposure. It is therefore essential to wear waterproof gloves when handling, as well as protective overalls or clothes that maximise skin coverage. Any cuts on the body must be kept clean and covered. Gloves that come up and over the wrist are highly recommended to protect this area. Safety glasses should be worn, especially when mixing, limewashing, harling, throwing, using a render gun, or plastering/rendering above your head. If skin contact does occur, the area should be washed immediately with soap and water and then rinsed with vinegar, which, due to its acidity will counteract the alkalinity of the lime and hence decrease the potential for burning and drying of the skin. When mixing up dry hydrate powders, goggles and a dust mask should always be worn. Lime powder will affect the eyes, and also the lungs and mucus membranes of the respiratory system if inhaled. If you do end up inhaling a large amount, seek fresh air immediately and thoroughly irrigate the nose and throat with water. Mixing is best carried out in the open air so that dust can escape quickly and easily.

Left: Protective gear worn to protect against the lime. *Right:* It is essential that suitable gear is worn when working with lime to protect the skin, eyes and lungs (when mixing natural hydraulic lime powder).

Julie Haddow

Lime plasterer

Julie Haddow is part of the new generation of young lime plasterers. She was a SPAB (*Society for the Protection of Ancient Buildings*) fellow in 2000. This entails a six month period of travelling around Great Britain meeting contractors, architects and engineers. She runs her own lime plastering business in Somerset, and is among one of the most talented and knowledgeable of her generation.

What training process did you go through to get where you are today?

I had no formal training through the traditional route, i.e. a plastering qualification at a Technical College. At Art and Design College I learned how to model figures in clay and plaster, take moulds – both plaster and silicone – and cast in a variety of different materials. These processes are perfect for repairing decorative plasterwork and are not generally taught in any depth at Technical Colleges. All of my lime training has been gained by working alongside experienced plasterers and from my own trial and error. Most of my real learning has come from watching someone else and then having a go myself.

Can you share a few tips?

There are four key factors:
* ***Adequate key***
By the term 'key', I mean an irregular surface that the lime plaster can grip onto. This can be a roughly pointed stone wall ready to take a first coat of plaster, or the key applied to a scratch coat with a wire scratcher. If you have provided a mechanical key for your lime to stick to, you are half way there. The surface must also be free from dust and debris. Dust acts as a barrier. Use an air compressor, a hand brush or a hose – always plaster onto a clean but damp surface.

* ***Understanding suction***
Any porous building material – be it cob, brick or stone – will literally 'suck' the plaster onto its surface. The problem is that if you don't wet the wall down enough before you apply your plaster then it will carry on sucking until all the moisture is gone and the plaster detaches from the background. We want to use this suction to our advantage and be in control of it. If you apply a wet material to a damp wall, you will get good

adhesion. By wetting down you are reducing the suction, but if you over-wet the surface you will kill the suction altogether. Play around with this aspect: each background material is different, and weather conditions also play a part. Likewise, if you have a large wall to plaster you might overly wet it to give yourself more working time. With lime plastering, you are not working with a chemical set as you are with cement and gypsum plasters, i.e. a predetermined setting time. You have to create your own working times by controlling moisture.

* ***Learn to trust your own judgement***
Have a play, find out yourself what works and what doesn't work – MAKE MISTAKES. Watch as many other plasterers as you can, and ask them questions – most tradesmen are only too happy to impart some of their hard-earned experience to someone who appreciates the trade. Lime is a different material from standard cement and gypsum plasters, but the techniques are very similar.

* ***Wisdom for your body***
Learn to use both hands for plastering right from the beginning. Plastering is a tough trade, and using both limbs can save you from injury. If you do suffer from any repetitive strain injuries such as tennis elbow (which is very common amongst plasterers), take up yoga – this practice stretches out all those contracting muscles.

If I had my time over again I would get trained in plastering through the conventional route and then I would pester a conservation company or a lime-plastering firm for a job. Any kind of plastering is good experience. I love plastering: it has presented me with some of the biggest challenges in life, and at the same time has given me so much joy and satisfaction. I have the utmost respect for time-served tradesmen who take their craft seriously.

If lime is accidentally splashed into the eye, it should be irrigated immediately with clean water (distilled is best). Irrigate the eye for up to 15 minutes if a lot has gone in. A dilute solution of weak sugar water is also recommended because it is slightly acidic and will help negate the alkalinity of the lime. It is advisable to seek immediate medical attention if the eye remains irritated.

Making up a lime-aggregate mix

Lime-aggregate mixes can be made in a variety of ways. The method chosen will depend on what size loads you are mixing, which type of lime you are using (a powdered natural hydraulic lime or a non-hydraulic lime putty), how much time you have, how much labour you have available, and the available budget. As with all traditional building methods, it can be executed inexpensively with simple hand tools, but this is fairly labour-intensive. At the other end of the spectrum are the more time-efficient methods using specialist mixing machines. It is also possible to use simple, inexpensive and easy-to-obtain machinery. As long as all the correct procedures are observed, a good mix can be achieved whichever of the above approaches are taken.

There are also currently many excellent specialist lime suppliers across the United Kingdom who can provide ready made non-hydraulic lime-aggregate mixes, suitable for most plastering/rendering purposes. These ready mixes are available in 1 tonne sacks and 25 kg buckets. All that is necessary is for the mix to be 'knocked up' (see below) immediately prior to use. It will have been mixed using appropriate methods and equipment, which ensures a consistent quality product. This option can be cost-effective and eliminates the sourcing, selecting, gauging and mixing of the other materials.

The aim of mixing

Before embarking on mixing up your own lime mortars, it is useful to understand what the exact objectives are that you are aiming to achieve in the mixing process. The aim of mixing is to bring about the intimate coating of lime around every grain of aggregate. It is also to achieve full homogenisation of all the different ingredients and to arrive at the correct consistency for spreading on the wall. These must be achieved with the correct amounts of water, as this will have implications on the overall performance of the mortar once dried on the wall. It is also important that there be consistency throughout every batch produced. Care must therefore be taken in how the different ingredients are measured out, and that there is a consistency of materials used for the duration of the project.

Different mixing methods

The following information presents guidelines on how to mix up lime-aggregate mortars in a variety of methods, from the most simple to those using specialised equipment. With any of the methods used, it is essential that:

- The materials are accurately measured.
- Appropriate aggregates are used.
- The right proportions of the different materials are used.
- The lime is mixed for the correct length of time.
- The water is added in the correct amount and rate.
- The materials are added in the correct sequence.

Water

The importance of paying attention to the amount of water used and the rate at which it is added cannot be underestimated. If too much water is added to a lime mortar mix, the potential for large amounts of shrinkage and hence cracking in the drying plaster/render is increased. This is because there will be a large volume change in the mortar as the water exits. It may also lead to poor bonding between the mortar and the substrate, which will manifest in the mortar slumping off the wall once it has been applied. Too much water will also diminish the strength of the mortar. It will prevent the aggregate particles from locking tightly together and will leave an excessively open structure when dry. On the flipside, too little water in the mix will make it dry and crumbly and difficult to spread on the wall. It may also inhibit the chemical reactions (carbonation and hydration) which initiate the curing of the lime. Adding water to a powdered hydraulic lime should be carried out cautiously and in very small amounts. This is because the more the ingredients are mixed, the softer and wetter the materials will become.

This is also true when mixing lime putty, which should not in fact, need the addition of any water at all – the moisture being liberated from within the putty structure should be sufficient to make a creamy workable mix. If water is necessary, because the ingredients won't mix together even after a long period of mixing (when using a drum mixer for example), only very small amounts should be used. If too much water is added and the mix turns soupy, however, it should be stored to allow it to stiffen before use.

There are a couple of simple and quick tests that can be done to determine whether your lime mortar has been mixed enough. These are to ensure that there is adequate moisture to make it easy to spread onto the wall and that adequate cohesion has taken place between all the ingredients.

Test 1
1. Take a small handful of lime mortar and drop onto a hawk from roughly 100mm (4") above.
2. Turn the hawk upside down quickly.
   The mortar should remain stuck to the hawk for at least 5 seconds.

Test 2
1. Create a ball of lime mortar roughly 100mm (4") in diameter.
2. Drop from waist height onto flat ground.

A mortar which is of a good consistency should not crumble, and should spread roughly from 150 – 160mm (6 – 6 $^1/_2$") on the ground.

Accurate gauging for consistent batches of mortar
It is very important to maintain an accurate system for measuring out the different amounts of aggregate, lime and any other materials being used. This will ensure that consistent mixes are produced. The most accurate system is to weigh the materials before mixing, but this can be impractical and tedious on a worksite. Good results can be obtained by volume measuring through the use of a sturdy gauging bucket. It should be strong enough to take the weight of the sand when full. Under no circumstances should a shovel be used as a method of gauging, because it will provide inconsistent results, affecting the quality of the mix.

Maturing non-hydraulic lime putty mixes
Traditionally, mixes made with coarse aggregates are known as 'coarse stuff'. These are used for backing coats or external finishing coats. Mixes made with fine aggregates (sand) are known as 'fine stuff' (or 'setting stuff'). These are generally used for internal finishing coats.

All mortars made with non-hydraulic lime putty can be used immediately after mixing, but the material is much improved if it is stored for at least a couple of days before use. The best material will be obtained from storing it for weeks, months and even years. The action of storing the mixed material encourages the lime to come into closer contact with the aggregate, and hence fully envelop the aggregate particles. This will make the mix easier to use and perform better.

To store the material, it should either be wrapped tightly in polythene or stored in sealed buckets or tubs. It should not be exposed to water, freezing temperatures, or to the air.

Mixing by hand the traditional way
(for non-hydraulic lime putties)

Lime-aggregate mortars were traditionally mixed by hand in a large, shallow wooden box using a variety of tools that were designed to thoroughly chop, beat and literally ram the lime and aggregate together. These actions serve to mobilise the stiff lime putty and help to spread it around the surface of each grain of aggregate. All mechanical mixing methods must aim to emulate this as much as possible. This method can be used for mixing non-hydraulic lime putties only.

To reproduce this method in a modern context, a large shallow plastic plasterer's bath can be used to mix small batches. For larger batches, an open-ended bay can be created using three strong boards, fixed securely together onto a clean flat board laid on the ground. The three side boards should be roughly 300mm (1') high and be able to withstand impact from the tools ramming the sides from within the bay.

The best tools to use are a square shovel, a dutch hoe, a pull hoe and a heavy tamper. The handle of a pick axe, or a 4"x2"' piece of wood will work well for ramming and beating. It is not sufficient to simply turn the materials over with a shovel.

1. Pour off excess water sitting on top of the lime putty.
2. Whisk the lime putty vigorously in a bucket (with a whisk attached to a powerful drill; a normal drill may break because it is not able to cope with the torque required), or beat it in a bucket with a pick-axe handle or piece of 4"x2"' timber (at all times protecting the eyes). This is carried out before being placed in the plasterer's tub or on the board to make it more malleable and easier to work.
3. Take roughly half the total amount of putty to be mixed and spread it across the bottom of the tub/board. Cover with roughly a quarter of the total amount of sand to be used. With the back of a clean square shovel, and using downward pressure, smear and press the sand into the lime putty and then chop and turn over. Repeat this action until the sand and lime are fully integrated.
4. Spread the mixed lime putty and aggregate out across the tub/board and add the rest of the putty. Layer this with another quarter portion of sand. Repeat the above actions of pressing, smearing, chopping and turning until well integrated. Continue until all the sand is added.
5. When all the sand has been added, the mix will feel stiff, and will get increasingly harder to work. At this stage, a drag or hoe can be used to chop the mix into smaller sections and then pushed against the sides of the bay or tub. The mix should then be pummelled with the hoe, by using a repeated downward chopping action, and then the action of pushing and pulling the material away and toward you.

Use a combination of the above methods and tools to achieve a thoroughly mixed material, which should also be soft and workable. It will take up to 20-30 minutes or more for an adequate mix to be made.

Adding hair

If the material is to be used immediately, the hair should be added at the end of the mixing process. The lime-aggregate mix should be spread out into a thin layer on the board or in the tub, and the hair sprinkled thinly over the mix. The hair should be evenly distributed by turning over the mix repeatedly with a shovel.

If the material is to be stored for more than one month, the hair should not be added until immediately before the lime mortar is to be used.

If the lime-aggregate mix is to be stored for any length of time, it must always be 'knocked up' immediately prior to use. This is because the mix may become crumbly and stiff with storage, and this process will restore the plasticity without the need to add water. The knocking-up process can be done by hand in exactly the same manner as described above.

Mixing non-hydraulic lime putties in a standard drum mixer

Many specialist lime suppliers and contractors will recommend not to use a standard drum (cement) mixer for making up non-hydraulic lime putty mixes. The main argument put forward is that they do not allow the lime and aggregate particles to be adequately and intimately squeezed together, and brought sufficiently into contact with each other. Also, because the lime putty is generally quite stiff before it has been mixed, and because the addition of water is not advantageous, the putty will have a tendency to stick tenaciously to the sides of the drum, making it very difficult to mix with the other ingredients. However, the specialist mechanical lime mixers (pan mixer and mortar mill) are expensive (although they can be hired), and are most suitable for making up large batches. It is therefore generally accepted that, with some simple procedures to improve the contact between the lime and aggregate, good non-hydraulic lime putty mortars can be successfully mixed in a drum mixer.

1. Remove excess water on top of lime putty.
2. Work the putty with a high-powered drill with a whisk attachment or piece of wood (as described in point 2, p.113), before adding to the mixer.
3. Add the whisked lime putty and aggregate to the mixer in the correct proportions in alternate batches. Mix until fully integrated. This should take around 20-30 minutes.

To assist mixing:
1. Tilt the mixer forward slightly by placing bricks or timber under the back two legs. This will help the lime and aggregate to fall off the paddles more easily as it rotates. Alternatively, it is possible to purchase cement mixers with the facility to tilt the drum using a geared wheel (easily available from most building supply stores and catalogues).
2. To induce compressive action into the procedure, thus emulating the squeezing actions of the more specialist mixers and the ramming/beating actions of hand-mixing, place a couple of medium-sized stones or scaffolding clips (which will not break down as easily as the stones) into the rotating mixer.

It will also be necessary to occasionally scrape the material off the sides of the drums and paddles. Don't try to do this whilst it is rotating, as there is a risk that your arm could get caught in the mixer.

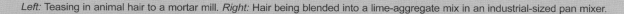

Left: Teasing in animal hair to a mortar mill. *Right:* Hair being blended into a lime-aggregate mix in an industrial-sized pan mixer.

If after 10 minutes, the lime putty and aggregate are not combining, a very small amount of water can tentatively be added to encourage softening of the putty and full homogenisation of the two ingredients.

Stored material can easily be 'knocked up' in the mixer for about 5-10 minutes before use, or until workable. The hairs should gradually be teased in at this stage.

Mixing non-hydraulic lime putty mortars in a mortar mill (a.k.a. a roller pan mixer)

The mechanical mortar mill is the crème de la crème of lime mortar mixing machines. Most specialist lime suppliers make their non-hydraulic lime putty mixes with these machines. For information on the benefits and functioning of these machines, refer to Chapter 2. Add the lime putty first and mix for around one minute. Add the aggregate mix for four-five minutes, until a workable, homogenous mix is achieved. Add hair either at the knocking-up stage, if the material has been stored, or at the end of the mixing process, if to be used immediately.

Mixing non-hydraulic lime mortars in a pan mixer (a.k.a. a paddle mixer)

A pan mixer falls somewhere between a drum mixer and a mortar mill both in terms of cost and efficiency (refer to Chapter 2 for more details). The full amount of lime putty should be added first and mixed on its own for a few minutes. The aggregate should then be added in small amounts and mixed for roughly ten to twelve minutes before being ready. A very small amount of water may be necessary to get the mix fully incorporated. The addition of hair requires the same process as above.

Mixing natural hydraulic lime mortars

Natural hydraulic limes can be made efficiently in a standard drum (cement) mixer. Because they come in a dry powder, it is necessary to add water to get the desired consistency. Also, the aggregate

and lime do not need to be squeezed together to achieve an intimate bond, as is necessary when using lime putty. For these reasons, the mixing processes are more straightforward. Hand-mixing can be done in a wheelbarrow or plasterer's tub, using a shovel and hoe. A mortar mill or pan mixer can also be used to good results.

There are two methods for mixing powdered natural hydraulic limes. It is possible to either dry mix the aggregate with the lime first and then add the water to achieve the desired consistency; however, this is a dusty option. Alternatively, the water can be added to the mixer first, and then alternate batches of lime and aggregate added. This will minimise dusting from the lime. Water should still be added cautiously. Add only that which is required to mix the ingredients together, and to make it wet enough to spread on the wall.

Unlike non-hydraulic lime putty mixes, mixes made with natural hydraulic lime must not be stored once mixed for more than 24 hours. This is because once mixed with water, the hydraulic set can take place almost immediately (depending on the strength of the natural hydraulic lime). The weaker NHL2 mixes, however, behave more like a putty and it can be advantageous to make them up the day before use. This will help the mix to 'fatten up', making it stickier and more workable. It must be knocked up before use. When using NHL3.5 or 5, only make up enough for 3-4 hours of work.

Mixing natural hydraulic lime mortars in a drum mixer

This method involves mixing all of the dry ingredients first before adding water. This is recommended because the abrasive nature of the dry aggregate assists with breaking down the agglomerated lime particles, which because of their fineness have a tendency to clump together. To avoid dusting, a piece of polystyrene foam can be held over the opening until water is added, the ingredients can be lightly sprayed with water to moisten the surrounding air.

1. Add alternate batches of dry ingredients to the mixer.
2. Rotate for about ten minutes.
3. When the dry ingredients are fully incorporated together, start to add water slowly. Add a small amount at first, and then allow the mix to rotate for at least five minutes. This is because the mix will get considerably more plastic and hence wetter as the mixing continues.
4. Mix with the water for about twenty minutes, then turn off the mixer for another twenty minutes to allow the lime to swell, improving the contact between the ingredients.
5. Turn the mixer back on and briefly mix, before teasing in hair if required.

Making a lime-aggregate mix for harling

Harling mixes need to be of a more liquid consistency so that they can be effectively cast onto the wall. They should be made in exactly the same way as a normal mortar mix, and then watered down to make a suitable slurry. The mix can be watered down with lime water, a thin limewash, or just pure water. It can be further mixed in any type of mixing machine, or by using a whisk attached to the end of a high-powered drill in a bucket. It should be thin enough so that it flicks easily and evenly onto the wall, and slides off the trowel smoothly, whilst still maintaining a form.

Mixes for use with a render gun

Mixes for use with a render gun also need to be slightly more liquid than those applied by hand. If the mix is too stiff it will not blow through the outlet holes in the hopper. To get the right consistency requires experimenting on site with the render gun. Like harling, it is acceptable for the mix to be more liquid, because the force at which it is sprayed onto the wall drastically improves its adhesion and compression. As the material hits the surface, the air is expelled, which similarly facilitates a more intimate bond. This is also true of the harling method. Additionally the air that forces the mortar onto the wall acts to dry the mortar slightly before it hits the wall. These both minimise the potential for cracking, as would be the case if a trowel-applied mix was too wet.

Adding a pozzolan to a lime-aggregate mix

If adding a pozzolan to the mix it should be added at the final stage, after the mix has been

Making up a natural hydraulic lime-aggregate render in a drum mixer. **Note: Please wear protective goggles, gloves and dust mask!** *Left to right:* Adding aggregate; Adding hydraulic lime powder; Aggregate and lime mixing together.

prepared as described above. It must be made up immediately prior to use because of its hydraulic setting mechanism. All pozzolans come as a dried powder, and therefore need to be mixed with a minimum amount of water and made into a liquid paste before being added. Mix the pozzolan with the other ingredients with whichever mixing method is being used, until it is fully incorporated. Use the mix immediately.

Recipes for lime mortars

There are many variations of ingredients and mix ratios for making up a lime mortar. The factors that must be considered when determining these are:

1. The substrate the material is being applied onto, e.g. hard masonry, soft crumbly masonry or brick, cob, straw bale, etc.
2. Type of aggregate being mixed with the lime binder, i.e. fine or coarse, and what particle size range is present.
3. The lime binder to be used, i.e. non-hydraulic lime putty or a natural hydraulic lime.
4. The coat the mix will be used for, i.e. stipple coat, base coats or finishing coat.
5. Levels of exposure/dampness present in the area to be rendered/plastered.

6. Method of application to be used, i.e. harled, trowelled, etc.

It is difficult to provide a definitive set of mix ratios/blend of ingredients for every possible scenario. However, it is possible to set out some parameters for situations at the extreme end of each spectrum:

1. When rendering or plastering below ground level or in areas that are constantly damp, a natural hydraulic lime or a non-hydraulic lime putty with a pozzolanic additive should be used.
2. When plastering/rendering onto soft materials such as cob, wattle and daub, soft brick or stone etc., or when plastering internally, a non-hydraulic lime putty is appropriate.
3. For external rendering onto soft materials, but where there are high levels of exposure or prolonged dampness, an NHL2 or lime putty with a small amount of pozzolanic additive should be used.

Provided that a good quality lime and well selected aggregates are used, the standard lime-aggregate mortar mix ratio is:

Adding water gradually and in small increments; Lime, aggregate and water mixing together (approximately 20 minutes); Teasing in hair; Mix until the hair is fully incorporated.

Base coats/external finishing coats
1 part lime : 3 parts coarse aggregate with fibre

Internal finishing coats
1 part lime : 1 part aggregate/1 : 2 with no fibre
(depending on surface texture desired)

Sand void ratios

The above mixes are arrived at by the assumption that a well selected aggregate is used. The amount of lime binder added to the aggregate should completely fill the voids between the aggregate particles, and should thoroughly coat each grain. Most well-graded aggregates, regardless of their size, tend to have a void ratio of around one third, hence a 1 : 3 (lime : aggregate) mix is generally the standard. For fine work (internal finishing coats) a 1 : 1 or 1 : 2 mix is often used. The higher amount of binder allows for a much smoother finish. A lime-rich mix should be applied very thinly so that shrinkage cracking is minimised. Many old internal finishing coat plasters consisted of neat lime without any aggregate added, applied very thinly.

If sourcing your own aggregates (and not from a specialist lime supplier), there is a basic test that can be carried out to determine the exact ratios of lime-to-aggregate required. This test was first determined by Vicat, a leading researcher into lime, in 1837. It has been used successfully ever since and is known as the 'sand void ratio test'. For information on how to carry out this test, please refer to the aggregates section in Chapter 2.

The general rule is that top coats should be weaker, or at least no stronger than base coats (i.e. base coats should consist of a higher ratio of aggregate to lime binder than the finish coats). This is to prevent creating tensions between the coats. These tensions could lead to cracking or complete delamination of the finishing coat from the coat beneath it.

For base coats, the lime to sand ratio should never be weaker than 1 : 3, but can be as high as 2 : 5

(1 : 2.5) depending on the aggregates being used. A harling mix is often made very lime-rich, i.e. 1 : 1.5, for maximum adhesion to the wall surface.

Some suggested mixes for a range of different circumstances

Mix ratio guidelines:
The different coats (base coats and finishing coats) should adhere to two basic principles:
a) The aggregates should generally be coarser in base coats and external finishing coats, and finer for internal finishing coats, subject to the strength and fineness of the work necessary.
b) The plaster/render mix should generally be stronger in the base coats and get progressively weaker toward the finishing coat (see above).

Mixes for external use may include:
a) Coarse aggregates should be used in an external finish coat for improved weathering.
b) External renders will often have variations with the aim of making them more resistant to the elements, e.g. using a natural hydraulic lime or adding a pozzolan to a non-hydraulic lime to impart hydraulic properties.

Natural hydraulic limes should be carefully selected with an understanding of their general properties and suitability in different circumstances.

NHL2

The weakest, most porous of the hydraulic limes, and the closest in strength and breathability to a non-hydraulic lime putty. Ideal for use on soft building substrates in an exposed situation, or where there is prolonged contact with moisture. For soft earth materials it is not advisable to go stronger than an NHL2.

NHL3.5

Slightly stronger than an NHL2 and therefore suitable for external rendering onto solid masonry (softer stone and brick) in a moderately exposed environment.

NHL5

The strongest and least permeable of the natural hydraulic limes. Ideal for rendering sound and hard masonry (dense, impervious brick, stone and concrete block) and when in severely exposed environments. Also good for rendering in wet environments, such as below water and below ground level. Note: the British hydraulic lime currently on the market is slightly less strong than the French and other European brands. This should be taken into consideration when selecting.

Non-hydraulic lime putty

a) Without a pozzolan: suitable for all internal plastering except where there is potential for the wall to take some knocks, such as in public spaces or in children's bedrooms. Appropriate for exterior walls that are suitably sheltered.

b) With a pozzolan: suitable for external rendering in moderately exposed environments, or onto a weak backing such as soft stone, friable brick or cob in an exposed environment.

Lime-to-aggregate ratios when using natural hydraulic limes

Hydraulic lime mortar mixes are generally specified with a higher lime content than non-hydraulic limes, such as base coats 1 : 2 (maximum 2.5). This is because they contain less calcium hydroxide and are therefore less workable. Natural hydraulic limes are therefore traditionally described as being able to carry less sand than a non-hydraulic lime.

Approximate lime-aggregate coverage rates

Scratch coat: 25 litre (5 gallon) container will cover 2.5m^2 applied at a thickness of 10mm.

Straightening coat: 25 litre (5 gallon) container will cover 4m^2 at a thickness of 6mm.

Finishing coat: 25 litre (5 gallon) container will cover 6m^2 at a thickness of 3mm.

Above: Scouring the lime render finishing coat.

Left: Floating on a finishing coat .

Right: Hand-applying an earth plaster base coat, onto which a lime render finishing coat will be applied for weathering protection.

Applying lime renders and plasters

There are three important stages, which must be carried out with equal diligence for the successful application of a lime plaster or render:

1. Pre-application – preparing the walls.
2. Application – applying the lime plaster/render.
3. Post-application – carrying out appropriate aftercare.

As is always the case with traditional building skills, there are many different techniques for successful application, including regional, historical and preferential variations. We have described general sequences and techniques, which cover all the key elements to plain lime plastering and rendering.

Straight or curvy?

The methods that we describe don't place a great deal of emphasis on producing walls that are perfectly straight and true, especially when plastering/rendering an old earth or masonry wall, or when using materials that lend themselves to organic shapes, such as straw-bale walls and wattle and daub. In these cases, there is a preference to follow the natural shapes and slight undulations of the substrate below. One of the many beauties of lime and other natural finishes, is how complementary they are to soft, slightly rounded shapes. It is also true, that when using the softer lime- and earth-based finishes, a rounded corner is stronger than a sharp junction, which means that it will not easily chip. This is not to say that perfectly straight walls cannot be achieved, and indeed would be more desirable when plastering/rendering onto a flat surface such as wood fibre board or brick, but that in the right context, the natural character of the walls should be allowed to speak through. We do not therefore advocate the use of metal stops and corner beads (along with the fact that they can rust over time and bleed into the plaster, and cause cracking due to differential movement). If perfectly straight walls are preferred rather than an undulating surface, it is necessary to apply more dubbing-out coats to eliminate deep pockets. Traditional tools that are used to aid the straightening process include the floating rule and the darby. These are scraped along the surface of freshly applied lime mortar, to even the surface to a level plane. The action of scouring with a wooden float will also reveal high and low spots, to indicate where extra filling out is necessary.

The coat system

Lime plasters/renders can be applied in one, two or three coats, depending on the level of protection needed, the desired aesthetic outcome of the finished wall, and the condition and nature of the wall beneath. We have described the process for standard three-coat work, but less (or more) can be carried out if required.

Sometimes it is necessary to apply a pre-coat known as the 'stipple coat'. This is a very thin coat consisting of a lime-rich, aggregate slurry (3 parts lime : 1 part sand). It can either be sprayed or harled onto the wall, and left as a rough texture. It can provide a variety of functions:

1. When used on friable, crumbly surfaces, such as old cob, soft brick or soft stone walls, it will consolidate the surface and provide a key for subsequent coats to adhere to.
2. On thirsty backgrounds, such as earth, soft brick, soft stone, or concrete block, it will help to control suction (how quickly the backing draws moisture out of the fresh lime mortar) for subsequent coats, and thus minimise shrinkage and consequent cracking.
3. On dense, impervious masonry, where there will be no suction between the backing and the lime mortar (essential for adequate bonding), it will provide a mechanical key for subsequent coats. The force of the throwing or spraying will engender a successful bond.

4. On very flat surfaces such as smooth concrete blocks, modern engineered bricks or smooth earth blocks, it will provide a key for subsequent coats.

Traditionally, the different coats have been named depending on the function they provide within the plastering/rendering system. For example, the first coat is often called the 'scratch coat' because it provides the key for the subsequent coats to be securely attached.

The second coat is often called the 'straightening coat' because its purpose is to even out any minor and major irregularities in the wall, to provide an even plane for the finishing coat.

The third coat is often called the 'finishing coat' because it is the final, decorative coat that provides the desired aesthetic and functional outcome.

There are two schools of thought about how long you should wait between coats before applying the next one. These are as follows:

1 Allow the previous coat to dry only up to the 'green hard' stage (resists indentation from a knuckle, but is soft enough to be scratched with a fingernail). This entails leaving it for up to one week before applying the next coat, depending on the drying conditions.

The positive attributes:
- Better bonding can occur between the coats.
- Less thorough dampening of the wall surfaces are necessary for good bonding between the coats.

The negative attributes:
- It will take longer for the base coats to fully carbonate (if using a non-hydraulic lime putty) and gain their full strength.
- There is a risk of further shrinkage in the base coats that could affect subsequent coats.

2 Allow the base coats to fully dry and start carbonating. This entails leaving the coat to dry/cure for up to three weeks before applying the next one.

The positive attributes:
- There should be no more shrinkage in the base coats.
- The carbonation process will have started making the base coat stronger.

The negative attributes:
- More thorough dampening is needed between the coats to ensure adequate bonding, meaning that there is more dependence on a good mechanical key (scratching up) between the coats.
- There is a much longer period needed between the coats for the completion of the work, which will have implications for how long the scaffolding is up (costs), and to the schedule.

The above points referring to the carbonation of the mortar are more pertinent when using non-hydraulic lime putties than when using natural hydraulic limes. The waiting times can thus be reduced when working with NHLs.

A recommended middle ground between the two schools of thought entails waiting longer before applying the straightening coat, because this coat will be buried deeper, and will hence have less access to the air for carbonation to occur; and waiting less between application of the finishing coat onto the straightening coat. The straightening coat is closer to the surface, and will have more opportunity to access the carbon dioxide in the atmosphere for full carbonation and strengthening to occur.

Pre-application: preparing the walls
The overall performance and successful application of a lime plaster or render is dependent on the success of the bonding of the first coat to the wall

substrate. It is therefore of vital importance that the wall is prepared in a manner that will optimise this bonding. For information regarding wall preparation, refer to Chapter 1.

General lime rendering/ plastering application processes

Refer to Chapter 2 for specific information on the application techniques described below. The application techniques below outline the most common techniques used at each stage of the process. This does not, however, mean that these exact techniques must be used. Everyone must find their own rhythm, and use methods and tools that suit their strength, level of experience, and preference. It is, however, necessary that certain rules are observed, such as adequate compression and not applying the mortar when it is too wet. As long as these and other rules are observed, it is possible to arrive at them in whichever way suits the individual.

1. Preparing the material. If using a non-hydraulic lime mortar that has been stored for maturation, it should be knocked up and hair added, immediately before use. If using a pozzolan, it should be added to the mix at this point. If using a natural hydraulic lime, mix up immediately before work is to begin.

2. Dampening the wall. Dampen the wall immediately prior to application with a fine mist sprayer. Do this a couple of times if the wall is really dry. Allow the water to sink into the substrate before applying the mortar.

3. Applying the stipple coat (optional). If applying a stipple coat, further work the mix to a slurry by adding water. This can be applied with a harling trowel or a render gun. A stipple coat should be no thicker than 3 - 5 mm ($^1/_8$ – $^7/_{32}$"). Wait for at least two days to allow the stipple coat to dry and cure, before applying the scratch

coat. This coat is not appropriate if applying onto lath or reed mat. The stipple coat should not be scratched up, nor pressed back with a trowel as the natural rough stipple provides the key for the next coat.

4. Applying the scratch coat. Dampen the stipple coat (if applied), before applying the scratch coat. The scratch coat can be applied with a hawk and laying on trowel, thrown on by hand, harled on, or sprayed on with a render gun. Refer to Chapter 2 for guidance on each of these methods. Once applied, the scratch coat must be 'scratched up' using a comb scratcher to create a key for the next coat. If applied using the latter two methods, the natural stipple can be left, which will provide an excellent key in itself. Alternatively, the mortar can be pressed back with a trowel, and scratched as above.

If working in hot, dry conditions the scratch coat should be misted down at intervals, to prevent it from drying out too quickly, and covered with damp sheeting if exposed to direct sunlight. If working in rainy conditions, the new work should be protected from driving rain, either via the overhang from scaffolding or by hanging some form of sheeting to protect it.

Minor hairline cracks in the scratch coat are acceptable. Larger cracks are an indication that something has not been carried out correctly or there is structural movement in the building (see troubleshooting guide at the end of this chapter). If possible, they should be worked back with a wooden float (see below regarding scouring), or the mortar removed and reapplied, if severe.

5. Applying the straightening coat. The function of the straightening coat is to create the exact profile that you want the wall to take. This coat may not be necessary if you have a relatively flat wall, or if an undulating wall is preferred.

Applying lime renders and plasters

Dampen the wall substrate as necessary before work begins.

Apply scratch coat using a steel 'laying-on' trowel or other tool of your choice.

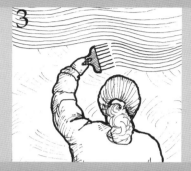

Scratch up damp plaster with a comb scratcher roughly 1-2 hours later.

Apply the straightening coat onto the pre-dampened scratch coat.

Scour the straightening coat using a wooden float once it has firmed up.

Scratch up the straightening coat with a 'devil float'.

Apply the final coat onto the pre-dampened straightening coat.

Scour the final coat using a wooden float once it has firmed up.

Finish as desired and carry out necessary aftercare.

Before application begins, any protruding bits of mortar should be scraped off with the side of a trowel. Dampen the scratch coat immediately prior to working, as before, and if warm and dry, dampen as you go. If the scratch coat is very dry, dampen the wall about one hour before work begins as well.

6. **Scouring the straightening coat.**
Once the straightening coat has firmed up, it is advantageous to scour the mortar with a wooden float. For an explanation of its functions and benefits, and for technique guidelines, refer to Chapter 2.

The scouring process produces a fairly flat and consolidated surface, lacking in key for the finishing coat to adhere to. To create this key, a 'devil float' should be used. A devil float is used at this stage for scoring the mortar instead of a comb or lath scratcher, because the indentations made are less deep. This is necessary because the finishing coats are thinner than the preceding coats, and a deep score may show through this final finish, or may cause cracking along the lines of the key.

7. **Applying the finishing coats.** The straightening coat should be allowed to firm up before applying the finishing coat. The finishing coat is best applied when the straightening coat is 'green hard'. It may be necessary to gently mist the straightening coat at intervals after its application, to prevent it from drying out too quickly, and to aid carbonation.
For top quality work (usually for conservation work), the finishing coat is best applied in two thin coats, at a total thickness of 3 mm ($^1/_8$") (1.5 mm ($^1/_{16}$") each). The first coat takes up the key and suction of the straightening coat, the second coat amalgamates into the first, providing a smooth, fluid finish. For less formal and external work it can be applied in one thicker coat.

The straightening coat should be lightly scraped with the edge of a steel trowel and lightly brushed to remove any protruding plaster/ render created by the devil floating.

Thoroughly dampen the wall before working. Apply the first coat using a steel laying-on trowel as before. A wood skim float can also be used to provide a rougher surface for keying in the second coat. Take care to really compress the lime into the key beneath. Do not overwork. Because it is so fine and the coating so thin, a little will go a long way.

Allow this first coat to firm up very slightly for roughly one hour (it could be as little as ½ hour, depending on drying conditions). The first coat should still be tacky to the touch. Lay the second coat into the first, ensuring that full contact is made between the two so that they amalgamate into one.

8. **Scouring the finishing coat.** The second coat should be allowed to set up, and then scoured with a wood float to help compress and tighten as before, to provide a durable, hard finish. Mist the wall lightly as you go if necessary. This step is not easy to achieve on undulating walls and can therefore be eliminated.

9. **Finishing work.** Differing finish textures can be achieved with a variety of different tools and techniques. These different finishes are for aesthetic as well as functional purposes. The main differences are between those intended for internal and external use. For guidance on which finish to use when, and for technique guidelines, refer to Chapter 2.

Post-application: essential aftercare

For a non-hydraulic lime mortar to fully and effectively carbonate, and for a natural hydraulic lime to achieve a successful hydraulic set, it is imperative that:

Bill Sargent

Traditional plasterer and pargeter

Bill Sargent is a practising master lime plasterer and pargeter, who comes from a long family line of traditional lime plasterers. He has helped to reinvigorate the art of pargeting across the UK, and is one of the most well-respected authorities on the craft. The craft of pargeting involves the formation of three-dimensional raised designs on external walls. It is a practice that is used throughout the world. In the UK, it is traditionally created by forming relief work in the lime render finish.

Has the way that you work with lime and your approach to pargeting changed in any way from your forefathers practices?

My approach to the work is the same now as when I started. The system I use is the same as my grandfather's. We always mix the sand and lime in a 3:1 ratio. One mixed tonne per 25 yards of finished wall 'two coats'. This is then covered for at least 30 days to allow the lime to bond with the sand to reduce cracking. Plastic sheets are used for this. I always put chopped straw in the mix. I am still the only lime plasterer I know who does this. I suppose you could say I work in a style that would not be out of place in the Edwardian Era.

Please give us a short history of the practice of pargeting in the UK, and the significance of some of the most common pargeting designs.

Henry VIII brought over the Italian Stuccoists to work on one of his royal palaces (all gone now). This is the first recorded exterior freehand work that I know of. However, I am sure that simple designs were in use before this time, people being what they are. Later, the Flemish migrants came over to the UK bringing along the craft with them. It was not long before local craftsmen started to imitate their work.

Most of the old work I have repaired is very similar to church carvings, stone carvings on churches, etc. These people did not travel far so the church was a strong influence on them, and nature of course.

Please could you give a brief breakdown as to how the pargeting process is carried out.

Pargetting is usually done in 2 coats of exterior render. When the top coat has been floated, I draw on my design with a small tool (small trowel) and start to build up, i.e. model the work. I can usually build up to 50mm (2") in place. If it is heavy work, a wire frame armature is used. This is filled with straw or I use twigs (traditional).

Please could you give our readers some tips for plain lime plastering work.

When plastering onto wood lath, soak your laths well before use. Dry laths will warp and expand and damage your work.
Always bond your laths every 37cm (15").
Leave a gap. A lot of failure is because laths are too close.
Leave your lime-aggregate mix to sit for at least 30 days before use. This stops work shrinking and cracking.
Always use lots of fibre – use ½ kilo per barrow of hair and 1 bucket of chopped straw. I use chopped straw because it acts as a fibre, plus it holds moisture. This allows for the render to cure slowly and holds moisture for the next coat.
Always cover the backing coat with hessian and keep damp (this is achieved by misting it down regularly). The slower it sets, the better the job.
Never over-scour the top coat – it will fail if you do. Float when still green, in a circular motion to compress the aggregate, then sponge with a damp sponge to create a smooth finish (external).
For an internal skim coat I always use a 1:1 (1 part lime : 1 part aggregate) mix of kiln dried sand and putty. Apply one coat, then lay down trowel to finish. Then run up with a rubber float. Next trowel off the fat, which could craze on the surface if not taken off.
Always make sure you use sharp sand with no rounded aggregate in it, and that the lime is well slaked and at least three months old.

1. Adequate protection of the new work is maintained for a certain period of time.
2. The rate at which the mortar dries out is controlled as much as possible. A lime mortar that dries slowly will carbonate into a strong crystalline form, as opposed to a soft, weak, chalky form.

To understand why this is so vital, please refer back to the sections in this chapter, which explain the processes of carbonation for non-hydraulic lime mortars, and the hydraulic setting mechanisms for natural hydraulic limes. The most common reason for failure in new lime work is due to its exposure to adverse weather conditions before being fully carbonated. Natural hydraulic limes, though less vulnerable in their early days, still require tending and protecting, albeit to a lesser extent. This is especially the case for the weaker hydraulic limes.

Protection of new work

New work must be protected from wind, strong draughts, direct rainfall and strong sun. This is so that the rate of drying is consistent, and so that the plaster/render does not dry too quickly, nor get saturated and wash away.

If using fixed scaffolding, the shade and protection created by the scaffolding boards will help to protect the walls from the brunt of the elements. Scaffolding should therefore be kept up for an extra three weeks after external rendering work has been completed, in most cases. Fixed scaffolding can also be used to hang hessian sacking or debris netting in front of new external render work to protect it from the more extreme elements. The sacking/netting should be set back from the render sufficiently to allow adequate circulation. Old sheets can also be used. Sheets or hessian can be kept damp if weather is excessively hot to help maintain a moist environment for the curing render. In hot weather, it is best to avoid using plastic sheeting, because condensation may be transferred onto the wall. This may prevent drying.

If not using fixed scaffolding, protective sheeting can be hung from guttering or attached to roof eaves, with an adequate air gap.

Ensure that all gutters and drainpipes are operating effectively to avoid channels of rain from running down the face of the wall and ruining the new render.

Controlling the rate of drying through gentle misting of new work

The aim of misting the new work with water is to ensure that it does not dry out too quickly, and for non-hydraulic limes, to ensure that adequate carbon dioxide is carried into the full thickness of the plaster/render for carbonation. For natural hydraulic limes, misting with water will provide the moisture necessary for a strong hydraulic set.

For both interior and exterior work with non-hydraulic lime, the wall should be gently misted at least twice a day for one week after work has been completed. For natural hydraulic limes this can be reduced to about four days. This should be increased if work is drying out quickly. Monitor closely.

Any small cracks that start to appear should be caught early on. If the wall has been kept adequately moistened, it should be possible to press the cracks back in with a damp sponge or sponge float, and then finished with the same technique used at the time of finishing. Although not an ideal situation, any cracks that will not yield to being re-worked can be filled with 'fine stuff' if not too excessive or large. The area concerned should be dampened, prior to application, with a damp sponge. Squeeze the 'fine stuff' into the crack and work it tightly into the seams with the sponge, to create a seamless finish. Any minor cracking can be filled in with the multiple applications of limewash to follow. Some minor cracks may even repair themselves because of lime's ability to self-heal.

For internal work, heating should be kept on a steady, low heat, or not on at all. In all cases, avoid cycles of hot and cold temperatures. Circulation should be encouraged to aid the curing process, but avoid direct draughts from open windows. Do not use heaters to force dry new work externally or internally.

Although weather can be unpredictable, the best precautionary measures that can be taken for optimum curing is to plan work around ideal weather conditions. Lime work is best carried out in late spring to early summer, and late summer to autumn, when the weather should be moderate. Of course, schedules do not always work out as planned, and you may find yourself forced to work in less than ideal situations. If this is the case, as long as temperatures are not 5^{0}C (41^{0}F) or lower, or above 30^{0}C (86^{0}F), it is possible as long as sufficient attention is paid to ensure that the above points are carried out diligently.

By far the best type of weather for external lime work is mild, with a very light drizzle. This will prevent too rapid drying of the render. The drizzly rain has the added advantage of carrying carbon dioxide into the render in the form of carbonic acid, thus ensuring optimum conditions for the carbonation of non-hydraulic lime.

Applying lime render/plaster onto wood lath or reed mat

The main difference between applying lime onto wood lath and solid wall substrates, is in the application of the first coat – the 'pricking up' coat – onto the lath. The application of the remaining coats is very similar to the general techniques onto solid walls. Lime is normally applied in three coats onto the lath. It is vitally important that the wood laths are thoroughly wetted the day before application, and then about fifteen minutes before work commences. Failure to adequately do so will result in excessive cracking as the dry wood quickly draws the moisture from the plaster/

render. The lath could also potentially swell once the mortar is applied, causing excessive cracking.

The application of the 'pricking up' coat onto the lath must be carried out effectively, as it provides the key onto the lath that holds itself and all the subsequent coats in place.

The mortar must be pressed on with enough pressure so it is adequately squeezed through the gaps in the lath, where it subsequently hangs over to form the key. These are known as 'nubs', and act as hooks to grip onto the back of the lath and anchor the plaster face in place. The pressure must not be too forceful, however, so as to squeeze too much material through the gaps, causing the nubs to fall off under their own weight. For similar reasons, the pricking-up coat must not be overworked.

Tips for application of the 'pricking up' coat:
1. Always start from the top of the wall and work down, so as not to knock off nubs formed below.
2. Work in a diagonal upward stroke.
3. Work with an even, direct pressure, slightly reverberating the trowel to work the material between the laths.
4. Always have enough mortar on the trowel to allow for a suitable amount to be pressed through the lath spaces.
5. Adding suitable amounts of hair to the mix is vitally important in creating a strong background, and for the formation of the nubs. Slightly more hair should be used in the 'pricking-up' coat than in subsequent coats.
6. The 'pricking-up' coat should never be scoured or devil-floated as this would apply too much pressure onto the lath, causing damage to the nubs and undermining the key.
7. The scratching of the 'pricking-up' coat should solely be carried out using a 3 or 4 pronged lath scratcher because it will cut less deeply than a comb scratcher, whilst providing the appropriate key for the subsequent coats.

Tom Woolley
&
Ian Pritchett

Tom Woolley is an architect, builder, researcher and teacher based in Northern Ireland. He was Professor of Architecture at Queen's University Belfast from 1991-2007, and is now acting as a professorial advisor to the new sustainable architecture course at the Centre for Alternative Technology in Wales. He is editor of the *Green Building Handbook*, author of *Natural Building*, and a forthcoming *Guide to Hemp and Lime Construction*, to be published in 2008.

Ian Pritchett is a leading authority on hemp-lime construction in the UK, as well as a manufacturer of hemp-lime and general lime products.

What are the basic ingredients of a hemp plaster?

TW: *Hemp, aggregate and a lime-based binder.*

IP: *Aggregate is usually sand.*

How is a hemp lime plaster/render different from a normal lime plaster/render? Why use it?

TW: *The hemp acts as insulation, so hemp lime plasters are ideal for upgrading the thermal performance of solid wall buildings. It can also be used for its decorative appearance.*

IP: *The hemp and lime is also quite robust and can thus be used externally as well as internally. It adheres well to most natural masonry materials, as well as straw bales and earth.*

What kind of finish can I expect to achieve?

TW: *It can be finished quite rough (like woodchip wallpaper), or smooth with bits of hemp showing. It can also have a fine lime finish applied to completely cover it.*

What is the availability of the material?

TW: *Where can you buy the ingredients? Through* Lime Technology/Castle *outlets or* St Astier *outlets.*

IP: *The range of materials will, most likely, also be available through* Wolseley *builders merchants.*

What are some sample plaster/render mixes?

TW: *Although it can be mixed from scratch using lime, it is normal to use a pre-mix of the binder and aggregate, then mix in the hemp shiv.*

IP: *The premixed binder ensures quality.*

Do I need to use a specially prepared hemp hurd with the lime?

TW: *The finer grades of hemp shiv are better for finer finishes.*

What kind of lime do I use?

IP: *Experts in France have been working on hemp and lime for 15 years and have developed pre-formulated binders. Both* Lime Technology *and* St Astier *have these products. Some people ask why spend more on using such a proprietary patented product when you can mix up 'any old lime'. The answer is simple: using the proprietary product guarantees success!*

What are the environmental benefits of using a hemp lime plaster/render over using a plain lime plaster/render?

IP: *Using hemp means that the plastering includes an insulation material, thus improving the thermal performance of the building. The insulation material is a crop-based renewable product which has absorbed carbon dioxide in its production.*

8. Scratching should never be carried out in the same direction as the lath, as this will cause cracking along the line of the laths. Scratch diagonally at a 45 degree angle to the lath, creating a diamond hatch pattern, 25 mm (1") apart from one another.

9. Application of a lime mortar directly onto lath should never be by means of harling, spraying or throwing, as the crucial nubs created on the back-side of the lath will not be formed.

Three steps to applying the 'pricking-up' coat onto wood lath and reed mat

For subsequent steps please refer to the general application steps above.

1. Pre-wet the laths (not reed mat) with water the day before application, and then again about 15 minutes prior to work commencing.

2. Apply the pricking-up coat 10mm ($^3/_8$") in thickness using a steel laying-on trowel and hawk.

3. Allow the plaster to firm up for a few hours (depending on the atmospheric conditions). Using a lath scratcher, scratch the surface of the mortar in a diagonal lattice pattern.

   Allow the pricking-up coat to dry and harden for up to one week (depending on atmospheric conditions). Mist the surface lightly with water if the mortar is drying too rapidly.

Applying lime onto straw-bale walls

Straw-bale walls can be plastered in a number of different ways. It is possible to either use lime for all coats, or to substitute the scratch coat and/or straightening coat with an earth plaster and then use lime for the final coat. It is also possible to use an earth plaster for all coats, but this is most suitable for internal plastering, dry climates or extremely sheltered areas. This is due to the less durable nature of earthen plasters against the elements, and hence their inability to adequately protect the straw bales (see Chapter 4 for more information on this).

Using an earth plaster for the base coats and lime for the finishing coats has some advantages and some disadvantages. Traditionally, this method has been used on earth and masonry walls in the UK, and throughout the world. This system can be used successfully on straw-bale walls as long as the inherent weaknesses are understood and steps are taken to minimise these.

Advantages:

• Earth plasters have a much lower environmental impact than the production of lime, and can largely be made on site and from local materials.
• Earth plasters are much less expensive than lime, although when making and mixing your own it will take up more time and labour.
• Earth plasters are very suitable to be used on straw bales because of their ability to self-seal, and because of their hydrophilic (water-loving) nature (see Chapter 4), thus protecting the bales from moisture.
• Earth plasters need less time to dry and cure, and can therefore speed up the plastering/ rendering schedule. (Although base coats must be completely dry before application of the final coat, and this may take at least a few weeks to achieve, especially in damp weather and in internal areas).

Disadvantages:

• Earth and lime have different rates of expansion and contraction. Earth plasters have much greater flexibility, and will therefore move more than lime during changes in temperature and humidity. This means that there will be a high chance of differential movement between the two materials, potentially causing cracking in the lime top coats, especially at the corners, where two walls join at right angles.
• Earth and lime will bond less well than earth on earth or lime on lime, so there is a potential for

Left: Lime render applied onto a straw-bale studio. *Right:* Traditional French lime render applied onto an ancient timber frame structure.

delamination of the lime finishing coat from the earth base coats.

Steps to minimise or eliminate these potential problems:

- Use curved corners instead of right angles to minimise friction at the corner trouble-spots.
- Increase the tensile strength of both the lime and earth plasters by adding lots of fibre to the mixes, to accommodate differential movement.
- Ensure that the earth plaster coat is left very rough or keyed up to provide a good mechanical key for the adhesion of the lime onto the earth.
- Ensure that the earth plaster is very well dampened before applying the lime coat, to provide good suction between the two materials. This can be enhanced using lime water or by applying a coat of weak lime wash onto the earth plaster immediately before application of the lime.
- Ensure that the lime is pressed firmly into the earthen plaster during application, and by subsequent scouring with a wood float.

For applying earthen plasters onto straw-bale walls as base coats, refer to Chapter 4.

Preparing straw-bale walls for plastering

Preparing the straw-bale walls for plastering is essential for successful results. This involves trimming the bales and stuffing the crevices between the bales. This has been covered in Chapters 2 and 4.

The coat system for straw-bale walls

The coat system for applying lime onto straw-bale walls is very similar to other walling systems already discussed, but with a few exceptions. Before applying the scratch coat, an initial thin coat of a lime-aggregate slurry is applied to the bales using a render gun or by hand. Its function is to engender a good bond between the lime and straw, and to create the key for the subsequent scratch coat. A steel trowel is less suitable for this job because it does not enable the lime to be thoroughly worked into all the crevices between the pieces of straw, ensuring a good bond.

The hands are perfect for really working it in, and a render gun will achieve this via the force with which it is sprayed on. A render gun finish can be worked in with a trowel, but will then need to be sufficiently roughened up to provide a key for the next coat. A hand-worked coat should be left very rough, with the finger marks and stubby bits of straw showing through. These will provide the key for the next coat.

Harling

The term 'harl' refers to any coarse mortar (i.e. lime mixed with coarse aggregates) which is thrown onto the walls of a building, generally

132

Left: New cob house with internal lime finishes and relief work. *Right:* Pigmented lime render in Saint-Antonin-Noble-Val, France.

on the external face. There are many regional variations throughout the UK, and the name 'harling' is technically the Scottish term for this method. Other regional terms include 'roughcast' in the south of England, 'scatt' in the south-west and 'wet-dash' in Cumbria. Generally the technique is the same, with slight variations between different regions. The effect created is a rough, stipply textured surface.

Harled coats can be used in a number of ways. As previously described, it is an excellent method to use on friable wall surfaces such as old cob, brick or stone walls, as a 'stipple' coat (pre-scratch coat) to consolidate the wall and provide a good key, before applying subsequent coats. It also serves well as a base coat onto dense, impervious stones, bricks, or concrete blocks to provide a mechanical key for the scratch coat, where bonding to the substrate via suction between the lime and the wall would be absent. Similarly, for very smooth, flat wall substrates which lack adequate key for the scratch coat to attach into, a harled stipple coat will provide the necessary key. It can be used internally as well as externally.

A lime finish thrown on in this way achieves the above attributes because of the superior contact gained from the force of the application. This provides an excellent bond between the mortar and the wall substrate. It also ensures optimum compaction of the mortar, due to the expulsion of air as it is thrown.

In addition to the above, a harled finish can be used as an external finishing coat in severe weather situations (hence its common use in Scotland). When used in this situation, the open, rough, texture of the harl finish works to slow down the rate of water runoff down the face of the wall. This is compared with a flat, smooth render surface, which could encourage large quantities of water runoff to be deposited in vulnerable areas, such as the base of the wall. Additionally, the ability of lime finishes to absorb, hold and release excess moisture, thus preventing penetration into the wall, is enhanced due to the increased surface area inherent in the stippled 'harl'.

An external harled finish can be achieved in one of two ways: either by building up a series of fairly thin harled coats to the desired thickness, or by applying one or two trowelled (i.e. flat) render coats first, and then applying a final harled finish on top. A harl mix can be made with a non-hydraulic lime putty, with or without a pozzolan, or a natural hydraulic lime, depending on the conditions in which it is to be used. The lime should always be mixed with coarse aggregates to achieve the rough texture. Mix as described in the mixing section above. A harled finish can be achieved using a harling trowel, which is specifically designed for the job. A render gun can also be used to cover large expanses of wall in a shorter time period. For detailed guidelines on both application techniques, refer to Chapter 2. This is messy work, especially for beginners, so wearing goggles, gloves, protecting exposed skin and covering floors, drainpipes, doors and windows etc., is essential.

Application of a lime mortar onto wattle and daub

Applying lime onto wattle and daub panels is a simplified version of what has been previously described in the general application techniques. Wattle and daub panels generally only need one coat of a lime plaster or render. For successful application, three principal rules should be observed:

1. Adequate keying-up of the daub.
2. Adequate wetting of the daub prior to application.
3. Adequate hair should be present in the lime mix for maximum tensile strength – allowing for movement within panels in the timber frame.

Traditionally, the daub on the wattle was ingeniously keyed using a small wooden peg no larger than the little finger. This was used to create downward pointing holes roughly 25 mm (1") deep. These holes provide an anchoring point for the lime coating to hook into. They should be created when the daub is still wet, and then allowed to firm up and dry with the daub before lime application.

Prior to application of the lime coating, the daub should be sprayed with a mister, allowing the holes to fill with water. This water should be given time to penetrate into the daub mixture, which creates sufficient moisture enabling the lime to dry out very slowly (traditionally, external was simply a thick daubcoat and lime wash). This will develop a strong plaster/render, with very little shrinkage and cracking, and should minimise the amount of aftercare necessary. A fibre-rich lime mix will help the plaster/render to accommodate the movement of the timber frame, preventing cracking. It will also help to prevent shrinkage of the plaster/render away from the edge of the timber panel.

Applying lime onto conventional plaster board

Conventional plaster board is not an ideal surface for the application of lime plasters. It is best to use an alternative backing material, an assortment of which are described below and in Chapter 1, or use wooden lath or reed mat. If plaster board is your only option, it is necessary to apply a primer first, to provide a sufficient bonding between the lime and the substrate. Such primers can be purchased from some specialist lime suppliers (see naturalbuildingresources.com) or can be home-made (see Chapter 1). Before applying the primer the joints between the boards should be taped and scrimmed. After the primer has been applied (as per manufacturers' instructions), lime plaster coatings can be applied as per the general instructions above. Normally, however, only a scratch coat and finishing coat is necessary because the wall surface is flat.

Applying lime onto mineralised wood wool, wood fibre and clay board

All these alternative backing materials provide excellent alternatives to plasterboard, and excellent surfaces onto which lime mortars can be applied. They each contain either an excellent mechanical or physical keying mechanism within their structure. Lime mortars can be applied directly to their surfaces after pre-dampening as normal. The board joints should be prepared as per instructed in Chapter 1. Again, the straightening coat can be eliminated due to the flatness inherent in the boarding. General application details should be followed. ∎

MEDIUM TO DENSE MASONRY

Sheltered positions / internal applications

COAT	THICKNESS	TYPE OF AGGREGATES	TYPE OF LIME	FIBRE	MIX RATIO
Stipple coat (optional)	3.5mm	sharp/gritty 3 - 0.075mm	NHL3.5 / 2 or putty or putty + pozzolan	No No Yes	1 lime : 2 sand 1 lime : 2 sand 1 lime : 2 sand + 10% pozz
Scatch coat	10 - 15mm	sharp/coarse 3.35 - 0.075mm	NHL3.5 / 2 or putty or putty + pozzolan	Optional Yes Yes	1 lime : 3 sand 1 lime : 3 sand 1 lime : 3 sand + 10% pozz
Straightening coat	8 - 10mm	sharp/coarse 3.35 - 0.075mm	NHL3.5 / 2 or putty	Optional Yes	1 lime : 2.5 sand 1 lime : 2 sand
Top coat	3 - 5mm	sharp/fine 1.18 - 0.075mm	NHL3.5 / 2 Putty	No No	1 lime : 2.5 sand 1 lime : 1 sand

Moderate to severe exposure

COAT	THICKNESS	TYPE OF AGGREGATES	TYPE OF LIME	FIBRE	MIX RATIO
Stipple coat (optional)	3.5mm	sharp/gritty 3 - 0.075mm	NHL 5 or putty + pozzolan	No No	1 lime : 2.5 sand 1 lime : 3 sand + 10% pozz
Scatch coat	10 - 15mm	sharp/coarse 3.35 - 0.075mm	NHL5 or putty + pozzolan	No Yes Yes	1 lime : 2 sand 1 lime : 2.5 sand 1 lime : 2.5 sand + 10% pozz
Straightening coat	8 - 10mm	sharp/coarse 3.35 - 0.075mm	NHL5 / 3.5 or putty + pozzolan	No Yes	1 lime : 2.5 sand 1 lime : 2 sand
Top coat	3 - 5mm	sharp/fine 1.18 - 0.075mm	NHL 3.5 or putty + pozzolan	No No	1 lime : 2.5 sand 1 lime : 1 sand

SOFT BRICK AND STONE & EARTH WALLS

Sheltered positions / internal applications

COAT	THICKNESS	TYPE OF AGGREGATES	TYPE OF LIME	FIBRE	MIX RATIO
Stipple coat (optional)	3.5mm	sharp/gritty 5 - 0.075mm	Putty	No	1 lime : 2 sand
Scatch coat	10 - 12mm	sharp/gritty 3.35 - 0.075mm	Putty	No	1 lime : 2.5 sand
Straightening coat	5 - 10mm	sharp/gritty 3.35 - 0.075mm	Putty	No	1 lime : 3 sand
Top coat	3 - 5mm	sharp/fine 1.18 - 0.075mm	Putty	No	1 lime : 1 sand

Moderate to severe exposure

COAT	THICKNESS	TYPE OF AGGREGATES	TYPE OF LIME	FIBRE	MIX RATIO
Stipple coat (optional)	3.5mm	sharp/gritty 5 - 0.075 mm	NHL 2 or putty + pozzolan	No No	1 lime : 1.5 sand 1 lime : 2 sand + 10% pozz
Scatch coat	10 - 12mm	sharp/gritty 3.35 - 0.075mm	NHL 2 or putty + pozzolan	Yes Yes	1 lime : 2 sand 1 lime : 2.5 sand + 10% pozz
Straightening coat	5 - 10mm	sharp/gritty 3.35 - 0.075mm	NHL 2 or putty + pozzolan	Yes Yes	1 lime : 2.5 sand 1 lime : 2 sand + 10% pozz
Top coat	3 - 5mm	sharp/fine 1.18 - 0.075mm	NHL 2 or putty + pozzolan	No No	1 lime : 2.5 sand 1 lime : 1 sand + 10% pozz

STRAW BALE

COAT	THICKNESS	TYPE OF AGGREGATES	TYPE OF LIME	FIBRE	MIX RATIO
Stipple coat (optional)	3.5mm	sharp/gritty 3 - 0.075mm	NHL2 / 3.5 or putty	No No	1 lime : 1.5 sand 1 lime : 3 sand
Scatch coat	10 - 15mm	sharp/coarse 3.35 - 0.075mm	NHL2 / 3.5 or putty	No Yes	1 lime : 2 sand 1 lime : 2.5 sand
Straightening coat	8 - 10mm	sharp/coarse 3.35 - 0.075mm	NHL2 or putty	No Yes	1 lime : 2.5 sand 1 lime : 2 sand
Top coat	3 - 5mm	sharp/fine 1.18 - 0.075mm	NHL2 Putty	No No	1 lime : 2.5 sand 1 lime : 1 sand

Moderate to severe exposure

COAT	THICKNESS	TYPE OF AGGREGATES	TYPE OF LIME	FIBRE	MIX RATIO
Stipple coat (optional)	3.5mm	sharp/gritty 3 - 0.075mm	NHL3.5 or putty + pozzolan	No No	1 lime : 2 sand 1 lime : 3 sand + 10% pozz
Scatch coat	10 - 15mm	sharp/coarse 3.35 - 0.075mm	NHL3.5 or putty + pozzolan	No Yes	1 lime : 2.5 sand 1 lime : 2.5 sand + 10% pozz
Straightening coat	8 - 10mm	sharp/coarse 3.35 - 0.075mm	NHL3.5 or putty + pozzolan	No Yes	1 lime : 3 sand 1 lime : 2 sand + 10% pozz
Top coat	3-5mm	sharp/fine 1.18 - 0.075mm	NHL3.5 or putty + pozzolan	No No	1 lime : 3.5 sand 1 lime : 1 sand + 10% pozz

LATH & PLASTER AND REED MATS

COAT	THICKNESS	TYPE OF AGGREGATES	TYPE OF LIME	FIBRE	MIX RATIO
Scatch coat	10 - 12mm	sharp/gritty 3.35 - 0.075mm	Putty	Yes	1 lime : 3 sand
Straightening coat	5 - 10mm	sharp/gritty 3.35 - 0.075mm	Putty	Yes	1 lime : 2 sand
Top coat	3 - 5mm	sharp/fine 1.18 - 0.075mm	Putty	Yes	1 lime : 1.5 sand

Moderate to severe exposure

COAT	THICKNESS	TYPE OF AGGREGATES	TYPE OF LIME	FIBRE	MIX RATIO
Scatch coat	10 - 12mm	sharp/coarse 3.35 - 0.075mm	NHL 3.5 or Putty + Pozzolan	Yes Yes	1 lime : 3 sand 1 lime : 2.5 sand + 10% pozz
Straightening coat	7 - 10mm	sharp/coarse 3.35 - 0.075mm	NHL 3.5 or Putty + Pozzolan	Yes Yes	1 lime : 2 sand 1 lime : 2 sand + 10% pozz
Top coat	3 - 5mm	sharp/fine 1.18 - 0.075mm	NHL 2 or Putty + Pozzolan	No No	1 lime : 2.5 sand 1 lime : 1.5 sand + 10% pozz

Troubleshooting guide

Common problems with lime plaster/render and their solutions.

Fault:
Lack of bonding to substrate or between coats. Light hollow sound when tapped. Bulging or slumping during application.

Possible causes:
1. Inadequately prepared wall substrate i.e. dusty, loose material on surface, friable wall surface.
2. Inadequate dampening of wall surface prior to application or oversaturation of wall substrate.
3. Inadequate key.
4. New work exposed to freezing temperatures when still wet.
5. Plaster/render applied too thickly.
6. Lack of adequate compaction and compression of each coat.
7. Plaster/render slumps/bulges during application.
8. Salt crystallisation.

Solutions:
1. (i) Ensure wall substrate brushed down with a stiff brush/broom to remove all loose material before work commences.
   (ii) Apply a stipple coat to consolidate friable surfaces.
2. (i) Ensure wall substrate and all previous coats are dampened prior to application and the day before, if it is a thirsty background.
   (ii) Allow walls to dry out before application.
   (iii) Allow dampening of water to soak in before application.
3. (i) On flat, smooth substrates apply a stipple coat.
   (ii) Carry out adequate scratching-up techniques before

application of subsequent coats.
4. Do not work if it will be 5°C (41°F) or below in the 1-2 months after application.
5. Observe correct thicknesses (see chart overleaf).
6. (i) Ensure proper compaction at time of application.
   (ii) Scour sufficiently where appropriate.
7. (i) Too much water in mix.
   (ii) Wrong sands or aggregates used – grain too rounded, not well graded.
   (iii) Inadequate key.
   (iv) Applied too thickly.
   (v) Inadequately dampened.
8. See fault below.

Fault:
White splotches on surface. Efflorescence (salt crystals showing up on surface). Damp patches.

Possible causes:
1. Salt present in aggregates used, in water or wall substrate.
2. Damp patches due to presence of salt, drawing moisture from air into wall.

Solutions:
1. (i) Ensure that washed aggregates are used
   (ii) Use clean potable water.
   (iii) Normally occurs when building fabric has been covered in a non-breathable wall finish, i.e. cement. Remove cement, allow building to release excess moisture. A sacrificial clay/lime poultice may need to be used to draw out the salts. Seek specialist advice.
2. As above.

Fault:
Powdering. Flakiness. General weakness of plaster or render. Crumbling.

Possible causes:
1. Rapid drying out of new work preventing adequate curing (carbonation/hydration).
2. Insufficient amount of aggregate.
3. Inadequately matured non-hydraulic lime putty used.
4. Too much water in mix.
5. Lack of adequate compaction and compression of each coat.
6. Improperly stored/damaged or old NHLs used.
7. Overworking lime coat with steel trowel during application process – brings out the fat of the lime to the surface creating a thin crust of lime devoid of aggregates. When drys and hardens, creates a weak, crusty surface.

Solutions:
1. (i) Curing is at optimum in moist warm conditions, encouraging slow drying out. Ensure adequate protection set up for optimizing the curing process.
   (ii) Ensure adequate misting of new work, post-completion.
   (iii) Do not render/plaster in 5°C (41°F) or below, or above 30° C (86°F) for at least 1-2 months post-completion.
   (iv) Leave scaffolding in place to protect new work for 2-3 weeks post completion.
2. (i) Ensure correct sands/aggregatess used i.e. not soft, rounded, and of one grade. Should be sharp, coarse, and well-graded.

(ii) Ensure that no silt or topsoil is in the sand or aggregates used

3. (i) Ensure that putty has been matured for at least three months (any good lime supplier will have done this already) for complete slaking of all quicklime material.
(ii) Store coarse stuff for a minimum of 2 days to encourage amalgamation of putty and aggregate particles.
(iii) Store with film of water, sealed in airtight containers.

4. Follow correct mixing procedures so no excess water is necessary to make the mix workable.

5. (i) Ensure adequate compaction at time of application.
(ii) Scour sufficiently where appropriate.

6. Do not use bags that have been exposed to moisture, that are ripped or damaged (they will begin to prematurely start to cure) or stored in excess of 6 months.

7. Do not overwork with steel trowel. Apply in direct, vigorous, strong strokes.

Fault:
Cracks in surface of render in excess of 1mm ($^3/_{64}$") (crazing or small cracks are OK in the scratch coat). Anything more than 2mm ($^3/_{32}$") could potentially be movement within the sub-structure of the building and should be monitored.

Possible causes:
1. Wrong ratio of lime to aggregate used, i.e. too lime-rich or not enough lime.

2. Wrong type of aggregate used, i.e. too rounded, not well graded.
3. Too much water used in mix.
4. Wall substrate of previous coat not adequately dampened or too wet.
5. Differential movement in backing materials.
6. Movement in structure of building.
7. Plaster/render coating applied too thick.
8. Plaster/render coating inadequately compacted into wall substrate or previous coat.
9. Lack of adequate protection and aftercare of fresh work.
10. Insufficient setting between coats.

Solutions:
1. (i) Seek advice from specialist lime supplier.
(ii) Do sand-void ratio test.
(iii) Carry out series of sample test patches.
2. (i) Seek advice from a specialist supplier.
3. Inadequate or inappropriate mixing. Non-hydraulic lime must be adequately worked so that additional water is not needed to be added to the mix.
4. Ensure correct dampening takes place immediately before work and as work progresses. For very thirsty backings you should wet the day before. Allow damp or newly constructed walls to dry out before applying new coatings. Allow pre-dampening water to soak in before application.

5. (i) Ensure different materials in substrate are tied together with appropriate materials.
(ii) Use a well haired plaster to improve tensile strength and minimise cracking.
6. Allow new-build structure or repairs to adequately settle/dry before applying renders and plasters.
7. (i) Refer to guide for appropriate thicknesses (overleaf). Dub out hollows in successive layers – not in one go – using pinning stones where necessary to decrease the amount of lime needed.
8. (i) Ensure proper compaction at time of application.
(ii) Scour sufficiently where appropriate.
9. Take all necessary precautions to ensure plaster/render does not dry out too quickly, including:
(i) Plaster at the right time of year and in correct weather conditions, not too cold or hot.
(ii) Leave fixed scaffolding up for 2-3 weeks post-completion for necessary protection.
(iii) Adequate misting of wall post-completion.
10. Allow for sufficient time between coats for hardening, drying and curing.

Monitor cracks for continuing movement in building and consult a structural engineer if cracks widen and persist. If building is stable, repair large cracks present in finish coat by opening out crack on either side by roughly 2mm ($^3/_{32}$") and fill with identical lime mortar mix.

4 Earth-based plasters & renders

Chapter 4

Earth plasters (also known as clay plasters) are currently enjoying a revival, after a long history of use in traditional buildings around the world. This resurgence is partly in the form of using home-made, locally resourced materials, and partly due to an emergence of ready to use, pre-manufactured earth plasters from both the USA and Europe. In this chapter we will use the term 'plaster' to denote both internal and external work.

Earth plasters, prepared at their most basic level, from clayey subsoil, aggregates and a natural form of fibre, would have been the first method of weatherproofing for primordial structures. This would have been due to the abundance of the necessary materials and the special qualities of the clay, specifically its ability to become plastic and malleable when wet, and hard and water-repellent when dry. Earth plasters have been used all over the world, in all climates, since shelter building began.

In the UK, earth plasters were routinely used on internal wall surfaces alongside lime, up until the end of the nineteenth century. Their regular and common use was due to the local abundance of the materials, and the fact that building lime and good quality aggregates were comparably expensive and sometimes difficult to obtain. Often they were used as an undercoat, to even out the wall surface before receiving a top-coat of lime plaster/render or limewash. Throughout the rest of the world the use of earth in plasters also has a rich history. In both Africa and the Americas, the application of earth plasters onto earth structures was traditionally women's work. The term 'enjarradora' is the special name given to women in the south-west states of

Below left: Earth plasters have been used in this bathroom to help regulate humidity. *Below right:* A beautiful external earth finish.

The natural earth plasters of this home create a warm, inviting atmosphere. Earth finishes by *Crocker Ltd*.

America who carried out these earth plastering techniques. Their methods of application and the materials used were highly specific from region to region, and indeed these traditions are still very much alive. In Africa, special relief work and painting carried out in earth plaster onto individual homes (known as 'litema') still remains a culturally significant way for people to decorate their homes and define their identity within the wider community.

There are many benefits to using earth plasters. They are porous, which means that they allow a building structure to breathe, so that it can act like a third skin around the building and its inhabitants. Earth plasters also have a thirst for moisture. This means that they can function to regulate levels of relative humidity in the atmosphere. They can safely absorb and hold moisture vapour within

their molecular structure when relative humidity levels are high, and then release it back into the atmosphere when relative humidity levels drop. As well as providing good quality internal air for the inhabitants, this mechanism also serves to protect the building fabric from moisture. Due to clay's thirst for moisture, and ability to hold onto it, this will also help prevent moisture from reaching materials that provide the structure of the building. It will also actively draw moisture away from these materials if they do get wet. For this reason, earth finishes are the perfect option for structures made of the softer, breathable materials, such as earth, straw-bale and wood. Earth plasters are now also being used in museums and galleries because of these characteristics, to regulate humidity and hence help to protect old and new works of art. An example of this is the Museum Kuppersmühle in Germany.

Earth plasters, if made without synthetic additives, are entirely non-toxic, making them ideal for those with chemical sensitivities. They even have the ability to absorb toxins from other materials and bind odours, such as cigarette smoke, to decrease levels of indoor pollution. Research is also currently being carried out in Germany into their ability to screen electromagnetic radiation, such as from computers and mobile phones (see *Modern Earthbuilding: Clay Plaster and Design*, Training course CD-Rom). On a more subjective and unquantifiable level, earth plasters generally feel good. They are soft to the eye, and can moderate temperature swings, making walls feel warm in winter and cool in summer. They also work acoustically to soften and round off sound, making them conducive to creating peaceful, calm spaces.

Like most materials made from 'natural' ingredients, they demand to be used respectfully and appropriately. They are often not generally conducive for external use, unless positioned in a very sheltered area, used in a predominantly dry climate, or in conjunction with special building design details, such as an external wrap around porch (see Chapter 2). If making an earth plaster from materials sourced on site and/or locally, the user must be prepared to become his or her own detective, to test and feel their way to a good mix through trial and error. If prepared this way, they can be inexpensive, but labour- and time-rich. The alternative is to purchase a ready-made, premanufactured earth plaster, which requires only the addition of water. These will provide consistent and excellent results (as long as all other due considerations are carried out effectively), but can be more costly.

It is very important to be aware that there are wide variations in clay over the world. For this reason, different craftspeople working with earth plasters will sometimes hold different opinions on recipes and methods of application. There is therefore no one formula that can be prescribed for success in all situations. This is perhaps one of the most exciting reasons to embark on using earth plasters.

Earth plasters are both dynamic and timeless. They can be used to create the most exquisite, contemporary, fine plaster finishes, but are equally at home in rustic, 'organic' and traditional environments. Clay subsoil, the main binder for creating these finishes, far from being just the earth beneath our feet, is an intelligent and chemically complex material. Yet at the same time it produces a finish that is easy to handle, and safe and simple to use. Capable of being applied in many different situations, the use of earth in buildings could make a very significant contribution to creating structures that are healthy, long-lasting, and which tread gently on the planet.

How earth plasters work: their science and mechanics

The formation of soil

Clay is but one element which makes up the soil covering the earth's surface. The science of soil formation is a complex subject. It brings into play many different elements that come together to form different types of soil in different parts of the world. To simplify this complex subject: soil is formed over time, due to the disintegration of the rocks making up the earth's crust. They are weathered both mechanically and chemically. Mechanical weathering involves the action of wind, agriculture and extreme weather conditions, such as heating and freezing. These act to shatter the rocks apart into smaller components. Chemical weathering involves the action of rainwater, charged with acids, which seeps into the soil and works a transformative magic to break up the parent rock and turn it into earth.

Clay is a mineral component of the soil. It predominantly originates from the weathering of feldspar. Feldspar is one of the most common minerals in the earth's crust. Clay is found in a band of soil known as the subsoil, so named because of its relative position underneath the topsoil. The topsoil is formed from organic material, derived mostly from decaying vegetable matter. It is the fine, dark, organic layer in which gardens are cultivated. The topsoil is not suitable for making an earth plaster with.

Along with clay, the subsoil also consists of particles of sand and silt. Sand, silt and clay are classified according to their particle size. These can be defined as (although authorities differ slightly): gravel 2mm to 75mm; sand 0.05mm to 2mm; silt 0.002mm to 0.05mm; and clay less than 0.002mm. Soils vary with regard to their proportions of sand, silt and clay, and this will have implications for the suitability of the soil for use within an earth plaster. For the purposes of making a sound earth plaster, the soil must consist of at least 10-20%clay minerals, and silt should be present in quantities of no more than 25% of this clay element.

The chemistry of clay

Clay minerals are present in a wide variety of forms. They belong to a large family and can be characterised by their layered, crystalline structure. There are three main members within the clay family, known as kaolinite, illite, and montmorillonite, with other transitional forms occurring within these: examples of these include kaolin, mica, and smectite respectively. These different clay mineral groups vary with regard to their chemical make-up, and hence all behave slightly differently when they come into contact with water. This behaviour is an important determining factor when selecting suitable clay for making up an earth plaster. This is because it has direct implications for how much the clay will expand and contract with water, which has a direct correlation with how much an earth plaster will shrink as it dries, how much cracking will occur in its dry state, and how it will interact with water once applied to the wall as a protective finish. To understand which of these clays are most

suitable for use in an earth plaster, and to understand how clays behave when they come into contact with moisture, it is advantageous to become aware of some of the more basic chemistry involved in their functioning.

Clay minerals derived from feldspar consist predominantly of microscopic particles of aluminium and silicon dioxides. These aluminium and silica molecules are shaped like plates, which are alternately stacked on top of each other. The alternate stacking between the aluminium and silica platelets creates an electrostatic charge between them. This electrostatic charge chemically attracts water into the spaces between the platelets. This is why clay is considered to be hydrophilic or, 'water-loving'. When present, this water acts as a bridge between the aluminium and silica platelets, bonding them tightly together to form a cohesive structure. When the spaces between the platelets are filled with these fine films of water, the platelets have the ability to slide over one another. This is why clay feels so smooth to the touch and is easily worked and moulded when wet. Clay also expands when the spaces between the platelets are filled and contracts when the water exits and the clay dries.

The presence and organisation of the aluminium and silica platelets determines a clay's tendency to attract and absorb water into its structure. These differences can be exhibited by the distinct behaviours between the main clay groups mentioned above. This is why some clays are more stable, and hence more suitable for clay plasters, than others. Bentonite, for example, is a very unstable clay. It will absorb large amounts of water into its structure, and expand and contract excessively (causing it to crack when it dries).

Clay has the ability to relinquish any absorbed moisture as quickly as it was taken on. This is through the process of evaporation. When the water evaporates from the body of the clay,

Earth plasters are highly versatile and can be used to create a wide range of finish effects, as shown in artist Roxanne Swentzell's adobe Tower Gallery shown above, in New Mexico, USA. Finishes by Athena and Bill Steen and family.

A range of elegant, natural earth finishes.

the platelets are pulled closely to one another, hence the characteristic nature of clays to shrink when they dry. Beneficial to anyone working and sculpting with clay however, is that the platelets will remain in the same shape that they have been moulded into, even when they dry. Unlike other binders used for plasters and renders, such as lime and cement, clay does not undergo a chemical transformation as it dries and cures. This means that it can be indefinitely re-wetted and reworked, and ensures that it can be infinitely recycled as a building material. It does, however, also mean that, though good for areas of high humidity (water vapour), it cannot be used on walls that come into direct and prolonged contact with liquid water.

The mechanisms of earth plasters as a wall finish

The mechanisms with which clay minerals react with water can have beneficial implications for their use within an earth plaster. This is specifically the case when building with breathing materials, which rely on finishes that will avoid the build-up of moisture, through their ability to similarly breathe. As has been established above, clay will absorb moisture into and out of its open pore structure. Unlike lime, however, which is also a breathing material, clay will self-seal itself on contact with moisture. This is because of the tendency of the water molecules, coming into contact with the clay, to bind themselves to the surface of the clay platelets and cause them to expand. This swelling closes up the spaces between the platelets, preventing the further passage of moisture through the full thickness of the earth plaster. The moisture is held here until conditions are dry enough for it to evaporate safely out. This prevents the moisture from being wicked into the underlying structure, as would be the case with cement, and can be the case with lime. The traditional method of using clay to line a pond provides a clear demonstration of this process at work (see p.33).

This mechanism makes earth plasters resistant to water, meaning that they can to a certain extent resist the passage of moisture through them (unless exposed to a constant flow of liquid water). This must not be confused with the concept of being 'waterproof', which would imply that moisture was unable to penetrate into its structure at all, like a waterproof paint.

When and where to use earth plasters
The self-sealing ability of earth plasters is highly beneficial for their interaction with moisture vapour (small molecules of moisture suspended in the air) where there is a gradual and gentle feed of moisture into its structure. This is why they are excellent in humid conditions, such as in bathrooms and kitchens. When an earth plaster is exposed to consistent driving rains (moisture in the form of liquid water), however, the clay in the earth plaster will become saturated, and hence its water-storing function will be overridden. In this circumstance, the earth plaster will inevitably begin to deteriorate, as it moves from a dry state into a plastic state and ultimately into a liquid state. At this point the clay molecules will be forced apart and the plaster unable to hold its form.

An earth plaster can be used externally, as long as there is enough time between rain showers for the plaster to fully dry out, and as long as other building design details are in place. There are also certain ingredients that can be added that will go some way to improving durability (see below). In the damper climate experienced in many parts of the UK, it is not generally recommended that they be used except in special circumstances (see Chapter 1). In all cases, an earth plaster should not be used as the final protective coat for a weather-facing wall (facing south-west in the northern hemisphere), as repeated maintenance will be needed to ensure that it continues to function as a protective coating to the wall substrate below it. A top-coat of lime render can be applied onto base coats of earth plaster to improve weathering. Numerous coats of limewash, or another type of breathable paint, applied directly to the earth plaster will also add protection, but these will similarly need regular maintenance.

When an earth plaster is used internally in areas where there is direct contact with liquid water, it must also be protected. An example of this would be covering the area around baths, sinks or showers with ceramic tiling, or oiling and waxing the plaster.

The hydrophilic (water-loving) nature of clay also means that it will absorb moisture from building materials, such as wood and straw, and then allow it to safely evaporate into the atmosphere. This will help to retard premature decay. Additionally, it can act as a protective barrier, preventing excessive amounts of water from accessing these materials.

The other ingredients present in an earth plaster

Clay is not the only ingredient present in an earth plaster. If it were, an inherently unstable material would ensue. It would be in a constant state of taking on water and expanding, and then relinquishing this water and contracting. If this were the case, an excessive amount of cracking would occur in the dry material. This would create a weak plaster, unable to fulfil its protective function. The additions of aggregates and fibrous matter are therefore vital for stabilising the clay in order to provide a durable and well-functioning covering. With the addition of these ingredients, it is possible to create a plaster that can benefit from the positive attributes of the clay without being dominated by them.

The next two sections will describe the functions of these additions, and the proportions in which they are needed. It will also assist you in being able to make an educated choice in selecting clay that is suitable for making an earth plaster.

Selecting suitable soils

If you decide to create an earth plaster with material that has been sourced on-site or locally, it is essential that you test this material first to assess its suitability for use. Always take small samples of the material to be tested before accumulating large amounts. Not only is it necessary to determine the grain size distribution of the soil (the proportions of sand, silt and clay present), but also the suitability of the clay mineral element present (if any). Due to the unique chemical composition of different types of clay, they will all behave differently with regard to:

1. Their expansiveness – how much water they are capable of absorbing, and therefore how much they will shrink and crack upon drying.
2. Their adhesion qualities – how well they can bind the other materials of the plaster together, and then stick them to the wall.
3. Their compressive strength – how strong they are.

All of these potential variables will affect the overall performance of the material once applied to the wall.

Testing for the material's suitability must be carried out in two stages:

1. Simple field tests to ascertain the proportions of sand, silt and clay in the raw material. This will illuminate what, if any, modifications will be needed in order to make a good earth plaster.
2. Carrying out tests and applying sample patches on to the substrate to be covered, with the modified raw material, i.e. with the addition of sand, fibre or any additives. This will help to ascertain the strength and binding powers of the material and determine what further amendments may be needed for the mix, before committing it to the full area to be covered.

Top left: Clay-rich subsoil (left hand), topsoil *(right hand)*. Topsoil is not suitable for plastering with. *Top right:* Hemp and straw fibres for use in earth plasters. *Middle:* A range of earth plaster mixes. *Bottom:* Clay-rich subsoil ready to be sieved.

We have also included some anecdotal evidence and interesting tests carried out by various individuals and research establishments. These can help to develop your overall understanding of the functions and behaviours of each of the components making up the earth plaster, and also to provide an understanding of how to alter the amounts of these components for specific circumstances.

It is important to remember that not all clays are suitable for building with. There are various levels of accuracy that can be obtained when testing for a soil's suitability. This is dependent on the sophistication of the methods and equipment used. Testing should begin simply and only get more sophisticated if results are not clear, if you lack confidence in your ability to read the results, or if more accurate data is required. The more practical experience gained, the more it is possible to trust your judgement using simple observations and tests. The levels of assessment are:

1. Observing the history of vernacular buildings with earth in your area, both as a walling material and as a finish. This should indicate the potential suitability of the soils in the area, for use as a building material. If there is no history of earth building in the area, however, this does not necessarily indicate that the soils are not suitable for making an earth plaster.
2. Testing soils using simple observations in the field.
3. Testing soils using simple apparatus.
4. Testing soils through the services of a laboratory at a university to provide very accurate and precise data. The Earthen Architecture Department of Plymouth University and the Architecture Department at Bath University specialise in testing soil samples for building purposes.

Clay-rich subsoils are sticky and plastic when wet.

Composition of a basic earth plaster mix

- The ideal basic earth plaster mix contains 10-25% clay and 75-90% well-graded aggregate.
- Earth plaster containing between 5-30% clay should work well in most circumstances.
- Silt should not be present in proportions greater than 25% of the clay element.

A clay-rich subsoil will mould into a sausage shape when wet.

A suitable earth will stick to the bottom of a down-turned palm when flattened against the palm.

To obtain accurate samples:

1. Always use soil from the sub-strata (not topsoil).
2. Remove large stones from the sample.
3. Test several samples from the same site.
4. Break up large lumps to provide consistency.

Testing soils in the field

To access the subsoil, in most circumstances the first 500 mm (20") of topsoil should be removed. There is often a distinct difference in the texture and colour between the threshold of the two. The topsoil will generally be dark and crumbly, whereas the subsoil will tend to be of a more compact texture, and may be of a lighter, golden brown colour, depending on the specific minerals present in the soil. Clay can be found in a variety of colours including greys, greens, pinks, purples, yellows and reds. Remove a sample of the soil to carry out some simple tests on the spot first, and then collect some samples to be taken away for further testing with simple apparatus. Always take at least three samples from any given site, from different locations, at least 30 metres (99') apart. Soils can differ in their composition widely within very short distances. These samples should be placed in labelled containers, with a record of the date and the exact location and the depth at which it was taken.

Use all of the senses of sight, touch, smell and taste to make initial observations about the composition of the soil.

1. Sight – what does it look like?

- If the shovel leaves shiny marks in its track it indicates the presence of clay.
- Form a moistened ball of the sample subsoil. Cut with a knife. If the cut surface is shiny it indicates that there is clay present; if dull, it indicates the presence of silt.

2. Touch – how does it feel between the fingers?

- Take a small sample of subsoil and remove the largest grains of gravel. Crumble between the fingers. How does it crumble?
  High clay content: hard to crush, lumps or concretions, very fine particles.
  High silt content: easy to crush into a slightly sticky powder, fine particles.
  High sand content: feels rough and gritty to the touch, doesn't hold form.
- With the same sample: spit on it and roll it between the fingers and the palm of the hand.
  Clayey soil: will feel sticky between the fingers and slightly greasy and smooth to the touch.
  Silty soil: may also feel sticky when wet, but not as sticky as clay.
- Squeeze a sample of the wet soil between the thumb and index finger, and pull them apart.
  Clayey soil: will stick together
  Sandy soil: will not feel sticky to the touch at all.
  Silty soil: will easily come apart
- Try to mould the moistened sample into a ball.
  Clayey soil: will stick together well and hold its form. When flattened against a down-turned palm it should stick. It should roll easily into a long sausage shape.
  Silty soil: will imitate clay in its ability to hold its form when moulded into a ball, but will not stick to a down turned palm, and will not hold its form when rolled into a long sausage.
  Sandy soil: will do none of the above.
- After handling the soil, rinse the hands gently with water.
  Clayey soil: hard to rinse off and may produce a soapy sensation.
  Silty soil: hands will rinse clean easily.
  Sandy soil: the presence of the rough grit will be felt and the hands will rinse easily.

3. Smell

This test should assist in detecting the presence of organic matter, and can indicate whether you have reached the subsoil strata. A freshly excavated sample from the subsoil should be odourless or smell slightly minerally.

The presence of organic matter will be detected by a musty, damp smell. It helps to moisten the sample prior to smelling.

4. Taste – the 'nibble test'

Do not carry this out if you detect that the soil is contaminated.

Not exactly tasting, but to detect the texture of the sample soil between the teeth.

Crush a small amount of the soil between the teeth.

Clayey soil: sticky, smooth.
Sandy soil: gritty and grinding.
Silty soil: smooth but not sticky.

Sausage test

To determine the cohesive properties of soil, i.e. how much clay is present.

1. Discard particles larger than 6mm (¼") from the sample.
2. Moisten the sample and mould between the hands into a plastic state.
3. Roll the sample between the hands to create a sausage shape, to a diameter of 30mm (1¼ "), and roughly 150mm (6") long.
4. Place the sausage in the palm of the hand and push it gently off the edge.
5. Observe at what point the sausage breaks. Measure the broken piece.

Results:

125mm (5") or less = low clay
125-250mm (5-10") = medium clay
250mm or more (10") = high clay

Ball-dropping test

1. Pack a handful of the moistened sample into a tight ball, 40mm (1.75") in diameter. The soil should be as dry as possible, but wet enough to form a cohesive ball. Remove stones and particles greater than 12.5mm (½").
2. Drop the ball from waist height onto a flat surface, and analyse the form in which it has landed.

Results:

- Flattens into a pancake = high clay content.
- Crumbles, shatters, falls apart = high sand content.

An ideal mix will hold its form when it hits the ground.

Let the ball dry, then drop it from table height:

1. Ball crumbles into bits and sand: too lean or sandy.
2. Shatters into pieces without crumbling: medium clay and is usable.
3. Remains whole: high clay content.

These simple field tests should provide enough information to indicate whether the soil is worth testing further. A soil that appears to have too much of one ingredient (i.e. too much clay), can be modified by adding an external source of the ingredient(s) lacking.

A soil that contains an unsuitable type of clay, such as bentonite, which is highly expansive, will not be suitable for use. This may not be obvious

The ball-dropping test: Drop the ball from waist height onto the ground. If there is too much clay in the earth it will flatten into a pancake *(left)*. Add more sand. If there is too much sand it will crumble *(right)*. Add more clay.

when testing in the field, but will become apparent once it has been made up into a sample plaster and tested on the wall, and via additional testing procedures, such as the 'box test' below.

Tests using simple apparatus
Test 1 below can be carried out with the raw material, or with the addition of aggregate. Do not add fibre for these tests, as it will help to prevent shrinkage, thus potentially masking the true nature of the material.

1. The Box Test
To test the percentage of potential shrinkage in the clay or an earth plaster mix.
- Use a series of long wooden boxes, which are at least 250 mm (10") long, 50 mm (2") thick and 50 mm (2") wide.
- Fill each box with a damp (same consistency as would be used when plastering a wall) earth plaster test mix, using different ratios of clay and aggregate in each box. Compact the material well into each box.
- Allow each box to dry thoroughly, then push all the material to one end of the box and monitor how much shrinkage has occurred in each mix.

To measure the amount of shrinkage that has occurred, measure how much the material has shrunk away from the wood along the length of the box. Divide this amount by the length of the box and multiply by 100 to find the percentage of shrinkage, e.g. 9mm shrinkage in a box 300mm long (inside measurement) = 3% shrinkage. Anything more than 3% shrinkage indicates that it is necessary to add more aggregate to the earth plaster mix. If the bricks do not hold their form at all and crumble apart, this indicates that there is not enough clay in the mix.

2. Sedimentation test
Clay and silt particles are too small to be identified through a process of sieving, though coarser

particles such as sand, gravel and stones (the aggregate) can be easily distinguished using sieves with different mesh sizes. This is discussed in detail in Chapter 2. To identify the proportion of clay and silt particles present in a given soil, a simple sedimentation test can be carried out. It must be noted, however, that this test will only provide a very rough estimate and should be used more for the purposes of identifying the presence of clay than for providing accurate data on the exact proportions of clay, silt, sand and gravel. It is best carried out in conjunction with the other tests, and not as a definitive test in its own right. It works on the principle that, when a given sample is mixed with water in a glass jar, and then left to settle out, the largest particles will settle at the bottom and the finest on top (the clay). To improve the accuracy of this test, the resulting sample should be assessed and measured when it is dry, because the clay expands when in a wet state. This can be achieved by carefully pouring off the clean

water

clay (1 hour to several days)

silt (10 minutes or less)

sand & aggregate (10 seconds)

Mark the jar at the positions at which each element has settled, to interpret the rough percentages of aggregates, silt and clay in the sample.

water without disturbing the sample and then allowing the jar to rest in a warm place with the lid off so that any remaining moisture can evaporate. When the sample is dry, a reading can be taken (see diagram above).

- Extract 3 or 4 different samples of subsoil.
- Place samples in different jars with tightly fitting lids, roughly 1/3 full.
- Add clean water to just below the top of each jar. A teaspoonful of salt added to each sample will help to break the soil down more quickly.

- Place the lids tightly on the jars and shake vigorously for 30 seconds.
- Place each shaken jar on a level surface where it will not be disturbed for at least 48 hours, and allow sedimentation to occur.

Observe the initial settling out of the samples. If there is clay present, the liquid in the jars will remain cloudy for at least a few hours, and up to several days. Refer to the diagram for information on how the other particles present in the samples will settle out.

Suggestions for modifying soils if necessary
If tests illuminate that the sampled soil contains not enough, or too much of one ingredient, it is possible to alter the relative proportions by adding an external source of the lacking component. If a soil is lacking in the vital binding clay element, there are various external sources that can be drawn upon:

- Add an external source of a clay-rich subsoil, excavated from another site.
- Add a bagged clay, such as kaolin, purchased from a pottery supply store. These can also be used as a finish in their own right.
- Purchase a fine brick dust from a brick manufacturer.
- In some areas or countries, road base may provide a suitable material.
- Consider using a pre-manufactured clay plaster.
- Add flour paste and/or manure (see below) to increase the stickiness and binding power of the soil. Do not rely on this option if the soil contains no clay at all. It should only be used to support a soil that is just short of the ideal proportion.

It is advisable to re-test the soil once any amendments have been made, and to carry out the sampling procedures described below, before committing the earth plaster to the wall. Before describing how to make up sample test batches, we will discuss the other essential ingredients necessary to make an earth plaster.

Other ingredients and additives for earth plasters

Any plaster or render, whether made out of earth or another material, should be made up of three basic components:

- a binder
- a structural filler
- water

Some form of fibre is also generally added to base coats, and sometimes to finishing coats. Sometimes additives are added to make a plaster more stable, and to enhance its performance under certain conditions.

In the case of making an earth plaster, the clay acts as the binder, the aggregate is the structural filler, and water activates the binding characteristics of the clay. The fibre gives reinforcing strength. The following provides a breakdown of these different components, and explains the additional materials often used in conjunction with earth plasters.

Clay as a binder
Clay acts as an adhesive and a binding agent. Its stickiness when wet allows it to stick to and wrap around the particles of aggregate and fibre, and hold them together. It enables the mix to adhere well to the wall substrate, and be worked into a smooth, continuous coating. Its characteristic behaviour as it dries ensures that the structural ingredients are held together even when it loses its moisture.

Unlike lime and cement, clay does not undergo a chemical transformation when it dries and cures. This is beneficial in that it can be forever re-combined with water, re-worked and re-used. This is good for novice plasterers, in that it allows for longer application sessions without the pressure of the material setting and becoming unworkable. It is also easier to amend work that has not turned out well on first attempts.

Above left: Dry clay and aggregate mix for an earth plaster. Above right: Sieving dry clay through a sieve set up at a 45 degree angle.
Middle left: Straw can be used in earth plasters to provide tensile strength. It must be chopped into short lengths for ease of application.
Bottom left: Kaolin clay can be used to make earth plasters. Below: A pre-manufactured earth plaster. It simply needs the addition of water.

Ed Crocker

Specialist in earth plastering

Ed Crocker is one of the founding members of *Cornerstones*, a non-governmental organisation in Santa Fe, New Mexico (USA). Cornerstones is a group which empowers Hispanic and Native American communities to sensitively restore their ancient adobe public buildings and sites. Ed Crocker also founded and runs an international architectural conservation and historic preservation firm in Santa Fe, New Mexico, that specialises in earth architecture conservation and repair.

Could you please give a short introduction as to how you got started with earth plasters and other traditional construction methods and materials?

My earliest passion and my first job was in archaeology. That is also the field in which I took my formal, academic training. Here in the south-west (USA), the archaeology involves the investigation of stone and earthen walls, often with an earthen render. In the course of many seasons in the field, I was involved not only in the excavation of earthen buildings, but in their conservation.

Many years and two careers later, I found myself doing general contracting in Santa Fe. I hated it, but began to find a niche by working on some of the older and more important adobe houses here – many of them on the state and national registers. It was during this time when I was underpinning the bell tower on the Santuario de Guadalupe, that I was approached to help organize the NGO that came to be known as Cornerstones.

For the next 13-14 years I planned and ran workshops in architectural conservation based on community involvement in public buildings and sites. Those included the historic churches in both Hispanic and Native American communities and, in the latter, kivas and clan-houses. The broad experience I gained resulted in a desire to disseminate the information. To this end, I have presented much of the experience at conferences and symposia, and write a monthly column called Understanding Adobe *for the local newspaper.*

Could you please give a few suggestions to a novice earth plasterer regarding materials, techniques & wall preparation.

Earthen plasters are more than mud thrown on a wall; they are complex mixes that, to be successful, must take into account binders, aggregates, organics, skill level, substrate and aesthetics.

The most salient principles must begin with the observation that there is no "recipe" for a successful earthen render, period. The unique matrix of each location, each exposure, each set of local materials, the available skill levels and the ultimate aesthetic consideration will lead to a vast and mutable list of approaches.

Because of the many variables, it is essential (let me repeat, essential) that every job begin with test panels. These will help define and refine the mixes, colour, durability, texture and method of application. In my experience, no matter the level of experience on the part of the craftsman, a project is doomed to failure if the plasterer approaches a job based on experience alone. No two walls are ever alike, no two sets of materials will ever match identically.

From a purely technical viewpoint, I consider the following super-important: the aggregate must be carefully designed to include a range and generally even distribution of particle sizes; straw in an exterior render should be applied parallel to the ground; a well designed earthen render does not need synthetics to make it a success.

Do you make all of your own earth plasters from found material, i.e. not purchased from a building supply store?

When working with earthen plasters, the only materials we buy 'off the shelf' are straw, and the occasional bag of Type S hydrated lime that we use in quantities of 1-2% by volume, to enhance adhesion and cohesion. Other than that, we borrow (source) the clays and aggregates locally, depending on the colour and finish the client desires. We maintain stockpiles of clays that range in colour from a dark greenish-gray to a very earthy brownish-red.

Locating clay

As has been previously discussed, there are many different clays, each with unique properties. Not all are suitable for use within earth plasters. There are many different sources for obtaining clay to make a beautiful and well functioning earth plaster.

Locally sourced clay subsoils

Clay is produced predominantly from feldspar, which is one of the most abundant minerals across the earth's surface. This means that clayey subsoils are present in many areas of the UK (and the world) and ensures that it shouldn't be too difficult to locate a suitable deposit within a short radius from where it is to be used. If it is possible to obtain a clayey subsoil from the back garden, or from a local source, the overall cost for materials can be kept to a minimum. It also provides the most environmentally sound option, minimising transportation of material over large distances. It is also extremely rewarding and visually pleasing when the building materials used to create a structure are literally a part of their surroundings.

To identify possible areas where clayey subsoils might be present, look out for areas of the ground where water sits on the surface, or where it takes a long time for water to disappear after a rainstorm. This is because clayey subsoils are notoriously slow-draining. Clayey subsoils are also hard to dig. If it is not possible to locate a source in the back garden, there are other options available, such as locating subsoils that have been excavated from a building site nearby. It is usually possible to arrange for a lorry-load to be dumped at your site for little or no cost. Other places to enquire at are local quarries and local farms. Farmers are often knowledgeable about the composition of the soils in the areas that they work.

Some clays to avoid

Some clays from the montmorillonite family, such as bentonite, are very hydrophilic (water-loving) and hence are highly expansive. They crack severely when dry and cannot be rendered stable even with large amounts of aggregate and fibres. They should be avoided. Most kaolin clays are moderately stable, and can be used successfully. However, they do vary from source to source and should be thoroughly tested prior to use.

A word about silt

Silt is similar to clay, in that it consists of very fine particles. It is made up of very small particles of rock, which tend to mimic the characteristics of clay despite being chemically different. One main difference is that they are irregular and jagged, in comparison with the smooth platelet structure of clay. This mimicking is due to the fact that the same slippery sensation can be felt when it is mixed with water. This is because silt particles contain a very thin film of clay on their surfaces, which superficially attract molecules of water in a similar way to pure clay particles. Carrying out thorough testing will enable the imposter to be differentiated from the real thing. Up to 25% silt of the clay element is acceptable in an earth plaster. Any more than this will compromise the ability of the clay to bind the sand and fibre together. This is because the clay will use up its binding powers on binding the particles of silt together.

Aggregates

For an in-depth discussion of aggregates – their functions within an earth plaster, as well as a breakdown of the best type of aggregate to use – please refer to Chapter 2. To sum up the most important points: the aggregate should be clean, sharp (angular) and well-graded. Base coats and external finishing coats generally include coarser/larger grains, whereas fine, internal finishing coats are generally made up with finer, smaller grains.

Water

Without the addition of water to the mix, the clay binder will remain inactive and unable to perform its functions of first sticking the ingredients together and then onto the wall substrate. As described above, clay and water have a special relationship. When they come into contact a reaction takes place to chemically attract and bind water within its molecular structure. This affords clay its special abilities to be moulded and worked. Clay exists within a continuum of different states depending on how much water is present – from a solid state (dry soil), to semi-solid, to plastic, and finally to a liquid state. When making an earth plaster, it is necessary to add just enough water so that it can be easily worked and spread. For spraying earth plasters onto the wall with a hose or render gun, a more liquid state is required. Water should always be from a clean, potable source, and should not contain dissolved salts.

Fibre and reinforcing mesh

The benefits of adding some form of fibre to an earth plaster are numerous. The network of fibres, evenly distributed throughout the mix, serves to hold the plaster together, thus providing tensile strength. This allows for flexibility within the body of the plaster when dry, enabling it to accommodate natural movements within the building structure without cracking.

Tests carried out by Bruce King et al (see *Design of Straw Bale Buildings*), show that the ductility (the ability to remain coherent even when stretched, compressed or deformed) of the plaster is also improved with the addition of fibre. A 50mm (2") plaster cube was subjected to compaction within a compression-testing machine. The sample with no fibre proved to be brittle and deformed early on in the test. The sample with fibre remained coherent over a longer period of time.

Other benefits of adding fibre include:
- It helps to control cracking by providing numerous small, control joints to localise the effects of shrinkage and expansion in the mix.
- It allows a plaster to successfully span two different materials within a wall by absorbing

some of the differential movement occurring between the dissimilar materials.
- It can help to increase the water resistance of an earth plaster if used in large quantities in the finishing coat. The straw will cause the water to be more evenly distributed over the surface of the walls and will help prevent the water from running down the wall in a straight path, potentially cutting a channel into the surface of the plaster. Tests have been carried out by various bodies to confirm this, such as by the earth building organisation, *Craterre*. Please find links to these in the Resources section.
- A finishing coat with chopped straw (or other textured fibre) will also provide texture and beauty to the wall.

Plant fibres such as chopped straw, hemp fibre, and sisal are predominantly used in earth plasters, although animal hairs such as horse hair can be used (see Chapter 3). Wheat straw is the most durable for use within an earth plaster, but barley straw is softer and easier to work with. The addition of horse manure to a mix can be beneficial not only for the enzymes it provides (which improve adhesion) but also for the fibres naturally present.

All plant fibres must be clean, dry and free of mould. Any discoloured or musty-smelling material should not be used as it could transfer mould into the plaster. If using chopped straw, it is possible to purchase a commercially available horse bedding material, which comes already chopped. Alternatively, long strands of straw can be chopped up with a strimmer/weed whacker in a dustbin. A leaf mulcher can also be used. Different lengths of straw should be used in the different plaster coats. Generally, longer strands of 100-200mm (4-8") are used in the base coats, and smaller, more refined strands of 25-50mm (1-2") in finishing coats.

The use of fibre in the mix can have implications for the method of application. A high-fibre mix

Above left: Sieving straw for the finishing coat. *Above right:* The fine, sieved straw ready to be mixed into an internal finishing coat earth plaster. *Below left:* Processing long fibres of straw through a leaf mulcher to chop it to the desired length.
Below right: Adding the processed straw to the earth plaster mix.

Glass-fibre mesh being incorporated into an earth plaster base coat to cover a localised repair in the wall. Once worked in with the hands, it should be well compressed into the plaster with a trowel.

will be hard to apply using a render gun, because the straw can clog the spray holes. Hand or trowel application is therefore more suitable for high-straw mixes. Alternatively, where a well-fibred mix is needed but spray application is preferred, a reinforcing mesh can be used (see below).

Reinforcing mesh

As an alternative to adding a vegetable or animal fibre to the earth plaster mix, a natural fibre, woven or plastic welded mesh can be embedded into the base layers to provide similar tensile strength and structural reinforcement. Reinforcing mesh can be useful when the plaster skin plays an important role in providing structural support for the walls, as is the case for straw bales.

There are various types of reinforcing mesh available, including those woven out of natural plant fibre materials such as hemp, jute, hessian and coconut fibre. These are beneficial when working within an environmentally sensitive build, and where the use of natural materials is important. However, they can decay prematurely if used within a plaster that is continually exposed to high amounts of moisture. The alternative is to use a welded plastic mesh made out of high density polypropylene glass-fibre. Metal meshing is not recommended for use within an earth plaster due to its relative inflexibility. If used together, cracking may occur in the plaster, because the plaster is more subject to subtle movements created by temperature and moisture differences. More importantly, metal

meshing covered with a porous earth plaster will be subject to rusting, as moisture and air move in and out of the plaster. Even using a galvanised metal mesh will not protect against this. As Ed Crocker, a specialist in this field points out, "Remember the built-in fallacy of the argument favouring steel embedded in a permeable plaster . . . it is permeable. Moisture goes in and out with great facility. What causes oxidation? It is the mixture of steel with water and oxygen, and is greatly accelerated when the contact is cyclical. Galvanising does not contribute significantly to the longevity of, let alone prevent, rusting. At best, galvanising will add 15% to the life of the steel it coats."

The use of reinforcing mesh embedded within the complete surface of the plaster should need only be considered when high-fibre plasters are desired, but where machine application is favoured. Reinforcing mesh can also be used in situations where fibre is not desired in the finishing coats for aesthetic reasons, but where some form of reinforcement is required. Short fibre, up to 25mm (1") in length, can be used effectively in a render gun without choking the holes. Reinforcing mesh can also be used for a wide variety of other purposes with earth plasters, as described in Chapter 1. Reinforcing mesh must have openings that are wide enough to enable sufficient amounts of plaster to squeeze through and hence fully bond, with the underlying surface. For walls, these must be at least 4.5 x 4.5mm ($^3/_{16}$" x $^3/_{16}$") wide, and for covering joints in building boards at least 2.5 x 2.5mm ($^1/_8$" x $^1/_8$") wide.

Additives and stabilisers for earth plasters

There are many naturally occurring substances that can be added to earth plasters to make them more durable against certain elements, or to simply enhance their beauty. The benefits include increased protection against abrasion or moisture. Most of these are based on traditional recipes, drawn from around the world, and have a long legacy of tried and tested usage behind them. However, even with the use of additives, earth plasters ask to be used in some circumstances and not in others. For these reasons, additives must not be relied on to force an earth plaster to perform in an inappropriate setting. Additives must be used to enhance the plaster, in conjunction with other well thought-out practices such as appropriate siting and building design details. Additives should not be used in order to avoid the proper selection of materials, proper mixing practices and methods of application. It must also be remembered that an earth plaster's value lies in its vapour permeability and ability to regulate moisture. Any additive that works to stabilise the material should never be added to a point that interferes with these characteristics. Non-natural additives such as those based on cement, acrylic or petroleum products should never be added to an earth plaster, as they are functionally incompatible. They will inevitably close the pore spaces and trap moisture in the walls.

The most commonly used additives are those added to increase the water resistance of the earth plaster, and to improve durability when used in areas of high impact, such as public spaces. Most of the additives used to improve water resistance do so by surrounding the clay molecules to prevent water reaching them, thus preventing swelling and contraction of the material. Examples of these include plant latexes such as cactus juices (in parts of the world where they are available), boiled seaweed (in Japan), proteins such as milk products and casein powder, animal blood, animal excrement such as cow or horse dung and urine,

and plant oils such as linseed oil. Wheat flour paste is also a useful and simple additive. Lime has traditionally been used in conjunction with earth to make durable plasters, with improved compressive strength and weather resistance. One synthetic product that has been used successfully by some on earth plasters to impart a waterproofing effect, is 'water-glass' or sodium/potassium silicate. This is a synthetic, inorganic mineral binder made out of sodium or potassium silicate. It can be painted onto the finishing coat, giving the earth a slightly sheeny appearance. It works in very much the same way as a Gore-Tex coating, consisting of very small holes. These allow moisture vapour to migrate out, but prevent liquid rain from entering in. It does not appear to affect the plaster's vapour permeability, but evidence of its effectiveness is predominantly anecdotal at this stage. Another similar product that is being used successfully in North America on earth plasters, is 'silane' (also known as siloxane). This is a non-toxic material which can be brushed or sprayed on to the finished earth plaster. It acts similarly to 'water-glass', in that it can prevent water absorption, whilst at the same time remaining highly vapour-permeable. We have no personal experience with this material as yet, but it remains as a promising option for increasing the potential use of earth plasters externally.

Animal dung

Cow and horse manure are most commonly used, although other animal dungs have been used with success. They contain enzymes, potash and phosphoric acid, which improve the binding qualities of the plaster, making it sticky and adhesive. They also give body to the plaster and slightly improve water resistance when dry. This is useful when the soil being used is short of clay. Horse manure also contains fibrous matter, which can replace or enhance the addition of chopped straw or other natural fibres. Cow dung, on the other hand, has more beneficial enzymes than horse manure. Cow dung is best used fresh from the field, when it is still moist and its enzyme activity is strong. Manure that has been composted for a long time will have lost its enzyme activity. Horse manure needs to be broken up so that it mixes evenly within the mix. If it is dry and hard, it should be broken up and sieved through a 12mm (½") screen. Alternatively, the manure can be soaked in a small amount of water to make a thick slurry, before being added to the mix. In India, the fresh dung and clay plaster ingredients are often soaked in water together and fermented for at least twelve hours before use. This is known as 'Gobar plaster'. The soaking process works to improve the ion exchange between the clay minerals and the manure. Soaking the clay and manure together for 1-2 days will improve the plaster mix. Manure can be added in amounts up to 20-30% of the total mix volume. However, as always, it is best to carry out samples to see how it behaves in your mix.

Horse urine has also been used traditionally, to diminish cracking and increase resistance to erosion, when used in place of, or as part of the mixing water.

Wheat flour paste

This is the most common additive used with earth plasters. A simple recipe of cooked wheat flour or a natural wallpaper paste made from wheat starch will serve to improve binding between the ingredients, enhance adhesion onto the wall, increase water resistance, prevent dusting and improve workability. It is by no means essential, but is useful if using a sandy soil with a low clay content, or if test patches exhibit a tendency for dusting (especially if no paint or wash is to be used for final decorative purposes). A clear wheat flour paste glaze can also be brushed on to a finished plaster to improve durability and prevent dusting (see Chapter 5). A high-gluten flour, such as white wheat flour should be used (not wholemeal). For recipes and usage guidelines, see p.173.

Vegetable oils

Linseed oil can be added to the finishing coat of an earth plaster to increase water resistance and improve flexibility, making it more elastic and hence able to expand and contract more efficiently without cracking. As long as not too much is added, the oil is able to repel water and improve flexibility without diminishing the vapour permeability of the plaster. If too much is added, it can decrease vapour permeability to unacceptable levels. It can also cause the finishing coat to separate from the coat beneath. Very small volumes of around 4-8 tablespoons (¼ - ½ cup) per

Left: Adding wheat flour paste to a kaolin clay plaster mix to reduce dusting and increase binding power. *Middle:* Mixing a kaolin clay plaster in a bucket. *Right:* Adding oil to the kaolin clay plaster mix for ease of spreading onto the wall.

wheelbarrowful is the maximum amount that should be used. Small amounts of other vegetable oils, such as sunflower or olive oil, can also be added to an earth plaster mix at the mixing stage (for all coats) to make it slip smoothly off the trowel and easier to apply. A splash of oil to a mixer full of plaster is all that is required.

Milk proteins

Proteins from milk products can be added to an earth plaster to increase the binding qualities of the mix, make it more workable, improve water resistance and increase durability against abrasion. They are also said to provide anti-mildew actions. Such products include fresh, powdered or sour milk, quark (fat-free white cheese), buttermilk, fromage frais, yoghurt and casein powder (a protein extracted from milk). Milk products can be added in volumes of roughly 10% of the total mix and can be added at any stage of the mixing process. Mixes should be used immediately and should only be used in areas where normal drying conditions can be expected.

Adding lime to earth plasters

Earth plaster mixes can be rendered more stable by adding non-hydraulic lime putty. By adding the lime, the amount of water the clay attracts and holds onto is reduced, which minimises the amount of swelling and shrinkage that takes place. This can make an earth plaster more durable and resistant to erosion. This is obviously a benefit when applying earth plasters externally. The above is achieved due to a chemical reaction between the calcium hydroxide in the lime, and the minerals – silica and alumina – in the clay, in the presence of water. The clay minerals become complex calcium and aluminium silicates, forming cementitious compounds in a clay/lime matrix.

The amount of lime to add is dependent on the clay content of the soil. This will obviously differ from place to place, so thorough sampling is necessary. As a guideline, soils with a lower clay content require less lime (1 part lime : 9 parts earth, for example), whereas soils with a higher clay content (more than 20%) require more lime (1 part lime : 5 parts earth, for example). Adding too much lime can weaken the overall mix, because there will not be enough clay minerals to react with the lime.

Make an earth plaster mix as normal, and then add the lime slowly to the mix, to ensure that the lime is evenly distributed and well mixed in. Allowing the clay and lime mix to sit for a few days (covered up) will encourage the reaction to take place more effectively. Re-mix before use. Ensure that the material cures slowly once applied to the wall.

Health and safety when working with earth plasters

Unlike lime, which is a highly alkaline and caustic material, all the materials used to make an earth plaster are fairly benign and relatively safe to use. There is no danger of damage to the skin when handling materials with bare hands. In fact, the silky mud feels great against the skin. The only reason that you may choose to wear gloves is because with prolonged contact the clay can dry the skin out, and coarse aggregate particles can agitate the hands when applying the plaster by hand. In these circumstances, wearing waterproof gloves can make the experience more comfortable.

If applying an earth plaster with a render gun, some form of eye protection is essential. This will protect against splash-back, especially from small particles of sharp aggregate.

When preparing and mixing dusty materials for earth plasters, it is advisable to wear a mask and carry out all operations in a well ventilated, outdoor space. Large amounts of dust can be created from fine aggregate, straw and clays. All powdered clays consist of extremely fine particles of aluminium silicate and can cause lung damage if inhaled in large amounts for a prolonged period of time.

Left: A variety of sample earth plaster mixes with differing proportions of clay and aggregate. *Right:* The samples are applied to the wall to be plastered, allowed to dry, and then monitored for cracking, durability, adhesion and dusting.

Testing and sampling earth plaster mixes

It has been clearly established that no two clay subsoils are the same. All subsoils differ with regards to the nature and proportions of clay minerals present, as well as the proportions and grain sizes of particles of aggregate. For this reason, testing and sampling all earth plaster mixes before committing them to the wall is an essential and integral part of the plastering process. This process encourages the development of a familiarity with all the materials being used. This is necessary to minimise or eliminate the potential problems that can occur with earth plasters, such as cracking, failure to bond to the substrate and dusting.

Because of the unique characteristics of locally sourced clay subsoils, it is not possible to provide a set of standard recipes for the user to apply in all situations. In addition to the soils variability, there are other factors that differ from job to job. These also need to be considered when choosing the ideal ratios of ingredients to be used.

For example, differences may occur between:
• Methods of preparation.
• Methods of application.
• The wall substrate it is to be applied onto.
• Orientation of the wall substrate.
• The conditions in which it is to be applied.

Recipes also differ for plasters used in different circumstances (such as when increased weather resistance or durability against abrasion is necessary), and within the coat system (between base coats and finishing coats). Guidelines and suggestions will be provided to assist in evaluating suitable mixes and recipes for all these situations.

When using pre-manufactured clay plasters, it is possible to eliminate most of the testing and sampling procedures. Each batch comes ready selected in the perfect proportions, and one need only add water and apply. However, any products based on natural materials will never be coerced into full standardisation, and it is therefore still advisable to try out a few sample patches on the particular substrate on which it is to be used.

164

Guidelines for sampling earth plaster mixes

Please refer to the section on mixing and application on how to prepare a mix.

Samples should be carried out on a section of the actual wall substrate that you intend to plaster. Start experimenting as early on in the building schedule as possible, to allow for samples to dry thoroughly and reveal their true nature. This will allow ample time for amendments to be made and re-testing to be carried out if necessary.

Some guidelines for sampling:
- Ideally, samples should be made no smaller that 500mm x 500mm (20x20") for accurate results to be obtained.
- The plaster should be applied up to 12.5mm (½") thick for base coats, and up to 6mm (¼") thick for finishing coats.
- Always apply onto a sheltered section of the wall or in the actual location where it is to be applied.
- At least ten samples should be carried out initially, and then as many as it takes to arrive at the ideal mix.
- The wall substrate should be prepared properly before application, and misted down where necessary.
- Allow each sample to dry thoroughly before analysing. In a sheltered or internal space this can take some time. A lightening in colour is usually a good indication of drying, as well as feeling hard to the touch.
- Make detailed notes on the mixes used and the results obtained. To make this easier, scratch the mix ratio used into the wet sample with the edge of a trowel.

Starting point ratios

Start off with a sample that consists of just sieved clay earth, without anything added.

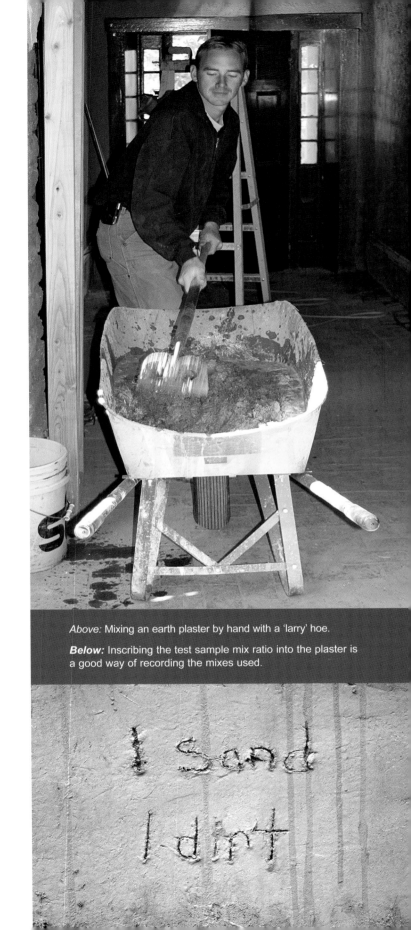

Above: Mixing an earth plaster by hand with a 'larry' hoe.

Below: Inscribing the test sample mix ratio into the plaster is a good way of recording the mixes used.

From here, proceed with the following:

High clay mixes:
   3 parts earth : 1 part sand,
   2 parts earth : 1 part sand.

Equal ratios:
   1 part earth: 1 part sand.

High sand mixes:
   1 part earth: 2 parts sand,
   1 part earth : 3 parts sand.

Sample the above mixes without the addition of straw first, and then do the next five samples in the same ratios with ¼ part straw (or other fibre) added. This selection of samples will also provide insight into the range of mix ratios that are sometimes used for the different coats. Examples include: a high clay content mix for the scratch coat; a higher sand than clay content for the straightening coat; and sometimes a higher clay content for the finishing coat (see below). This phase of testing is also useful for playing around with the amount of water needed to be added. As a general rule, just enough should be added to make the sample fluid and easy to apply, but not so much that the mix is sloppy. Prepare the small sample mixes in a bucket for speed and efficiency, using a spade, gauging trowel or whisk on a drill to mix the ingredients together. As well as the above test patches, it is helpful to carry out some of the tests described previously, such as the box test, and the ball drop test. These will support the information obtained from the sample patches.

Analysing the sample patches

Analysis of a particular mix begins at the stage of application, notably, how the mix goes onto the wall. Ideally it should spread on smoothly and with little effort, but it should hold its form once on the wall and not slump off. It should stick well to the wall, but not be so sticky that it sticks mostly to your hands or trowel and is hard to spread.

- If it is hard to spread: it may be too clay-rich and need the amendment of more sand; it may be too high in fibre content; or it may be too dry.
- If it is too sticky: it may be too clay-rich, and need more sand added.
- If it refuses to stick to the wall and spread into a cohesive mass: it may be too sand-rich, and need the addition of more clay to bind the sand and give it more body. It may also be too dry (add more water), or too wet – more fibre can be added to absorb some of the excess water, or more dry ingredients (sand and clay) can be added in the correct proportions. Alternatively, the mix can be left to stand to allow some of the excess water to evaporate. An inability to get the plaster to stick successfully to the wall may also be due to the fact that the fibre has not been evenly and thoroughly distributed throughout the body of the mix. Clumps of fibre will inhibit smooth spreading and adhesion to the wall.

Once the samples have thoroughly dried, it is necessary to assess their performance with regards to the following:
- Cracking, i.e. dry shrinkage
- Dusting, i.e. resistance to abrasion
- Adhesion i.e. binding strength
- Water resistance (especially if used in an area where water contact is likely)
- Hardness/durability

The following provides some recommendations for amending the mixes if the samples do not perform well. For a more detailed troubleshooting guide, refer to Chapter 3 (pp.138-9).

Cracking (dry shrinkage)

For the scratch coat, a small amount of cracking is to be expected, especially when using a high-clay mix to help it stick to the wall. It can even be beneficial to have some small cracks to provide points of key for the next coat. Excessive cracking or large cracks, as well as any evidence that the plaster is peeling away from the wall, deserves paying attention to, and the following should be considered:

- Improper sand, i.e. not coarse and/or well-graded
- Too much clay – add more sand and or/fibre
- Not enough fibre
- Too wet or too dry
- Applied too thickly
- Cured too quickly– in wind or direct sun, or wall substrate not adequately dampened prior to application

Dusting (resistance to abrasion)
A good earth plaster should not leave traces of dust on the fingers when rubbed, or crumble off the wall when agitated. It should resist indentation when scratched with a fingernail. If this is not the case:

- Too much sand or silt – add more clay
- Add animal manure or wheat paste to bind the ingredients together more effectively, especially if the option of adding more clay is not available
- Use a well-graded, sharp sand to provide a good skeleton to the mix

Adhesion (binding strength)
If the plaster fails to adhere successfully to the wall substrate, it is likely that there is not enough binding material to hold the ingredients together and stick it to the wall. Follow recommendations for point above (Dusting).

Water resistance
If an earth plaster is applied externally (which is not advised without correct building design details) and expected to come into contact with moisture occasionally, it may need to be stabilised to increase its water resistance. Test the sample patches by subjecting them to a light, steady spray of water from a hose, and observe how it behaves. Earth plasters that need to be more weather-resistant perform better with high amounts of fibre and aggregate, and benefit from the addition of stabilisers such as wheat flour paste, linseed oil, casein and other milk products. They can also be covered with breathable paints and washes to assist protection.

Hardness and durability
The hardness and durability of a plaster will determine how well it resists knocks from daily living, such as knocking a piece of furniture into the wall. This is again a function of the binding strength of the materials and their resistance to abrasion. These can be maximised by following the suggestions under 'Dusting' and 'Adhesion'.

Testing a lime finishing coat
If applying a finishing coat of lime onto an earth plaster, it is also advisable to carry out a test patch of the lime onto the earth plaster to see how it behaves. Particular areas to be observed include how well the lime bonds to the earth and the level of cracking.

Customising mixes for specific circumstances
NB: These mixes should always be tested as above.

1. **Flexible plaster for improved tensile strength.** Examples where this may be necessary include:
- When plastering below structural elements such as roofs and ceilings, which are subject to movement.
- If needing to apply the plaster when walls have not had time to dry out and are hence not fully settled.
   In these circumstances, add lots of fibre to increase tensile strength, and more clay. This should make a hard, elastic mix. The extra straw should counteract the additional clay.

2. **For application onto friable walls:**
   An extra clayey base with lots of fibre should help to consolidate the wall. Other measures, such as applying a 'stipple coat' (see Chapter 2), can also be used.

Wet-sieving a pre-soaked clay subsoil.

168

3. **For base coats providing support for finishes needing very hard surfaces.** Examples include highly polished and decorative rendering, such as tadelakt and marmorino, or when preparing a base for tile work. Use an extra-high-fibre mix.

4. **Increased weather durability for external use**
- Cow dung and wheat flour paste additives (as well as other suitable regionally available additives).
- More aggregate and straw for increased strength and erosion defence. Some practitioners recommend applying the straw parallel to the ground (with horizontal trowel strokes) to better shed water off the wall.
- Apply plaster more thickly (you need more fibre to counteract this) or apply more coats.

5. **Machine application:**
- Less fibre and shorter fibre lengths – less than 25mm (1") – to avoid clogging the holes of the gun. More aggregate can be added to counteract the lower volume of fibre. Use a reinforcing mesh, worked well into the base coats, if you need a high-fibre mix.

6. **Application during damp/wet periods or areas of low ventilation:**
- Avoid very high-fibre mixes because mould can result from the micro-organisms in the straw. If mould does occur, allow the plaster to dry, then brush with a stiff brush. Alternatively, a borax and water solution can be sprayed on (1 part borax: 4 parts hot water). Adding borax to the mix will help prevent mould from developing when a slow drying time is expected.

7. **Sculpting mix:**
- Wheat flour paste, lots of clay for extra workability and lots of fibre, so that the mix can be applied thickly without incurring cracking.

8. **Orientation of external walls:** (Northern hemis.)
- South-west/west wall: severe weather – full wrap around porch or a rain screen, if using an earth plaster.
- North/south-east/east walls: moderate weather – lime render finishing coat onto earth render base coats, or a thick – 50-75mm (2-3") – earth plaster (built up in layers) with multiple coats of limewash (or other breathable paint) on top.

Material preparation and mixing

When making earth plasters from scratch, out of locally sourced clayey subsoils, the preparation of materials and the mixing processes tend to be more time- and labour-consuming than the actual process of application. It is thus important to consider this in the overall building schedule, and to allow for adequate lead time to be able to carry it out thoroughly and effectively.

This part of the process presents the perfect opportunity to work, if possible, with a large team of people, drawn from friends, family and the wider community. Most of the processes do not require previous building experience, and all the materials are safe and non-toxic to work with. Sharing these processes among many people will considerably increase progress, and make it a lot more enjoyable.

The correct preparation of the raw materials, especially the clay, is vitally important for the overall quality of the earth plaster. Tests carried out by Gernot Minke at the University of Kassel, in laboratory conditions, proved that effective preparation, with regards to the method and duration of mixing, dramatically affected the binding force (how well the clay binds the other ingredients together and how well it sticks to the wall), the tensile strength (the ability of the plaster to remain cohesive under tension), and compressive strength (the ability to withstand buckling under downward pressure). One such test measured the binding force of earth samples from the same mix. One sample was mixed for ten minutes in a laboratory mixer and another for one minute. Both were mixed in the same mixer. The sample that was mixed for ten minutes had a 57% increase in binding force as compared to the one mixed for one minute. However, a further sample that was mixed for twenty minutes showed an 11% decrease in binding force, which suggests that there is an optimum mixing time.

"The 'secret' of loam (earth with clay, silt and sand) lies in the lamellar (plate-like) structure of the various clay minerals and their internal electrical attraction, which is activated only by water and by movement. This means that by kneading loam in a plastic state, the clay minerals are able to come together in a denser, parallel-layered packing, achieving greater binding force, and when dry, higher tensile and compressive strength." (Minke, *Building with Earth*, 2006).

There are many steps involved in preparing and mixing materials: sieving and soaking clay, chopping straw, preparing additives, and possibly sieving your own aggregate. There are many ways of carrying out each of these operations, depending on the size of the project, the available equipment, and how many people are involved. Whatever

the circumstances, good organisation is the key to a smooth operation, as well as devising and establishing systems where teams of individuals can be responsible for certain tasks. The placement of material stockpiles, in relation to mixing equipment and water supply, should also be well thought out, as this will considerably affect the amount of time and energy required for processing materials.

The following provides a breakdown of ways to prepare and mix earth plasters that should encompass most situations and scales of production.

Preparing clay

Raw, excavated clay usually requires preparation to break down heavy clods and to remove stones, gravel and debris. Traditionally, in places where winter climates were cold and there was sufficient frost, raw clay was weathered over the winter to break down the clods. It was dug in the autumn, moistened, and then stacked in a pile in the open. The action of freeze-thaw on the clay, as the frozen water expanded, caused the clods to disintegrate.

Clay needs to be further prepared by the two processes of soaking and sieving. The order in which the soaking and sieving processes take place will be dependent on the moisture content of the raw, extracted clay. If it is dry and crumbly, it will be easy to dry-sieve the material first, and

Left to right: Clay soaking in an old bathtub. Blending the soaked clay to break down large clods. Sieving the soaked and blended clay.

then soak it. If it is damp or wet, dry-sieving the material will be almost impossible, so soaking the material first is essential. This will help to break down the clods of sticky clay and turn it into a wet slurry. This slurry can then be poured through the sieve more easily.

Soaking

This is to hydrate the clay, making it sticky and workable, and help to activate its binding properties. Soaking for 12- 48 hours will enhance this property by increasing the electrochemical attraction between the clay minerals. Soaking can also help to break down small clods of clay, and assist in separating the clay particles from the sand, stones and gravel. These larger particles will fall to the bottom of the soaking vessel, making it easier to access the clay. Clay can be soaked in any watertight container, such as an old bath, a plasterer's bath, plastic or metal dustbins, buckets, or a pit. To construct a makeshift pit, straw bales can be set in a square or circle and then draped with a tarp.

- Break up large clods of clay before soaking (if it has not been previously sieved) with a spade, by stomping on it, or by using the flat edge of a sledgehammer.
- Fill the soaking container roughly $1/3$ full of clean water first. It is important that the clay is added to the water, and not the other way around,

otherwise the clay will not thoroughly dissolve in the water.
- Add the clay subsoil to the soaking vessel so that it is $3/4$ full.
- Add more water if necessary.
- To assist in breaking down the clay material, the soaked mixture should be either agitated and stirred with a spade, or mixed with a paddle on a drill.
- Cover the container so that the water does not evaporate or rainwater enter.
- If adding manure, it can be added at this stage, so that they soak together for at least 12 hours.

Sieving

This process is necessary to remove stones, gravel and unwanted debris from the clay. For base coats, which require larger aggregate particles, clay should be sieved through mesh with an aperture of 6mm ($1/4$") or 12mm ($1/2$"). For finishing coats requiring finer sand particles for a smooth finish, clay should be screened through a sieve with an aperture of 3mm ($1/8$") or 6mm ($1/4$"). After the clay has been sieved (if dry-sieved), it should be soaked for at least 24 hours, or longer if possible.

Wet-sieving method
If the clay was not dry-sieved prior to soaking, it needs to be poured through a 6 or 12mm ($1/4$ or $1/2$") screen after it has soaked. The raw material should be poured through the sieve after it has been soaked

Once sieved, the clay should produce a thick and creamy slip, the consistency of thick, chocolate custard. This provides the basis from which aggregate and fibre can be added to make an earth plaster, or which can be used on its own as a clay slip coat onto straw bales.

for 24 hours or longer. Depending on how well the material has broken down, the hydrated clay may require some manipulation to feed it through the mesh. Whisking the soaked material before pouring it through the sieve will make this process much easier. The easiest method for sieving the material is by placing the sieve on top of a bath, wheelbarrow or bucket in order to catch the material beneath. The resulting sieved mixture should be thick and creamy, and wet enough so that the other ingredients can be easily incorporated without the addition of too much additional water.

Dry-sieving method
There are different methods to dry-sieve clay. If the material is well broken down and dry, a large rectangular sieve, propped up at a 45° angle, makes it easy to shovel material through with an easy swing motion. Some form of sheeting needs to be placed on the ground under the screen to collect the sieved material and to keep it free of debris.

If the material is less well broken down, and has a high clay content, it will require more work and manipulation to feed it through the mesh. For this it is easiest to set the sieve up horizontally onto a bucket, barrow or bath, etc. The material can be worked through the mesh with a piece of wood, a brick or the hands. The sieved material can be used to make a mix in its dry state, but will be improved if soaked for 24 hours.

The process of sieving is best done well ahead of time and with many hands. It is by far the most time-consuming part of the earth plastering process. Once the clay has been both sieved and soaked, the material should have transformed into a thick and creamy liquid, known as a 'clay slip'. It is used as the basis for making earth plasters, as well as for use on its own as a pre-scratch 'slip' coat onto straw-bale walls. It can also be mixed with long straw for stuffing voids and crevices in straw-bale walls, before plastering. When making fine finishing coat plasters, the clay subsoil needs to be further sieved through a 3 - 6mm ($^{1}/_{8}$ - $^{1}/_{4}$") screen. This process will be made easier and less time-consuming if it has been screened through a 12 mm ($^{1}/_{2}$") sieve first.

Preparing straw
If using straw for fibre, it will need to be chopped into a variety of sizes (see above section on fibre). There are various methods that can be employed to achieve this:

1. **Strimmer** (weedwhacker)
   Place the straw into a clean dustbin roughly $^{1}/_{3}$ full. Turn the strimmer on inside the bin to chop the straw until it is at the desired length. It may need to be further sieved to get very short straw.
2. **Leaf mulcher**
   Feed the straw through the mulcher at least twice (more for shorter lengths). This is the most efficient option.
3. **Sieving**
   Straw can be grated through a 6mm ($^{1}/_{4}$") sieve, or cut by hand with scissors. These are slow processes, and highly inefficient. Use as a last resort.

Some brands of straw and hemp horse bedding consist of perfectly chopped strands which are ideal for use in earth plasters. Some contain a variety of strand lengths. The longer strands are ideal for base coats. For finishing coats, the straw can be sieved to remove the longer strands. Using horse manure also provides an excellent source of short fibres. It can be used on its own for finishing coats, and supplemented with an additional source for base coats.

Aggregate
Base coats generally require coarse, angular, well-graded grain particles of 0.9 - 5mm, and finishing coats require grain sizes of 0.01mm – 3mm. Aggregate can either be purchased to the correct specification, or can be sieved through a variety of mesh sizes to achieve the necessary gradings. See aggregates section, Chapter 1 for more details.

Preparing additives

Manure

Fresh cow manure can be soaked with the clay or added at any stage of the mixing process. Horse manure is best soaked separately at first, because it may require further sieving to break down the clumps of fibre. The fibre that is collected in the sieve can be teased apart and added back into the sieved manure.

Flour paste

Flour paste should always be added to the mix immediately prior to it being used. Add after the clay and sand have been mixed thoroughly together. Making wheat flour paste is a simple process, requiring a cooker or small stove with enough heat to achieve and maintain a rolling boil. It should be used immediately after being made, or can be kept for up to one week in a fridge.

Method:

1. Whisk together 1 cup of white wheat flour and 2 cups cold water into a smooth paste resembling thick pancake batter. Work out all lumps.
2. Bring 6 cups of fresh water to a rolling boil in a large pan.
3. Maintaining the rolling boil, add the wheat flour and water mix slowly to the water, stirring constantly.
4. Maintain the boil and stir constantly, until the paste becomes thick and slightly translucent. The paste is now ready to use. Allow to cool down before using.

Making wheat flour paste.

Making a sanded adhesion coat with wheat flour paste, manure and coarse aggregate.

The paste should be smooth and lump-free. Pass it through a sieve if any lumps remain.

The amount of wheat flour paste used in an earth plaster mix is dependent on the unique composition of the mix. It should therefore be tested in different ratios. As a general guideline, half a cup of wheat flour paste can be added to a 5 gallon bucket of earth plaster. If too much is added it will make the mix unworkable.

Making a clay slip and straw stuffing mix

This simply involves coating fibres of long straw with clay slip. These are used to stuff the holes and crevices within straw-bale walls. This helps to seal the bales against air leakage, and also helps with initial straightening of the walls before plastering.

Method:
1. Fill a container half full of clay slip.
2. Add fibres of long straw to the clay slip, ensuring that each strand is thoroughly coated in clay. It can be either dunked in, in handfuls, or allowed to soak for a little while. The latter will soften the straw, making it easier to work into the crevices.

Making an adhesion coat

An earth plaster will not stick well to wood or concrete. If these materials are embedded into the wall to be plastered, it is possible to apply an 'adhesion' coat first, to improve the bonding of the plaster. This 'adhesion coat' method was devised by Cedar Rose in North America. It consists of a mix of cooked flour paste, sharp, gritty sand and manure. It is useful for smaller spans of timber or concrete, under 450mm (1' 6").

This adhesion coat works to provide a key, via the sharp sand protrusions, for subsequent coats to attach to. It also prevents the wood or concrete from absorbing moisture too rapidly from the scratch coat, which could cause it to dry out too quickly, leading to a weak bond and excessive cracking. For more information on plastering over different materials within a wall, refer to Chapter 1.

Method:
Mix together in a bucket to form a paste:
- 2 parts cooked flour paste (see previous page)
- 1 part fresh manure
  (sieved through a 12.5mm (½") screen)
- 1 part sharp, gritty sand

Do not add any extra water: the flour paste should make the mix liquid enough to incorporate the ingredients together. It should be quite stiff, to ensure a thick enough coverage on the wood/concrete. It should be applied, once freshly made, with a paint brush. Apply roughly 3mm ($^1/_8$") thick, in one even coat. If the material being covered is particularly smooth, it may require a second coat to provide adequate tooth. Allow the first coat to dry before applying the second one. The adhesion coat will require stirring from time to time in the bucket, to agitate the sand and prevent it from settling on the bottom. The adhesion coat should be allowed to thoroughly dry before the scratch coat is applied.

Mixing earth plasters

Mixing can be carried out in a number of ways. As pointed out earlier, the mixing process will have an impact on the final quality of the plaster, and how well it performs. The mix must always be adequately stirred and kneaded so that the ingredients become well integrated. A good mix can be achieved by hand-mixing in a large or small container (an old bath, plasterer's bath, barrow, bucket, etc.), stomping it with your feet on a tarpaulin, in a pit, or on a clean mixing pad, and with a variety of mechanical mixers. As always, the chosen method will depend on preference, the amounts needed and the budget, labour and machinery available. The following descriptions provide information on the various methods that can be used. Materials must always be measured out accurately in standardised containers (your gauging device), such as a sturdy bucket.

Dry mixing versus wet mixing

If time is short, and the soaking stage omitted, unsoaked, sieved clay can be mixed together with the aggregate and then water added to achieve the desired consistency. This will not produce as high a quality of mix as when soaked clay is used, both in terms of its performance and its usability. Foot-stomping the unsoaked clay and sand (see below) will help to knead the clay and sand particles together, bringing them into more intimate contact with each other.

Hand mixing in a container

Mixing in a barrow or bucket is suitable for small amounts. An old bath or plasterer's bath is good for larger volumes: their long, flat shape works well for thorough mixing of all the ingredients. When mixing in any of these containers, a small lady's spade is invaluable for getting into the tight corners of the container. A pull or larry hoe (see p.165) also works well to push and pull the material around. The long handle can make it easier on the back. The whole body should be engaged with the movement – bending the knees and moving the arms and torso in a loose, fluid motion.

Mixing a pre-manufactured earth plaster in a bucket.

Method:

1. Add the clay slip (and soaked manure if being used) to the mixing container.
2. Add half the sand.
3. Thoroughly mix the clay slip and sand together.
4. Add ¼ of the remaining sand.
5. Mix until thoroughly incorporated.
6. Add remaining ¼ of sand.
7. Mix thoroughly.
8. Tease small amounts of straw into the mix in increments. Ensure that the straw does not form into clumps. Using hands to work the straw in is often more effective than using a spade or a hoe.
9. Work the mix for roughly 10 minutes, turning, chopping and stirring so that it is well mixed and aerated.

The resulting mix should be the consistency of thick cake mix. If using a clay slip, it may not be necessary to add any further water. If the clay slip is too watery from the start, and the resulting mix too sloppy, the mix should be left to sit until surplus water has evaporated and it has sufficiently stiffened. Alternatively, more dry, sieved clay, sand and straw can be added in the correct proportions to absorb the excess moisture. To test whether it is at the right consistency, a trowelful should be placed onto the hawk and then scooped and turned. It should form into a mound the length of the hawk. If it doesn't hold form, and slops all over the hawk, it is too wet. Also, apply some to the wall and observe how well it spreads on. Any additives, such as wheat flour paste, oil or casein are best added at the stage before the straw is introduced, to ensure thorough incorporation. The performance of the mix will be enhanced if the clay and sand, once mixed together, are able to stand for a couple of hours or more (overnight if possible). This will encourage the clay particles to thoroughly surround and coat each grain of sand.

Mixing with a whisk on a drill

The clay slip and sand can be beaten together in a container, using a paddle-mixer attached to a drill.

A heavy duty drill with a lot of power works best, especially for larger mixes. This method works well to aerate the mix and to thoroughly bind the ingredients together. Straw should be incorporated by hand or with a spade, to prevent the strands of fibre from getting entwined in the paddle. Mixing in straw is easier if the beaten clay and sand is transferred into a wheelbarrow before being added.

Mixing in a pit

For larger batches, earth plasters can be mixed in a shallow pit. The simplest method of creating a pit is by placing straw bales in a square or circle, and draping a large tarpaulin over the bales so the edges come out and over the bales. The edges of the tarp should be anchored down. A pit made in this way enables the mix to be either foot-stomped on the tarp, or turned over with a spade. If using the latter method, a piece of sturdy plywood should be laid at the base of the pit on top of the tarpaulin, to prevent puncturing of the tarpaulin.

Mechanical mixers

This is the best method for mixing large batches, especially when demand for speedy production is required. Several batches can be made ahead of time and stored in a large container until needed. This will allow the mixing crew to jump start production. There are a range of mechanical mixers available, each with their own advantages and disadvantages.

Drum (cement) mixer with rotating barrel
Drum mixers are the most common and inexpensive type of mixer that can be purchased or hired. They consist of a stand which supports a rotating drum with attached blades on the inside. These blades cut the material being mixed, whilst the rotation action folds and drops the material, helping it to mix evenly and thoroughly. Their main drawback for mixing earth plasters is that the stickiness of the clay can cause the material to accumulate on the sides of the drum, encouraged

Mixing an earth plaster in a plasterer's bath.

Top row left to right:
Sieving the soaked clay.
Adding well-graded, coarse aggregate to the sieved clay slip.
Mixing the aggregate with the clay.

Middle row left to right:
The aggregate has been fully incorporated into the mix.
Adding straw to the clay-aggregate mix. Stomping the clay helps to blend the ingredients together.

Bottom row left to right:
Mixing the straw in by hand is easier when it has first been added.
A final turnover with a shovel will ensure all ingredients have been thoroughly mixed.

Left to right: Adding half of the aggregate to the mixer. Adding clay slip to the aggregate. Adding the rest of the aggregate.

by the lateral forces of the spinning. This can hinder thorough mixing. It is less of a problem when using soaked clay rather than dry material. To overcome this, mixes can be made slightly wetter to encourage the material to slide off the blade and the sides. Adding a small amount of vegetable oil (a tablespoon full per mix) will also help prevent the material from sticking.

Another tip is to tilt the mixer forward by propping the back legs with pieces of timber or bricks. Drum mixers are also available with a geared wheel, to enable the drum to be set in a forward tilting position. The mixer can also be stopped periodically and the sides scraped with a gauging trowel.

Mixing with soaked clay in a drum mixer
1. Add half the aggregate.
2. Add all the soaked clay into the mixer and allow it to mix until fully incorporated.
3. Add the rest of the aggregate and allow to mix for a few minutes. Add a small amount of water to the mix if the sand and clay start to ball up.
4. Add a small amount of oil to the mix (1-2 tablespoons). Rotate until well mixed in.
5. Gradually tease in the fibre, ensuring no clumps form. Longer fibres – longer than 125mm (5") – may get wrapped around the blades, so it may be necessary to stop the mixer periodically and scrape them back into the mass of the material.

Shorter fibres should mix freely.
6. Rotate all the ingredients together for approximately ten minutes, by which time it should be thoroughly blended together into a thick, creamy mix.

Mixing dry clay in a drum mixer
Dry ingredients (sieved clay and sand) can either be mixed together first, before adding water, or a small amount of water added to the mixer first, and then the dry ingredients added in turn. The fibre should always be added last. Always add a little water at first, then mix for a short while, adding more if necessary. The more it mixes, the more liquefied it will become.

Mortar mill (roller pan mixer)
For information on mortar mills, please refer to Chapter 2. Add the clay to the mixer first. If using dry clay, this should be followed by adding some water to mix the clay into a liquid paste. Add the aggregate in small increments. Allow the ingredients to mix together for a short while, and then add more water if necessary. Gradually tease the fibre into the mix once the clay and aggregate are thoroughly incorporated. Mixing time is minimal – around four to five minutes – due to the squeezing action of the rollers. Their only drawback is that longer strands of fibre can get caught up in the scrapers. This should not be a problem with strands of 75mm (3") or less.

Left to right: Mixing the aggregate and clay slip together. Adding a small amount of vegetable oil to the mix. Adding the straw.

Pan mixer

For information on pan mixers, please refer to Chapter 2. They work very well to mix the ingredients together, but be aware that longer strands of fibre may get entwined around the mixing blades. Use the same sequence as above.

Mixing bagged clays

Bagged clays, such as kaolin, require less preparation than locally dug clayey subsoils. They come already ground up as lumpless, fine powders. Mixing is therefore very easy straight from the bag, though they can also be soaked in water first to hydrate the clay minerals. Mixing can be accomplished in the same variety of ways as described above. Flour paste is essential with a kaolin plaster, to fix the ingredients together and prevent dusting when dry.

Mixing pre-manufactured clay plasters

These come already blended with the perfect proportions of sand and clay, and require only the addition of water. They can be easily mixed in a tub or bucket with a paddle mixer on a drill, or mechanical mixers can be used for larger quantities. If fibre is desired, this sometimes needs to be supplied and added separately. As with home-made earth plasters, workability and performance improves the longer the mix stands before being used. Allow to stand for a minimum of 30 minutes before application. If adding extra fibre, do not store with fibre for more than one week. If the plaster becomes stiff after standing, it should be knocked up prior to use with some more water.

It is also possible to purchase one tonne sacks of ready-mixed earth plasters from select suppliers, thus eliminating the need for any preparatory work and mixing (see naturalbuildingresources.com).

Guidelines for storing mixed materials

As already discussed, mixing material and then storing it is beneficial for improving workability and performance. Allowing it to stand will improve the contact between the clay and sand particles, and will enhance the binding forces of the clay minerals. Having a stockpile of ready-mixed materials also means that the application process can run smoothly and unhindered, without having to wait for further batches of material to be mixed. The benefits of allowing the material to sit can be gained within 30 minutes, but are vastly increased the longer it can sit. Temple builders in Japan traditionally allow their earth plasters to sit for three years before using. If there is straw in the mix, it will keep for up to one week in a wet mix (less in warm weather) before microbial action kicks in and causes it to rot. This can lead to a mouldy plaster once applied to the wall. Always store the material in covered containers so that it doesn't get too wet or dry out.

Applying earth plasters

Working with earth plasters is a thoroughly pleasurable and rewarding experience. When well made, an earth plaster will glide smoothly across the wall in one easy motion, allowing for quick and efficient progress. It is a great medium for those new to plastering to work with, because of its slow drying time. This means that the plasterer is not having to work against the clock to apply and work the material before it sets. Working with earth also means that any mistakes can be re-wetted and easily reworked until an acceptable finish is achieved. The non-caustic ingredients within earth plasters also allows for a certain freedom when it comes to being able to touch and feel the material. From this, one can develop a stronger and more immediate sensitivity toward the material. As with all plastering mediums and techniques, the success of applying earth plaster depends on three stages, each of which must be given equal importance:

1. Pre-application: preparing the walls to be plastered.
2. Application: spreading the material onto the prepared walls and working it in.
3. Post-application: protecting walls whilst drying, paying attention to drying speeds and remedying problem areas.

Earth plasters can be successfully applied onto a wide range of wall surfaces. This includes most traditional and 'green' wall substrates, such as cob and straw-bale, but also includes some conventional wall substrates, such as plasterboard and concrete block, as long as certain preparatory measures are taken (see Chapter 2).

The coat system for earth plasters

Earth plasters are generally applied in several layers of thin coats to build up to the desired thickness, as opposed to one thick coat. The reasons for this are the same as for most plastering systems: earth plasters will crack if applied too thickly, will slump off, and may delaminate from the wall. Additionally, if one thick coat were applied which subsequently cracked, the cracking would occur throughout the full thickness of the coat.

Many different names are used to refer to the different coats. For the purposes of this book, we will use the same terms used in Chapter 3. These include: the first coat – the 'scratch' coat, so called because it is roughened up or scratched to provide a key for the subsequent coat; the second coat – the 'straightening' coat, so-called because it is applied to even out the wall surface and provide the shape and profile of the finished wall; the third coat – the 'finishing' coat, which serves as the final wall surface, used as a decorative finish in itself, or as a surface onto which coloured paints and washes are applied. For straw-bale walls, natural builders in North America have devised an additional pre-scratch coat, known as the 'slip coat'. This consists of a liquid clay slip, which is either sprayed on or applied by hand. Its function is to provide a solid surface on the bales, to which the scratch coat can strongly adhere.

Not all three coats are always required, especially when plastering onto substrates that already provide an even, flat plane. Examples include the building boards, such as clay board, as well as very straight walls made out of a homogenous material such as rammed earth, light clay, or rammed hemp-lime. Two or three coats are usually necessary where walls exhibit some or all of the following characteristics:

- On soft, flexible surfaces, such as reed mat and straw bales, to provide structural strength.
- On wall surfaces that are irregular and lumpy, such as old cob walls, stone walls etc.
- On walls that are composed of different materials, which are likely to expand and contract at different rates, such as where a lintel is to be plastered over.

- Where thick layers are required for extra humidity regulation, such as bathrooms and kitchens.
- Where reed mat or mesh (not metal) is to be used to bridge different materials in the wall, such as embedded timbers.
- When a very fine quality finish is required.

The different coats can be made up with varying proportions of the different ingredients – clay, aggregate, straw (fibre). This produces mixes that perform slightly differently depending on their role in the coat system. Generally aggregate sizes are: 0 - 5mm (0 - $^3/_{16}$") in base coats (or for an external finishing coat for weathering purposes); 0 - 3mm (0 - $^1/_8$") for finishing coat.

Clay slip bonding coat for straw-bale walls

Has no additional aggregate or fibre added. The high clay content makes it very sticky, so that it binds strongly to the straw substrate. Applied in a thin coating to cover the straw.

Scratch coat

With aggregate added, but generally a high clay content to make it stickier, so that it binds well to the wall substrate (or the clay slip coat for straw-bale walls). Moderate amounts of straw to provide tensile strength and to counteract the potential for cracking due to the high clay content. Some minor cracking is acceptable, because it can help provide key for the subsequent coat. Ensure that delamination of the material from the wall does not accompany the cracks. The mix should be made and applied fairly wet for ease of spreading and a good even coverage. The aim of this coat is to cover the whole surface with one uniform finish. Average thickness: 12.5mm (½").

Straightening coat

A higher sand to clay ratio and a higher amount of straw (fibre) added. The high sand ratio provides structural strength, and the straw provides additional tensile strength. This enables the plaster to be applied more thickly without extensive cracking, in order to fill out holes and crevices, and to bring the wall into a more even plane. For areas that need building out, a drier mix is preferred. For deep holes and crevices, where material in excess of 72.5mm (2.5") is necessary for straightening, the material should be applied in numerous thinner coats to build out to the desired plane. Allow each layer to dry before applying the next one. Average thickness: 25mm (1"), and not more than 50mm (2") in one go for filling out large holes and hollows.

Finishing coat

A slightly higher sand to clay ratio for external plasters, to take advantage of the structural strength of the aggregate and to provide resistance against erosion. Note, however, that there are certain types of clay, in some parts of the world, where it may be beneficial to add more clay in the finishing coat: for example when the clay has lime naturally present (i.e. 'caliche' in New Mexico), or when the clay is mildly hydraulic. This is why testing is essential, and no one way can be prescribed. For internal walls, a slightly higher clay to sand ratio is sometimes beneficial to help seal the plaster, and to provide a more durable, less dusty finish. Fibre is optional for internal walls, used mainly for decorative purposes.

Externally, straw will help to make the earth plaster more weather-resistant, encouraging the water to sheet quickly off the wall. The mix can be applied slightly wetter for ease of application and to provide an evenly coated, smooth finished surface. This coat is applied thinly, which will help counteract the higher ratios of clay (internal), and water. All materials should be sieved through a 3mm ($^1/_8$") screen to provide a smooth, fine finish, unless a coarser finish is desired for external use. Average thickness: 3mm ($^1/_8$") internal; 6 - 12mm (¼ - ½") external.

Remember to test all mixes before use.

Above left to right: Scooping the worked plaster onto the trowel and spreading it onto the wall with a firm upward stroke.

Above left: Applying an earth plaster straightening coat with a laying on trowel. *Above right:* Using a darby to straighten the earth plaster. *Below left:* Applying a kaolin clay plaster finishing coat. Below right: Sponging the kaolin plaster finishing coat.

How long to leave between each coat

Scratch coat onto a clay slip coat – straw-bale walls
Applying the scratch immediately onto the freshly applied wet clay slip will improve adhesion between layers. As the slip coat is so thin, very little cracking should be expected. On the other hand, waiting for the slip coat to dry thoroughly will ensure that it has fully bonded to the straw bales, providing a solid base on which to apply the scratch coat and all subsequent coats. A dry slip coat will need to be thoroughly dampened before application of the scratch coat. Both methods work.

Straightening coat onto scratch coat
It is acceptable for this coat to be less than thoroughly dry before applying the straightening coat. If the scratch coat is slightly tacky, it will enhance bonding between the two coats.

Finishing coat onto straightening coat
For best practice, the straightening coat should be thoroughly dry (especially if built out thickly in some places) before application of the final coat. This is to ensure that the final coat does not crack. This could happen if it is applied onto a coat that is still drying and shrinking. In all cases, each coat must be thoroughly dampened prior to the application of subsequent coats. This is to ensure maximum bonding, and to prevent the undercoat from drawing excessive moisture from the fresh coat as it dries.

Bonding between the coats
Earth plasters will bond well together without being scratched up. This is because a dried coat will become 'live' again once dampened down, activating its sticky clay molecules. This will provide ample suction to bond the coats together. Adhesion will, however, be enhanced if base coats are scratched or roughened up to provide grooves for the new coat to key into. Scratching up is essential when applying a lime finishing coat onto an earth base coat. Creating a rough surface with the hands works well, as does using a plasterer's scratching comb (see Chapter 2). This is best used for keying up the scratch coat, whereas a devil float is most effective on the straightening coat, to produce less deep incisions.

Wall preparation
As with all plastering techniques, correct preparation of the wall substrate before receiving the first coat is of the utmost importance. General wall preparation techniques are discussed in detail in Chapter 2. Also to consider in the pre-application stage are other essential preparatory measures, such as masking and protecting areas not to be plastered, reinforcing windows (reed mat around the reveals of straw-bale walls), erecting scaffolding where needed, and ensuring that the worksite is efficiently organised. These details are also discussed in Chapter 2.

Getting the material onto the wall
Below is an outline of the basic steps needed to be taken for applying earth plasters onto most wall substrates. Where wall substrates require specific techniques, these are outlined in the individualised steps following this section. This section should be used in conjunction with the application technique instructions also outlined in Chapter 2.

Earth plastering, more than any other plastering technique, allows for real freedom and flexibility in the approach one takes to getting the material onto the wall. Many techniques and tools work very well, including applying by hand, spraying on with a render gun, as well as application with standard and specialised trowels. Some methods work better in certain situations, and these are outlined below. Beyond this, there is no substitute for diving in and having a go, until a natural rhythm and personal system is developed.

Earth plasters should not be applied when temperatures are at 5°C (41°F) or below, as well as for one week after application. This will avoid possible problems associated with freeze-thaw in wet material, whereby the moisture in the plaster will freeze into ice crystals, causing the plaster to expand and then contract excessively as the crystals thaw. If the weather is cold and work is being carried out internally, prepared material is best brought inside 24 hours before work commences, to allow it to reach room temperature. There may also be issues with mould developing on the surface of the plaster (from the straw) if temperatures remain low (below 10°C/50°F) at the same time as it being rainy for one week or more. When applying material in hot and sunny weather, it is best to organise the work schedule so as to avoid too much direct sunlight hitting the walls. This can be achieved by working on the west side of the building in the morning, the east side in the afternoon, and the south side as the sun descends, or on a cloudy day. The north side can be done at any time. Newly constructed walls should ideally be fully dried out and settled before application of the first coat. A small amount of residual moisture is acceptable, however, and can in some circumstances even benefit the first coat of plaster, in that it will help to prevent it from drying out too quickly (earth walls, for example). The finishing coat should ideally be applied after the base coats have been allowed to settle for approximately one month (or as long as possible). This will allow any residual settlement in the building to take place. This can be monitored in the base coats, as any major settling movements will manifest as large cracks in the plaster. The base coats can therefore be used as indicators of what is taking place in the structure of the building.

General application steps

1. Dampen the wall substrate (if necessary)
Do this approximately one hour before work commences, and then 10 minutes before. The wall can also be dampened as you go.

2. Apply the scratch coat
Start at the top of the wall and work down, to prevent falling bits of plaster from damaging work carried out below. The aim of the scratch coat is to provide an even coverage over the whole wall substrate. The scratch coat is the ideal place to deal with any elements such as:

- Electrical cables and ducts which have been chased into the wall. If the chase is deeper than 50mm (2"), it is advisable to fill the area with an earth plaster mix, allowing it to dry before the scratch coat is applied.
- Heating tubes set in the wall (a system popular in Germany and Holland).
- Covering different structural elements, such as lintels, wood uprights and repairs to the wall.

For details on how to integrate these elements into the plastered wall with reed mat and reinforcing mesh, refer to Chapter 1.

If no fibre has been used in the scratch coat mix, when spraying on with a render gun for example, it is essential that a layer of reinforcing mesh is fully embedded into the full surface of the freshly laid scratch coat. If applying the earth plaster onto a fairly straight wall, the freshly laid plaster can be straightened up using a straight edge, darby or large smoothing float at this stage.

3. Scratch up the scratch coat (optional)
The scratch coat can be applied fairly rough to provide the key for the straightening coat. If applied by hand, the grooves left by the fingers should provide adequate key. If applied with a steel trowel, the surface is likely to be quite smooth, and additional scratching with a comb scratcher can help with bonding the next coat. If sprayed on with a render gun, the untrowelled stipple effect will provide a perfect key for the next coat.

4. Apply the straightening coat
The straightening coat can be applied onto the scratch coat either when the scratch coat is fully dry, or when almost dry. If it is fully dried (when

it has completely changed to a lighter colour), it is essential that it be thoroughly dampened before the straightening coat is applied. It should still be moistened very lightly even if slightly damp. The aim of the straightening coat is to define the shape of the wall. This may entail building out low spots, in which case a slightly thicker coat can be applied up to 25-50mm (1-2") thick. Large hollows may need to be built out in consecutive layers, allowing each one to dry before applying the next.

Before applying the straightening coat, areas of trim, such as around doors and windows, and anywhere that the plaster meets a different material, should be cleaned up. This involves cutting away any dried plaster that is not tightly pressed into the join. This is especially important around windows and doors, where a well sealed joint is essential for preventing the incursion of moisture in through the window trim. It is also beneficial to scrape or brush off, with the edge of a steel trowel or a stiff brush, any loose or protruding material from the scratch coat.

4. Scour the straightening coat (optional)
To produce a well compacted straightening coat, it can be scoured with a wooden float. The scouring action helps to consolidate, compact and compress the material into itself and into the scratch coat beneath. It also helps to even out the surface of the plaster, by knocking off high spots and moving material into low spots. This process is not essential, but is beneficial if carried out correctly. The plaster should be scoured when it has had time to firm up but is not fully dry (i.e. it resists indentation from a finger, but is dented by a fingernail).

6. Scratch up the straightening coat (optional)
Scratching up the straightening coat after it has been scoured will ensure that there is good key for the next coat. This can be done with a comb scratcher as above, but is best carried out with a devil float. The devil float will provide a shallower indentation, ensuring there is no cracking in the

finishing coat along the indentation lines, and that the indentations do not show through.

7. Apply the finishing coat
The finishing coat serves to provide a base onto which a decorative, breathable paint or wash can be applied. It can also be finished so that it provides a decorative finish in itself. In both cases it is important that the finishing coat is applied and finished in a way so that it not only provides an aesthetically pleasing surface but also performs with maximum durability and strength. The qualities necessary for this are that it is hard enough to be able to withstand some bumps and knocks, and that it dusts off minimally. The plaster is applied in a thin layer using the same techniques as above. Hand-application is generally not recommended because it is difficult to achieve a fine, compact surface. The finishing coat can be applied slightly wetter than the base coats. This allows for easy spreading to achieve a smooth surface. Due to the thinness of the coat, a little material will go a long way. As always, the previous coat should be misted down about 10 minutes before work commences, and as work proceeds if the moisture is quickly absorbed.

First apply the material in small sections, with the aim of getting it onto the wall. Do not spend much time on perfecting the surface at this stage. Once the material is up, go back over it using an open trowel edge (leading edge raised, and trailing edge in contact with the wall). Blend the smaller sections together, and begin to smooth the surface. If you are working over a large surface area, do this as you go. After the material has been applied, it should be allowed to 'firm up' slightly (pressure from the thumb will not leave an indent), and then worked in a variety of ways depending on the type of finish desired.

8. Optional scouring step
This should be carried out when the plaster has slightly firmed up. It is an optional step, but if

Applying earth renders and plasters

Dampen the wall substrate as necessary before work begins.

Apply scratch coat using a steel laying on trowel or tool of your choice.

Scratch up damp plaster with a comb scratcher when still damp.

Apply the straightening coat onto the pre-dampened scratch coat.

Scour the straightening coat using a wooden float once it has firmed up.

Scratch up the straightening coat with a devil float.

Apply the final coat onto the pre-dampened straightening coat.

Scour the final coat using a wooden float once it has firmed up.

Finish as desired and carry out necessary aftercare.

Applying a pre-manufactured clay plaster colour coat using a range of trowels and techniques. The areas not to be plastered have been taped to provide a clean plaster line.

Second from top, right: 'Bull-nosing' the corner – working the trowel horizontally across the corner to create a smooth angle.

Third from top, right: Using a plastic disc to create a smooth rounded corner.

carried out will further compact and tighten the plaster, preparing it for the finishing techniques and making them easier to carry out. It will also produce a more durable finished surface.

9. Carry out finishing techniques
The quality and texture of the finish is down to the timing (how soon it is re-worked after application), the tools used, and the particle sizes of the aggregate.

The finishing coat is also the place to refine any relief or sculptural work, either shaped by hand or carved out with sculptural tools. It should be carried out when the plaster is leathery hard. It is always best to trial a small area of plaster with the chosen finishing technique, to check for suitability and so that a practice run can be carried out. For detailed guidance on the finishing techniques, please refer to Chapter 2. To summarise the main finishing techniques:

Sponge finish: (external/internal)
This will produce a sanded, matt, slightly grainy or textured finish.

Wood float finish: (external/internal)
This will create a more open-grained, textured but very well compressed finish plaster.

Hard trowel/burnishing and polishing (internal)
This creates a very smooth and tight-grained finish.

Achieving different surface finishes with the addition of fibre and mineral additives
Various materials can be added to the finishing coat earth plaster mix to give special effects and to enhance the overall performance of the plaster:

- To achieve a reflective finish, large or small flakes of mica can be added in a proportion of up to 1%. The flakes should be wiped over with a damp sponge or brushed and polished to produce this effect.

- For a textured finish, the addition of finely chopped straw, hemp hurds and other vegetable fibres can be added, up to 15% in volume. For the finishing coats, all fibre material should be finely sieved for ease and success of application. All fibre should be well integrated at the mixing stage so that it is evenly distributed throughout the plaster finish.
- For a polished effect, marble dust can be added – around 10-20%. This is the ingredient added to classic Italian Marmorino lime-based plasters, to give them their characteristic glossy sheen. Marble powders can be sourced from pottery supply stores. For all mineral additives, particle sizes should be no greater than half the thickness of the plaster i.e. 2 - 5mm ($^3/_{32}$ - $^3/_{16}$"). If more than 10% mineral additive is introduced into the mix, it should be counted as part of the aggregate ratio.

To maximise the effect of these additional ingredients, the plaster should be polished or brushed when it has had time to firm up. Once it has fully dried, the surface can be further wiped over with a soft dry tile sponge and, when using mica, buffed with a soft-fibred dry cloth.

- Pigments can also be added to the finishing coat plaster. This is most appropriate for white or light clays such as kaolin. It is also the perfect opportunity to take advantage of the wide variety of naturally occurring coloured clays and sands that exist, providing unique and beautifully coloured plaster finishes.

If a painted finish is desired, it is essential that a breathable, natural paint or wash be used, such as a limewash or alis (clay wash).

Additional steps for application onto specific walling systems

Clay slip bonding coat onto straw-bale walls
The processes for applying earth plasters on to

straw-bale walls are identical to the standard application steps outlined above, with the exception of the clay slip coat. This thin coat (no aggregate added) is applied directly onto the bales before the application of the scratch coat. This is an excellent system devised by North American straw-bale builders. It works to create an initial bond onto the straw, achieved by its wet consistency and high clay content. This then provides a solid base onto which the scratch coat and all subsequent coats can adhere. Its benefits can be further appreciated when it is considered that the plaster system on a straw-bale wall provides substantial structural support to the walls.

The structural effectiveness is determined by how well the plaster is bonded to the wall, making the clay slip coat a beneficial part of the plastering process. The clay slip coat is by no means obligatory, but it is hard work trying to get an earth plaster to stick directly to the bales, and it will not create as good a bond with the straw. The slip coat can be applied by hand, but ideally should be sprayed on with a render gun. The latter method will provide a superior bond due to the force with which the plaster is sprayed, which enables the plaster to penetrate beyond the surface of the bales and into the nooks and crannies of the fibres of straw. If applying by hand, a cupped hand should be used to drag and compress the plaster into the straw. This should be followed by hand massaging the slip coat into the bales, to work the material into the crevices.

Owing to the wet consistency of the slip, it is not necessary to mist the bales prior to application. However, it is necessary to dampen the walls if omitting the clay slip stage and applying the scratch coat directly onto the bales.

Some argue that the scratch coat should not be applied onto the clay slip until the latter has completely dried. This is so that it can establish its bond with the straw, and so that all cracking (some cracking is to be expected with such a high clay content) has manifested and stabilised. The slip coat is then re-moistened before applying the scratch coat. The counter-argument is that by applying the scratch coat immediately after the slip has been applied, whilst it is still wet, a much better bond is forged between the two coats, and it is hence easier to apply. Experience shows that both methods work, and the chosen method should come down to personal preference and scheduling. If using reed mat to cover different and/or smooth substrates, the freshly applied clay slip coat provides a perfect bed in which to place the reed mat. It also means that when the scratch coat is pressed through the gaps in the reed mat, an excellent bond will be achieved between the two earth plaster coats.

Application onto reed mat and reed board
Applying earth plasters onto reed mat and reed board is similar to application onto straw bales. A clay slip coat can also be applied onto reed board to reinforce the bond and to make application of

Approximate earth plaster coverage rates

Scratch coat: 25 litre (5 gallon) container will cover 2.5 metres squared applied at a thickness of 10mm.

Straightening coat: 25 litre (5 gallon) container will cover 4 metres squared at a thickness of 6mm.

Finishing coat: 25 litre (5 gallon) container will cover 6 metres squared at a thickness of 3mm.

the scratch coat easier. This step is not as essential as it is for straw bales, however.

Application tips:
- The reed mat/board need not be dampened down prior to application.
- Extra care is needed to ensure that the material is pressed through the gaps of the reed.
- Only two coats are necessary: base and finishing coat. A well-fibred base coat is necessary to prevent cracking, or alternatively a reinforcement fibre mesh can be embedded into the wet base coat, to cover the full surface of the wall.
- For external applications onto reed board, a special glass-fibre reinforcement mesh is necessary to create extra stability.
- The joints between the board must be prepared as described in Chapter 2.

Application onto wood lath

Wood lath is not a suitable background for earth plasters, owing to the non-chemical curing nature of the plasters. This means that the essential hooking nubs that develop at the back of the lath will not be strong enough, leaving it vulnerable to failure. Lime plasters, which set and cure suitably hard enough, are a better option.

Application onto plasterboard

Earth plasters are ideal for application onto plasterboard to bring character and depth to their flat surfaces. It is only necessary to apply one base coat and a finishing coat, because the surface is so flat. It is possible to get away with applying just a finishing coat.

Earth plasters can be applied directly onto plasterboard as long as certain preparatory measures are taken to assist the plaster to bond to the inherently smooth surface of the plasterboard. It is also necessary to slow down the rate of absorption of the moisture from the plaster into the very thirsty board, which would create a weak bond as the plaster dries out.

Ways to enhance bonding onto plasterboard
1. Using wheat flour paste in the earth plaster mix. The glutinous wheat flour will act as a natural glue to bind and stick the plaster onto the plasterboard surface. The flour paste need only be incorporated into the first plaster coat, which is in direct contact with the plaster board.

2. Using a grainy mix like the adhesion coat, to provide a toothed surface for the earth plaster to key into. A mix of wheat flour paste, manure and sand will stick to the smooth surface, and will dry extremely hard. Variations of this include rubbing or brushing on a clay slip and coarse sand mix onto the wall. One coat is normally sufficient, but two or more coats can be applied if the material does not provide even coverage. Allow these grainy bonding layers to dry thoroughly before applying the first coat of earth plaster.

3. Using a purchased primer, which also contains coarse sands within a blend of binding agents that serve to stick the particles onto the wall surface, and then create a hard, durable body once dry. Most of these products use primarily 'natural' and non-toxic ingredients, which are breathable and safe to use, even for chemically-sensitive individuals. These grainy primers come ready to use, and are simply brushed or rolled on. Check manufacturers' guidelines for individual product application.

As well as applying a sanded, grainy primer or adhesion coat, it is necessary to prepare the joints between the boards, to prevent cracking in the plaster (see Chapter 2). Before applying any of the above methods, it is essential to ensure that the wall surface is clean, dry and free of grease and dust.

Aftercare
Earth plasters require a set of drying conditions that are not extreme in any one direction. To ensure optimum performance from an earth plaster,

it must dry out neither too quickly nor too slowly. A plaster that dries rapidly by direct, hot sunlight, wind or draughts is liable to crack. This is due to the sudden volume changes in the material, causing shrinkage in the material as the water rapidly evacuates.

On the other hand, a plaster that lacks sufficient warmth or ventilation will fail to relinquish its moisture before moulds start to flourish. This is most likely when organic vegetable fibres are present in the mix. For the above reasons, it is necessary to control the drying and curing process when necessary, to provide the optimum conditions for gradual and even drying.

General guidelines:
1. Always apply earth plasters within the correct climatic conditions. If freezing conditions suddenly manifest, the best course of action is to protect new external work with tarps or sheeting (with a suitable air gap to prevent condensation). For internal work, some form of heat source can be introduced on a low, even temperature to increase drying times.

2. If the weather is cool and rainy during the course of a week or more after new plaster has been applied, drying times can be improved through the use of dehumidifiers, maximum ventilation (open windows), and/ or by introducing an external heat source (on a low even heat). For external work, remove rain tarpaulin protection whenever possible to encourage air to circulate and carry away evaporating moisture. If mould does occur, it should be removed with a stiff brush or sprayed with a hydrogen peroxide or borax solution (1 part borax dissolved in 4 parts hot water). If there is a concern about the drying of the plaster before work commences, borax can also be added to the mix in the proportions of between one tablespoon and half a cup per mix.

3. Fresh, wet earth plasters will simply wash off if exposed to direct liquid moisture. Never apply in the rain, and keep tarped during rain.

4. Avoid the drying effects of direct, hot sunlight. If this cannot be avoided (by careful scheduling) protect fresh work with damp sheeting, hessian sacking or tarpaulins. Always maintain a suitable air gap of 300-600mm (1-2') between the wall and the sheeting. Misting the plaster lightly with water at regular intervals will help to slow drying times.

Repairing earth plasters

The beauty of plasters made out of earth lies in their ability to be re-wetted and instantly re-worked at any stage in their life cycle. This ensures that minor cracking that manifests in a finishing coat can be re-wetted and closed up with either a sponge or plastic/metal trowel. Similarly, any chips or damaged areas can be re-filled with fresh material and trowelled or sponged in until the edges are well blended into the existing plaster. Always dampen the damaged area and the area around it before refilling. Reserving some of the original plaster mix for such occasions is recommended. If a fibred mix has been used, dry into small 'cakes' to prevent moulding and rotting of the fibre, and simply remoisten and rework before use.

Troubleshooting guide

For guidance on remedying some of the common problems that one may encounter using earth plasters, follow the principles of adjustment outlined in the sampling/test batches section (pp.166-7). Referring to the troubleshooting guide in Chapter 3 (pp.138-9) will also provide insight and solutions into some of the most common problems encountered with plastering with earth. Many of the problems encountered when working with lime are similar to those that are experienced when working with earth plasters. ■

Lime- and earth-based paints & washes

5

Limewash
Casein paint
Alis clay paint

There is a large variety of lime- and earth-based paints and washes that can be successfully applied onto existing or newly rendered/plastered walls. The final painting process will serve to unify and beautify the surfaces, provide depth and colour (if chosen), and create the atmosphere and tone of the space. Natural paints can also aid in filling minor cracks and blemishes in the plaster or render and prevent dusting.

Finely plastered internal walls, especially those made with earth plasters, can be left unpainted, particularly if a final colour coat has been used or a decorative element such as chopped straw or mica flakes have been added to the final coat. Earth plaster coats can also be painted with a number of translucent glazes to enrich and preserve the earthy tones, whilst giving added protection.

As well as having a decorative function, paints provide an element of protection for the walls, especially on external surfaces. The paint finish acts as the first line of defence against climatic and environmental conditions, especially against the ingress of moisture. Thus the paint finish can serve to protect the render and wall substrate beneath from premature weathering. Most of the lime- and earth-based paints and washes described in this chapter achieve this protection in a different way from the synthetic waterproof paints commonly used in the conventional building industry. Instead of acting as a waterproof barrier against water, their protective role is primarily of a sacrificial nature: it is accepted that they will, over time, gradually erode and need to be replaced. This cheaper, less labour-intensive part of the building is therefore sacrificed to save the render and walls, whilst allowing the walls to breathe.

Below left: A window in South Africa finished with vibrant colours, using traditional techniques.
Below right: Museum walls finished with natural clay paints to regulate internal humidity and protect museum contents.

Of the utmost importance for buildings made out of porous materials i.e. that need to breathe to remain healthy – such as cob, straw bale, porous stone and brick – is that the paint or wash is of a compatible porosity to the wall substrate and/or render/plaster. This means that it will, alongside the plaster or render, help to facilitate a healthy exchange of moisture in and out of the walls. As described in Chapter 1, this is essential for preventing trapped moisture within the building fabric, which can lead to dampness, mould and ultimately potential failure of the structure. As well as not being functionally compatible, a non-porous paint will over time fail to adhere to a porous substrate. Moisture can get trapped between the paint and the wall surface, creating flaking and blistering, and ultimately complete delamination.

The history of paints and painting

Decorative painting has been practised since the Stone Age. This was in the form of cave paintings, which were used to depict stories and everyday life. The process involved the grinding up of natural pigments, such as ochres, iron oxide, manganese oxide and charcoal. These were made into a liquid paste with water and then painted or smeared onto the stone (generally limestone) with feathers, fingers or tufts of fur. Many such cave paintings survive in pristine condition around the world.

Paints used in the past by everyday folk were home-made and based on locally available ingredients such as clay, lime, milk (casein), eggs, blood, urine and earth pigments. These were based on regional traditions and tried and tested recipes, often passed down from generation to generation. For the wealthier classes of society, more expensive and rare ingredients were used to make up paints. This involved the use of rare pigments to produce extravagant colours, which were then mixed with expensive oils and resins.

The approaches used in regard to painting buildings – the philosophy and materials employed – have changed drastically over the past 80-100 years, particularly since the Industrial Revolution. Prior to the advent of mass-manufactured paints (from the end of the nineteenth century), professional decorators would mix each batch of paint on-site with simple ingredients. These produced the traditional paints, such as oil- and water-bound distemper (water, oil, whiting and natural glues), oil paints (linseed oil, turpentine and pigments), limewash (slaked lime and water) and milk paints (casein powder or milk). This tradition continued, despite the availability of ready–made products, until the late 1950s.

A quantum leap in the paint industry took place in the 1950s, during the post war construction boom. At this time, the first synthetic petrochemical paint was formulated. This set the stage for industrial paint manufacturing around the world. These synthetic paints, consisting primarily of synthetic oils and latex, were incredibly cheap and simple to produce on vast scales. This meant that paints made with simple and safe ingredients which had been used for hundreds of years – such as lime, milk, plant oils and clay – were replaced by the chemical formulations that still line the shelves of DIY stores throughout the world today. In recent years there has been a growing awareness of the direct links between these modern paints and major environmental degradation. The link has also been made with these products in creating a range of health hazards including cancers, chronic respiratory illnesses and even dementia.

A growing awareness of the hazards associated with synthetic paints, has encouraged the development of pre-manufactured 'eco-paints', which are now readily available on the market. These have been formulated using the best knowledge of the past – traditional ingredients and methods – alongside scientific research, to produce paints that are convenient to use

African women applying traditional paint finishes to their earthen homes.

and which provide consistent results. They are kinder to the environment, human beings, wild-life and the building fabric on which they are applied. The first paint of this kind was developed in the 1970s by the German scientist Hermann Fischer. He took simple ingredients and recipes that had been tried and tested for thousands of years, and came up with ways to enhance some of their properties. These formulations are continually being developed and improved upon. They have lead the way for the first phase of the EU directive (January 2007, second phase 2010), which sets out to limit the emissions of some of the most dangerous gases from conventionally-made paints. This has meant that even conventional paint companies

have been forced to change some of their most harmful ingredients, and be held accountable for their practices. There is, however, still a long way to go to make this a safe and ethical mainstream industry.

There is currently a strong and growing market for these new breeds of paints, as well as a growing amount of information and awareness surrounding the use of traditional, home-made paints. By making up your own paints from scratch, it is possible to have ultimate control over the ingredients being used to make the paints, as well as the colour and texture of the finish. These home-made, traditional paints are by far the most

'green' and safest option available. They are also often the most beautiful and effective when used on buildings made out of 'natural' and traditional materials. A large portion of this chapter is dedicated to sharing recipes and techniques for making and applying some of the most popular and beautiful traditional paints.

Paints – their ingredients and attributes

Understanding the main components that go into making a paint can help the painter gain awareness of two key things: to understand the potentially dangerous substances that can be present in some paints, and to learn what ingredients are necessary to make a successful home-made paint.

Any paint must contain the following:
* A binder
* A solvent or 'carrier'
* A pigment or 'colour' (optional)

The binder
The binder acts as a glue to stick the pigment (if used) to the surface of the wall. It must have the property of being able to dry out without losing its strength or binding power. It also provides the main body of the paint, and determines its texture and character.

In synthetic paints, the standard binders are normally synthetic chemicals such as acrylic and vinyl. These are products of the petrochemical industry.

In traditional home-made paints and good quality modern 'eco' paints, the binders can include (among others) lime, clay, milk protein (casein), egg, flour starch and linseed oil.

The solvent or 'carrier'
The solvent serves to dissolve and hold both the pigment and the binder in suspension within a spreadable, liquid form, until the paint is applied. It is therefore known as the 'carrier'. Once the paint has been applied, the solvent should evaporate to leave the dry binder and pigment intact on the wall. Many solvents that are used release volatile organic compounds (VOCs) into the atmosphere as the paint dries and the solvent evaporates. This is what creates the typical smell of a freshly painted room. It is these VOCs that are responsible for the majority of the environmental and physical damage created by paints.

For synthetic paints, the standard solvent is mineral turpentine, produced from crude oil.

In traditional home-made paints and good quality, 'eco-paints', solvents consist mainly of vegetable-based turpentine, from renewable plant sources such as citrus oil (made from orange peel), pine resin, water, alcohol and linseed oil.

The pigment or 'colour'
The addition of a pigment to paint gives it colour and can serve to hide or cover any surface blemishes in the wall. There are many different types of pigment available, which can broadly be characterised into natural and synthetic.

Modern synthetic paints are made up solely of synthetic pigments, which provide strong colours. Most 'natural' paints are made with earth pigments, which provide subtle, earthy hues.

Other ingredients:
Some paints (traditional, 'eco' and synthetic) also include additional ingredients to help fulfil specific requirements.

Examples include:
* Preservatives and anti-fungal agents, such as borax and clove oil (safe and natural) and formaldehyde (toxic and dangerous).

- Fillers to bulk the paint out, such as chalk, clay (natural and safe) and titanium dioxide (safe, but very destructive in its production methods).

The dangers of synthetic paints

Perhaps the most illuminating example of the dangers of synthetic paints from a health perspective is that in Denmark, 'painter's' or 'solvent' dementia is a fully recognized disease. Also, as far back as 1987, the World Health Organisation's international agency for research on cancer officially stated that occupational painters have a 40% increased risk of contracting cancer. Greenpeace has directly linked the increase in volatile organic compounds in the atmosphere to a decrease in the reproductive functions in human and wildlife populations.

On an environmental level, US research has concluded that VOCs in paint production create levels of smog in the atmosphere almost equal to that created by vehicle exhausts. It has also been proven that when one gallon of paint is thrown away and seeps into the earth, it has the ability to pollute 250,000 gallons of drinking water. Synthetic paints can have an impact on:

- Human health
- The health of the environment and wildlife
- The health of buildings made out of porous materials, including traditional buildings

Human health

The direct effects of the use of paint on human health come predominantly from the solvent element within the paint. Unless water is used, all solvents used in conventional paints emit volatile organic compounds (VOCs) into the atmosphere as the paint dries. These VOCs combine either with each other or with other volatile chemicals present in the atmosphere to produce very toxic chemicals. The most dangerous levels are found in the air whilst the paint is drying, and when the paint smell is at its strongest. However, some VOCs can offgas from a paint for many years, even when dry. If VOCs are inhaled into the body, they can create a plethora of minor and serious health problems to both the painter and to those inhabiting the painted space. The American Lung Association, for example, has linked contact with VOCs to eye and skin irritation, headaches, muscle weakness, lung disorders, nausea, irreversible liver and kidney damage and cancer.

The two most common solvents used in acrylic and emulsion paints, toluene and xylene, can potentially cause long term foetal damage and developmental problems. Many synthetic paint manufacturers have made a move to eliminate solvents and hence VOCs from their paints by using water as a solvent. However, this has generally meant that a large number of equally dangerous chemicals, such as glycol ethers, have been added to replace the functions previously carried out by the synthetic solvents. Hence a can of paint that is labelled 'low' or 'zero' VOC is not telling the whole story.

Synthetic paints are literally made up of a concoction of different chemicals, each having their own long list of potential related illnesses. Some of these are minor and short-lived, like headaches and nausea, others can be long-term and chronic, such as allergies created from statically charged, dust-attracting vinyl binders. Still others can be highly life-threatening, such as glycol ethers, asphalt and polyurethane, which can create cancers.

Damaging paint chemicals can enter the body through inhalation, ingestion, and direct contact with the skin. Once in the body, some of these chemicals are known to be bio-acccumulative. This means that they can build up in the cells and remain there, even to be passed onto future generations.

The environment and wildlife

Owing to the interconnected nature of all things, whatever impacts the environment also affects all living and breathing inhabitants of the planet, and hence the two cannot be separated. Environmental degradation from conventional paints occurs at all stages of its life cycle:

- The production of the paint itself, through the extraction and production of the ingredients.
- The toxic gases released from the paint once used.
- The afterlife of the paint – the ability of painted materials to safely biodegrade, the problems associated with the safe disposal of paint leftovers, and the pollution created by the run-off when cleaning brushes.

Paint production

The bulk of conventional paints are made up from products from the petrochemical industry, such as vinyl and acrylic. It goes without saying that oil dependency must be diminished as it is a non-renewable resource and is made with an incredibly energy-intensive process.

Titanium dioxide, which is a white pigment used in all synthetic paints to increase coverage and opacity, is one of the most energy-intensive and damaging of all ingredients used. Titanium dioxide is a natural mineral. To make it pure white, it must be purified by a process of cleaning with acids. These toxic acids are generally dumped into the environment. All these processes contribute vast amounts of CO_2 emissions into the atmosphere.

Vibrant limewash colours made from natural earth pigments, to enhance the surrounding landscape.

The release of toxic gases

The airborne VOCs released into the atmosphere once the paint is on the wall and begins to dry, accounts for 9% of all airborne pollutants and contributes to ground level ozone. The American Environment Protection Agency (EPA) rated paint as being amongst the top sources for indoor air pollution.

The afterlife of the paint

Any material that has been coated with a toxic paint will not easily or safely biodegrade into the ground, painted wood being the foremost example. All synthetic paints are toxic to wildlife in any quantity. Furthermore, the synthetic chemicals present in their formulations are persistent and will take millions of years to break down into safe components in the environment. This also includes any paint residue flushed into the environment through washing brushes.

Building health

All synthetic paints are non-porous, and do not breathe. They are also brittle and inflexible. Any paint used on a building made out of porous materials requires a paint that is compatible in terms of its porosity and ability to expand and contract in line with the natural movements of the building. If this is not observed, it can lead to problems with trapped moisture in the walls, flaking paint, damage to and possibly failure of the plaster/render and even of the walls themselves.

Why are synthetic paints so widely used?

It is hard to fathom why synthetic paints managed to replace and virtually eliminate the use of traditional paints, all within the space of a mere 60 years. This is especially hard to understand when it is considered that home-made traditional paints were generally made with safe, local materials that were compatible with the buildings they were being applied to. Hindsight can only be gained through time, and clearly convenience is a powerful lure. Most people were ready to relinquish what they saw as a laborious process, requiring a range of tools and ingredients. Most of the world was ready for all that was convenient, predictable, consistent and less labour-intensive. The new, modern paints were obviously well marketed and perceived as being convenient and easier to apply (one coat of conventional paint versus three coats of limewash). People were ready to be liberated from the necessary repainting required every few years. But times are changing again, and the growing awareness of the dangers of synthetic paints is encouraging a revitalised interest in making paints from scratch. This enables the painter to know exactly what ingredients are involved, as well as allowing a sense of personal satisfaction from being involved in the whole process. For those who prefer to be safe, healthy and life-supporting, but who want the convenience of a good quality, ready-made paint, it is also possible to look to the new generation of 'eco-paints'.

Paint preferences: In order to improve the welfare of living beings, buildings & the environment, try to use:

1. Home-made limewashes, clay paints, distempers, casein paints with natural earth pigments.

2. Mineral paints, and water and plant-based paints.

3. Paints made from plant and mineral ingredients using natural solvents.

4. Water-based synthetic paints.

5. Solvent-based synthetic paints.

Pre-manufactured 'eco' paints

The definition of what entails an 'eco' or 'natural' paint is fairly vague, and can be quite confusing. Most of the major conventional paint manufacturers now produce a line of paint, which they claim to be either 'low' or 'zero' VOC, 'breathable', and sometimes even 'natural' or 'eco'. Care should be taken before purchasing one of these paints. There is, however, an ever-increasing number of companies who are producing very good quality, versatile and authentic 'natural' paints. For a paint to live up to the name of being 'eco' or 'natural', the company producing it should adhere to the following principles:

- **Minimising impact on the environment**
  Renewable and biodegradable ingredients. Minimal or no off-gassing of toxic, ozone-depleting chemicals.

- **Eliminating danger to human health**
  Non-toxic and even life-enhancing ingredients, such as odour-absorbing clays and pleasantly smelling essential oils. Minimal or no off-gassing of toxic VOCs.

- **Maximising the health of a building**
  High vapour permeability, allowing buildings to breathe and thus help prevent damp and mould.

The most important test lies with the willingness of the company to provide comprehensive ingredient lists and production information that states exactly what materials are included in the paint and how they were produced. This is especially important for chemically-sensitive individuals, who may even be allergic to some of the 'natural' ingredients included. For example, some of the non-synthetic solvents used, such as citrus oil or vegetable turpentine, may also trigger allergies, although they are not nearly as damaging in the long-term as their synthetic counterparts. For this reason it is also necessary to ventilate any internal spaces being painted, even if using a safe paint. On the whole, it makes the most sense to opt for a paint company that uses simple technology and simple ingredients, drawn from traditional recipes and know-how. Also it is best, where possible, to support companies that are producing locally or at least within your country.

Currently, many of these 'natural' or 'eco' paints are slightly more expensive than their conventional counterparts. This is obviously because the market is still relatively small and therefore production is on a smaller scale (which is, however, quite often a good thing), and because the raw materials being used are of good quality and therefore more expensive.

To save on expense, and so that you know exactly what is going on your walls, it is possible to opt for making your own paint. This can be an easy and satisfying process. The rest of this chapter provides recipes and guidelines for producing 'eco-friendly', healthy, beautiful and cost-effective paints and washes.

Home-made natural paints

Most home-made natural paints are simple and easy to make. Many of them require inexpensive ingredients, which are easy to get hold of. Many of these ingredients include everyday household grocery items, such as wheat flour paste and skimmed milk. Other more specialist ingredients, such as linseed oil, casein powder and lime, are easily obtained from specialist suppliers.

The majority of the home-made paints described below consist primarily of a base (or binder) of either lime, earth (clay) or milk protein (casein powder). Certain additional ingredients can be added to these basic paints and washes, to enable them to function better in certain circumstances. Water is the primary solvent.

Pigments

All the home-made paints described below can be used in their natural state to produce a white or buff coloured paint. It is also possible to add colour through the use of pigments. The pigments can also be blended together to create unique and personalised colours. There are many different types of pigments, and not all are suitable for use in lime-based paints and washes. Also, some are highly toxic and energy intensive/polluting to produce. Broadly speaking, pigments can be categorised into:

Natural earth and mineral pigments

Natural earth pigments are literally derived from different coloured earth and rocks. They are first extracted and mined, secondly either crushed and ground, and then sieved. They are either used in their raw form or heated to produce different shades. The different colours are attributed to the different minerals present, such as iron oxides and manganese. Natural earth pigments normally dictate the specific regional colours of an area, as they will have been mined locally. This is why many traditional towns and villages sit so comfortably within their surrounding environment, as they are literally painted with materials from the earth and rocks around them.

The earth pigments are the most suitable for use in home-made paints because they are generally the safest and are the most compatible with lime. Lime is very alkaline, and some pigments will react negatively with this alkalinity. The most compatible, or 'lime-fast' pigments are those composed of the metal oxides, such as the yellow, red and brown ochres, raw and burnt siennas and umbers. All reputable lime suppliers and pigment specialists should be able to advise on the suitability of a pigment for use in a limewash. The mineral content of the natural earth pigments also makes them more resistant to the effects of ultraviolet light, meaning that they are less likely to fade over time.

The colours produced from the natural earth pigments are generally soft, subtle, earthy, and less bright than the synthetic pigments. Their crystalline structure causes light hitting the paint surface to be reflected in different directions, meaning that paints made with natural pigments provide a uniquely vibrant finish of unsurpassed richness.

Natural animal or plant-based pigments

Plant or animal dyes can be utilised as pigments in paints, but are not recommended because they will fade very quickly with exposure to light.

Synthetic pigments

These are made synthetically from chemicals to either replicate the natural earth pigment colours, or to extend the range of colours naturally available. Many pigments are derived from natural but very toxic heavy metals, such as cadmium and chromium, or from products of the petrochemical industry.

Many of these pigments are very stable and lime-fast, such as cobalt blue, emerald green, Indian red and cadmium yellow. They are thus suitable for use in limewashes. However, they are more toxic and energy-intensive to extract than their natural earth counterparts.

Preparation of pigments

Most pigments can be purchased ready to use in a fine powdered form. If using personally extracted coloured clays or pigments, or the pigment is coarse, it is necessary to grind it into a fine powder using a pestle and mortar, grinding mill or a rolling pin onto a hard surface. Dampening the material prior to grinding will prevent dusting and will assist with the grinding process. The more finely ground the pigment, the more evenly dispersed it will be in the paint, and hence the more uniform the finish achieved. If the pigment is not finely and evenly ground, streaks of pigment may appear on the wall.

Natural earth pigments are found in rocks and soils around the world in a range of colours.

Sculpture by Roxanne Swentzell.

Natural earth pigments need to be ground down to a fine powder before being added to paint.

Breathable finishes, such as limewash, should be used on traditional buildings to ensure that the building fabric remains healthy.

The ground pigment is best if it is soaked for 24 hours, or overnight in a small amount of water, to fully break down the particles of pigment before being added to the paint base. Alternatively, the pigment can be mixed with warm water in a sealed jar and shaken vigorously prior to being added to the paint. If the pigment does not dissolve easily in water, it can be mixed with a small amount of alcohol, such as vodka or another white spirit. Once added to the paint base, soaking the mixture for an hour or two will further help to disperse the pigment throughout the paint.

The fine powders of pigments can be hazardous when inhaled, so always use a mask and work in a well-ventilated space when handling.

Sampling

All pigments behave differently when added to a paint base, so it is always advisable to carry out a few sample patches on the substrate to be painted, before committing it to the entire wall. It is also very difficult to anticipate the final colour of the pigmented paint before the paint has been applied to the wall and fully dried. The colour in the bucket of the wet paint will be many shades darker than the dried paint on the wall, and the only way to accurately arrive at the desired colour is to carry out numerous tests. Take notes on each recipe, as it is easy to forget the exact proportions used in each mix.

Generally speaking, the more pigment added, the deeper the colour. However, there is a threshold amount that can be added to a certain amount of paint base, beyond which, the paint will be weakened, creating a powdery paint. This threshold is based on the percentage of pigment that can be held by a given amount of binder. This amount is 7.5-10% of pigment by weight of the binder. This threshold can also be ascertained through the test batches: if the dried paint or wash easily dusts off, the threshold may have been exceeded.

Mixing colours

Colours get deeper with each consecutive coat. Different and unique colours can be achieved by mixing various pigments together. Too many colours, however, will produce muddied tones, so stick with 2-3 colours at most. The standard colour wheel, used to provide insight into how different colours work together, can be a useful tool for helping to create a personalised colour palette. The general principles for mixing different colours are:

1. Start off with a single pigment and add consecutive colours, one at a time.
2. Start with the weakest colours first, then add the strongest.

Lime

Lime is the principal ingredient in limewash (it acts as the binder). Generally, a non-hydraulic lime putty is preferred for its pure white colour and because it produces a better consistency limewash. Natural hydraulic limes can be used where damp conditions prevail. However, the strength of the lime used should correlate with the strength of the plaster/render and wall substrate below (see Chapter 3). An NHL2 is generally best in these circumstances for making exterior limewashes. The cheaper hydrated 'builders lime' will not produce a good limewash, and its use is not recommended.

A well made limewash produces a highly effective, simple, inexpensive and beautiful finish. It creates a soft, matte effect that compliments and enhances old and new buildings constructed out of breathable materials. Like all building traditions utilising lime, it has been used for thousands of years to protect and beautify internal and external walls. Due to its mildly antiseptic qualities (because of its alkalinity) it has a rich agricultural history: it was used to help keep domestic and farm outbuildings healthy and safe. In many cultures around the world, the yearly limewashing of public

Basic limewashes

A basic limewash can be made out of either a non-hydraulic lime putty or a natural hydraulic lime powder.

1 Basic limewash with putty

Use as a general limewash for in- and outdoors.

Ingredients:

- 1 part mature lime putty (minimum 3 months, 6 months to 1 year old for best quality)
- 3 parts clean water

Mixing:

1. Fill bucket $1/3$ full with lime putty.
2. Add water gradually and whisk together using a paddle attachment onto a drill, until the consistency of full fat milk is reached.
3. Add pigment if desired (see below) and whisk thoroughly until well incorporated.
4. Can be used immediately, but will improve if left to stand for 1 hour or more. If it is standing for a day or more, more water may need to be added before use to thin it down to the desired consistency.
5. Whisk thoroughly immediately before use, and continue to stir at intervals throughout the application process.

Amounts and coverage:

6-8 m² per litre. Coverage may vary depending on the texture and porosity of the wall surface.

2 Limewash with hydraulic lime

Can be used where continual dampness is an issue.

Ingredients:

- 1 part natural hydraulic lime powder. Use the information in Chapter 3 to determine the correct strength required for the job. NHL2 produces good results in most situations
- 3 parts clean water

Mixing:

Always wear a mask when mixing natural hydraulic lime powder.

1. Follow instructions as per mixing lime putty to reach desired consistency of full fat milk, replacing the putty with natural hydraulic lime powder.

A limewash made out of natural hydraulic lime is best used immediately.

Amounts and coverage:

7-8 m² per litre. Coverage may vary depending on the texture and porosity of the wall surface.

Caution: Always wear protective gear when handling materials containing lime.

Limewash troubleshooting

1. Cracks and crazes:
- Wall not sufficiently dampened before application.
- Limewash made too thick.

2. Powders off the wall when dry:
- Limewash made too thick.
- Limewash applied too thickly.
- Too much pigment.

Making up limewash with mature non-hydraulic lime putty.

Clockwise from top left: The materials and tools needed: mature lime putty and water, and a range of brushes.

Adding 1 part of lime putty to the bucket (one third full).

Adding 3 parts water to the lime putty (roughly to the top of the bucket).

Mixing the water and putty together.

The mixed limewash should be the consistency of full-fat milk.

Limewash with casein / linseed oil

Either casein powder or linseed oil can be added to the basic limewash mixes for increased durability.

A Limewash with casein

Use when additional protection is needed.

Ingredients:

- 5 parts mature lime putty or natural hydraulic lime.
- ½ part casein powder.
- OR 4 parts milk curds
- Clean water (enough to make consistency of full fat milk).

Mixing:

1. Make basic limewash (full-fat milk consistency).
2. Add pigment to the lime if using.
3. If using casein powder (as opposed to curds), soak in a small amount of hot water for 2 hours.
4. Add limewash mix to casein solution and whisk (with a drill) together until fully incorporated.
5. Thin with water as necessary to achieve consistency of full fat milk.

Use mix immediately. Don't store more than 1 day.

Amounts and coverage:

6-8 m² per litre. Coverage may vary depending on the texture and porosity of the wall surface.

B Limewash with linseed oil

Use when extra water-shedding properties are needed.

Ingredients:

- One 3-gallon (15 litres) bucket of limewash (a standard builder's bucket).
- 2 tablespoons of boiled linseed oil (roughly 3-4% by volume).

Mixing:

1. Mix a basic limewash.
2. Add linseed oil, (heating the oil gently aids dispersion) and mix in thoroughly.

Best used immediately.
Mix regularly during application to prevent oil from separating from the limewash.

Amounts and coverage:

5-7 m² per litre. Coverage may vary depending on the texture and porosity of the wall surface.

Caution: Always wear protective gear when handling materials containing lime.

Making casein curds from skimmed milk

1. Leave a container or jug of skimmed milk in a warm place for a few days or until it starts to sour and the curd (solid material) separates out from the whey (the liquid material). The milk can be warmed gently on a stove to speed up this process, or a small amount of lemon juice or vinegar can be added.

2. Remove the solid curds and place in a muslin cloth in a colander, so that the whey can be squeezed out. Wash the curd thoroughly with clean water, especially if lemon juice or vinegar is used, to remove acidity.

Adding linseed oil to limewash

Linseed oil, in its raw form, will make limewash more durable and flexible, and encourage it to shed water more effectively. For this reason it is often used on external walls that are subject to heavy, direct rainfall. The linseed oil creates a fatty acid synthesis with the lime, to make lime soap. This fills the pores to a point that makes it more water-repellant, but still allows it to remain suitably vapour-permeable. Heating the oil gently before adding will greatly assist even dispersion throughout the limewash. Once added, the mixture must be thoroughly mixed and beaten, and continually agitated throughout the application process. This is to prevent the oil and water from separating over time. It is best to only add the linseed oil to the final coat of limewash, to maintain maximum breathability throughout the other coats. It is also best to ensure that any freshly applied lime plaster/render is fully dried and carbonated before application.

Adding pigments to limewash

Pigment can be added to any of the above mixes. As mentioned earlier, limewash can only carry a finite amount of pigment before it is weakened and left prone to powdering. Generally, 7-10% by weight of lime is considered the maximum.

This is why most traditional limewash colours are pastel. For more vibrant colours, an additional binder, such as casein should be added (see recipe above). Short of meticulously weighing each ingredient, experimentation and testing will give good indication as to whether the maximum amount has been exceeded. Signs to look out for are powdering, once applied and dried, a point at which the colour does not alter any further, and patchy areas of colour staining appearing on the wall once dried.

and private buildings was an important part of spring cleaning rituals (and still is, in some parts of the world).

Like a lime plaster or render, a limewash dries and cures into a water insoluble finish via the process of carbonation (as well as hydration, if using a natural hydraulic lime). It reacts with carbon dioxide in the atmosphere, to revert back to calcium carbonate, its original chemical form (see Chapter 3). No toxic fumes (VOCs) are released from the limewash as it dries out. Limewash is often said to produce a unique surface 'glow', especially when natural earth pigments are added. This is a result of the crystals of calcite ($CaCO_3$) that are formed during carbonation. These crystals absorb light and then reflect it back in duplicate. This is known as a 'dual refractive index'.

The main benefit of using a limewash, especially on buildings made out of porous materials, is its high vapour permeability and hence breathability. This is due to its micro-porous structure, which ensures that any moisture absorbed into the outer skin of the limewash or plaster/render is able to quickly and efficiently evaporate. This allows the walls to dry out, and hence prevents the accumulation of excessive and harmful moisture build-up within the structure. This also makes limewash the ideal finish for use in remedial situations in old buildings where dampness is an issue. Limewash will also successfully heal minor shrinkage cracks in the plaster/render, as well as evening out blemishes in the wall surface, especially when numerous coats are applied to build up protection. Limewash is also flame-resistant, and will prevent the spread of flames. It can be made washable if made well, and is not affected by ultraviolet light.

Areas of application
Because limewash is water-soluble, it is most suitably applied onto walls or backgrounds that are porous and hence water-absorbent. The ideal background is a freshly applied lime plaster or render. This ensures maximum bonding, colour fastness and durability. The porous nature of the limewash will enable a freshly applied lime plaster/render to continue carbonating, even when painted on immediately. Other excellent backgrounds include porous stone, brick, earth walls and earth plasters. Any non-porous masonry should be primed with a limewash and fine sand mix (silica sand works well), in a ratio of 1 part lime : 1 part sand. This should be evenly applied with a paint brush onto the surface and allowed to fully dry before the application of subsequent basic limewash mixes. Portland cement and concrete blocks will also receive limewash well, as they are highly absorbent materials, despite lacking vapour permeability.

Limewash will not adhere well to wood (unless it is unvarnished), metal, gypsum plasters or other smooth, polished surfaces. To remedy this, an intermediate bonding coat can be used to enable bonding to occur. These can either be purchased ready made from a specialist supplier (see www.naturalbuildingresources.com) or made up from a simple recipe listed in Chapter 4. Another option is to use a casein additive to the limewash mix, which acts as a glue to enhance adhesion (see recipe on p.210).

If using lime putty to make limewash, it is essential that a mature lime putty is used. This will ensure that all the lime has been fully slaked before use. A lime putty that is 6 months to 1 year old will produce the best results. However, most lime putty is supplied at a minimum of three months old, and this can be used to make a perfectly adequate limewash.

Some producers supply a read-to-mix lime paint that is made from natural hydraulic lime powder and pigment. It simply requires the addition of water and then blending. Lime putty-based washes, with or without pigments, can also be purchased in wet form ready to be applied.

Applying limewash

Always protect your eyes and hands with safety glasses and gloves as the lime is caustic.

Limewash needs to be applied in a minimum of three coats (five or six is best for newly painted walls), in order to develop depth and even coverage.

1. Dampen wall prior to application with clean water. If applying onto a freshly lime plastered or rendered wall, application with a pure limewash (basic mix) can be carried out 'al fresco'. The limewash is applied when the lime plaster/render is still wet and not fully carbonated. The porosity of the limewash will enable carbonation to occur simultaneously in both the limewash and freshly applied plaster/render. This can strengthen the bond between the limewash and the wall, and can intensify the colour.

2. Always agitate the limewash in the container before application, and regularly during application. This will prevent the ingredients from settling out, and ensure that the pigment is thoroughly integrated.

3. Use a wide paint brush 100mm (4"). For smooth walls, a short, stiff bristled brush works best. For 'knobbly' walls, such as old cob/stone walls or a harled finish, a longer bristled brush works well to access between the undulations, and to cover the larger surface area. Use a range of smaller brushes for edging and detailing.

4. Limewash is runnier than conventional paint, so care should be taken not to load the brush with too much material, otherwise it will drip excessively. By dipping the brush only half way into the limewash and squeezing out the surplus paint against the bucket edge, or flicking it a few times into the bucket, the brush will not become oversaturated.

5. Apply the limewash by brushing it vigorously into the wall surface, getting into all the nooks and crannies. Brush strokes can be in all directions, or in a tight circular movement.

6. Apply each coat thinly to prevent crazing and cracking, and avoid the temptation of going over areas already covered. The limewash will appear translucent on first application, and will only develop its opacity as it begins to carbonate (1 - 24 hours).

7. The first coat should be thinner than subsequent coats, which can be made progressively thicker.

8. Allow each coat to dry for at least 24 hours before applying subsequent coats. Mist each previous coat lightly before applying a new one.

Additives to enhance the performance of limewash

Limewash does not work like synthetic paint, which function to protect underlying materials by repelling moisture. A limewash acts more like a sacrificial layer, and though highly effective at protecting the underlying materials, will eventually weather and need renewal every few years, depending on exposure. For this reason, numerous ingredients have traditionally been added to the basic limewash mix to encourage it to shed water more effectively. Other additives can also be incorporated to enhance the adhesion and binding qualities of the limewash, and to increase resistance to abrasion.

Linseed oil

Linseed oil, in its raw form, will make limewash more durable, flexible, and encourage it to shed water more effectively. For this reason it is often used on external walls that are subject to heavy, direct rainfall. The linseed oil creates a fatty acid synthesis with the lime, to make lime soap. This fills the pores to a point that makes it more water-repellent, but still allows it to remain suitably vapour-permeable. Traditionally, a clarified animal fat called 'tallow' was added to limewash to perform the same functions. It was added during the slaking process because the tallow is a solid material at room temperature. The heat produced during slaking caused the tallow to melt and hence disperse easily amongst the lime. In modern practice linseed oil is a preferred alternative, not only because it is more convenient to use but because tallow considerably decreases breathability, and it can leave a bad, lingering smell for many months. It can also mould in damp conditions, and its water-repelling nature can make the application of fresh coats of limewash on top very difficult.

Exercise caution when purchasing raw linseed oil from hardware stores or builder's merchants, as it can include potentially toxic chemical drying agents. Good quality linseed oil can be purchased from specialist suppliers (see naturalbuildingresources.com). Heating the oil gently before adding will greatly assist even dispersion throughout the limewash. Once added, the mixture must be thoroughly mixed and beaten, and continually agitated throughout the application process. This is to prevent the oil and water from separating over time. The linseed oil should be added to the final coat of limewash to maintain maximum breathability throughout the other coats. It is also best to ensure that any freshly applied lime plaster/render is fully dried and carbonated before application. The decreased breathability may prevent full carbonisation.

Casein powder (milk protein)

When casein powder (an acid) is added to a basic limewash mix, it reacts with the alkaline lime to make a natural glue: calcium caseinate. This increases the binding capacity of the limewash, allowing it to adhere more effectively to the background. The calcium caseinate is relatively insoluble and does not considerably affect permeability as long as not too much is added. These are useful characteristics for external, exposed situations where improved weatherproofing and rain-shedding qualities are needed. It also makes a useful additive for applying limewash to difficult surfaces. In an internal situation, it also improves the ability to wipe the finished surface.

The limitation to using a casein additive is that, being a milk product, it can be susceptible to mould growth in damp areas, so it is best to choose another type of breathable paint in this situation. If adding casein to limewash, it should be incorporated immediately prior to its use to prevent moulding.

Casein

Casein is derived from milk protein. It can be added to limewash to enhance its properties, or used to create a paint in its own right. Casein can be purchased in powder form (see above) or used in the form of curds, made from skimmed

Top: A sculpted relief painted with pigmented casein paints. By Athena and Bill Steen.
Bottom: A pigmented natural paint on top of a micaceous plaster. By Carol Crews.

Applying natural home-made paints.

All bar middle right: White clay 'alis'.

Middle right: Limewash.

milk. Powdered casein is more potent and will produce a more durable paint. It is also more convenient and easier to mix.

Casein or 'milk' paints have a long and successful tradition of use throughout Europe. Milk was, and is, a readily available material, especially for rural communities, and it was recognized that it was not only suitable as a nutrient-rich food source, but also useful to make a protective wall coating. Ready-made casein or milk paints can be purchased from specialist suppliers or can easily be made at home with a few simple ingredients, to produce a range of different finishes.

Casein paints are vapour-permeable, and are therefore suitable on porous surfaces that need to breathe in order to remain healthy. They are fairly water-resistant, though not waterproof. They are lightly wipeable. They provide an excellent option for chemically-sensitive individuals, as they have a mild, non-toxic odour. Casein paint will produce a flat, matte paint finish with a slightly textured surface. Casein paint is very permanent. It will not need a primer, even onto smooth, polished surfaces, because of its highly adhesive qualities.

Using casein powder

Casein powder is a much more concentrated form of casein. One part casein powder is roughly equal to eight parts curds. A paint made from curds is much less permanent than using casein powder.

How to use casein paint

Casein can be added to water to produce a translucent glaze. This can be applied directly onto an earth plaster to protect it and decrease dusting, whilst allowing the natural earth-coloured finish to be maintained. Pigments can be added to this mix to produce a translucent colour glaze. To make a full-bodied, opaque paint, fillers such as chalk, clay, lime and pigments can be added. This will produce a soft, matte finish with a flat but rich texture, similar to limewash.

Additives to enhance the performance of casein paints

The addition of lime will increase weather-resistance and durability (see previous section), and make it suitable for external use. A pure casein paint should only be used internally as it will not withstand the elements. It should also be avoided in internal areas that are subject to a lot of humidity, such as bathrooms, kitchens and laundry rooms, as it will be susceptible to moulding. Linseed oil can also be added to make it more water-resistant. Casein paint will need to be used on the same day it is made, otherwise mould may develop.

Clay: alis clay paints

Clay, in the form of locally sourced subsoils, or bagged clays such as kaolin, can be used to make a thin clay paint. This is a tradition still much practiced in the south-west USA on the earth plasters of adobe structures. Such a clay paint is known as an 'alis'. It was traditionally applied by the 'enjarradoras' (native women plasterers of the south-west of America). The word 'alis' is derived from the Spanish word, 'alisar', which means 'to make smooth'. A handful of key North American natural builders have done much work with developing this practice. Carol Crews, a modern day 'enjarradora', is one such person, and has inspired us and many others with her beautiful work. A basic alis is made from mixing together finely sieved clay and water to create a slip that is painted or rubbed onto the wall in several layers. Different coloured clays can be used to create a variety of beautiful and uniquely coloured finishes. Alternatively a white clay, such as kaolin, can be used as a neutral base to which to pigments can be added.

Where to use an alis clay paint

Alis clay paints are highly breathable, and they therefore make a complementary finish for an earth plaster. As with an earth-based plaster, an

Casein paints

Casein is used to make a translucent wash, a primer, or an opaque full-bodied paint.

1 Casein wash

Use as a translucent glaze on top of an earth plaster.

Ingredients:

- 1 part borax
- 8 parts hot water
- 1 part casein powder (or 8 parts curds)
- 4 parts clean water
- Pigment (optional)

Mixing:

1. Add casein powder to 4 parts clean water and let sit overnight or for a minimum of 3 hours. Mix well with a paddle & drill to dissolve lumps.
2. Mix together borax and 8 parts hot water and agitate until dissolved. Allow to cool.
3. Add the borax and casein solutions together and mix thoroughly.
4. Prepare pigment as described above and thoroughly incorporate into the mix.

Amounts and coverage:

8-10 m² per litre. Coverage may vary depending on the texture and porosity of the wall surface.

2 Casein primer

Use as a primer before applying a casein paint to provide better coverage of casein paint.

Ingredients:

- 1 part borax
- 8 parts hot water
- 1 part casein powder
- 4 parts clean water
- Pigment (optional)

Mixing:

1. Add casein powder to 4 parts water and let sit overnight or for a minimum of three hours. Mix well to dissolve lumps.
2. Mix together borax and 8 parts hot water and agitate until dissolved. Allow to cool.
3. Add the casein and borax solutions together and mix thoroughly.
4. Prepare pigment as described above and thoroughly incorporate into the mix.

Amounts and coverage:

8-10 m² per litre. Coverage may vary depending on the texture and porosity of the wall surface.

Caution: Always wear protective gear when handling materials containing lime.

Applying a casein wash

- Follow the basic guidelines for applying limewash.
- Needs at least two coats for even coverage.
- Apply with a wide paint brush and small ones for detail work, brushing in all directions.
- Will dry on the wall in about one hour.

Applying a casein primer

- Again, follow the basic guidelines for applying limewash.
- Use a wide paint brush and small ones for detail work, brushing in all directions.
- Drying time is approximately one hour.

3 Casein paint

Use as a top coat.
Always use casein paints immediately.

Ingredients:

- 1 part casein powder (or 8 part curds)
- 4 parts lime putty*
- 4 parts water (and a bit more for later thinning)
- Pigment (optional)

Mixing:

1. Put 1 part casein powder in a bucket with 4 parts water. Mix well to dissolve lumps. Allow to soak overnight (minimum of three hours).
2. Add the lime putty to the casein solution and mix together thoroughly with whisk attached to drill.
3. Add more water as required to reach the consistency of full fat milk.
4. Prepare pigment as described above and add to the casein paint, mixing thoroughly.

Amounts and coverage:

6-8 m² per litre. Coverage may vary depending on the texture and porosity of the wall surface.

*Substituting borax for lime

Like lime, borax is an alkali, and can therefore be substituted for lime to produce the same binding properties. Using lime will produce a more water-resistant paint, whereas borax makes a better glaze emulsion.

Because borax is not white, it is a better option when wanting to produce a dark-coloured paint.

Mixing:

1. Dissolve 65g of borax in 1 litre hot water.
2. Mix the borax to the casein slurry, thinned with 12 litres of water.
3. Prepare pigment as described above and thoroughly incorporate into the mix.

To make a thicker, more full-bodied paint, a filler such as white kaolin, clay or chalk can be added (roughly 3 parts).

Casein paint troubleshooting

1. Dusts on the wall when dry – add more casein powder.
2. Cracks and peels when dry – add more water to the mix.

Applying casein paint

- Again, follow the basic guidelines for applying limewash.
- Apply two thin coats, or more if necessary.
- Wide paint brushes are best for the main body of work and small ones for detailing. Use wide brush strokes in all directions.
- Drying time is approximately one hour.

Alis clay paints

Alis clay paints are best for interior work, and are generally applied in two coats.

The recipes below are given as a guideline only, and should be refined by carrying out individual test batches on the wall. Each test patch should be allowed to dry fully before being analysed and amended according to the outcome (see page 224).

1 Base coat

Alis clay paints are very similar to earthen plasters, and exact recipes cannot be provided because of the many variations of raw materials.

Starter recipe:

- 1 part clay subsoil, coloured clay or a bagged clay (kaolin clay).
- 1 part finely ground mica or fine sand (silica).
- ½ part wheat flour paste.
- Pigment optional.

Mixing:

1. Make up wheat flour paste (see Chapter 4) and allow to cool.
2. Add roughly 2-3 parts cold water to every 1 part wheat flour paste, to make it liquid enough to enable easy integration of the remaining ingredients.
3. Add sand/mica and clay to wheat flour paste and whisk together, until a creamy, spreadable consistency is achieved like thick cream.
4. Add pigment when well mixed and mix evenly.

It can be mixed up in buckets, a wheelbarrow, plasterer's bath or cement mixer, depending on the amounts being made. Use immediately because the binding power diminishes the longer it sits, and the wheat flour paste will mould.

Amounts and coverage:

6-7m² per litre. Coverage may vary depending on the texture and porosity of the wall surface.

2 Top coat

Use the same recipe as for the base coat, except that the sand is omitted. Mica can still be used as a decorative element, and chopped straw can be added to provide texture.

Starter recipe:

- 1 part clay subsoil, coloured clay or a bagged clay (kaolin clay).
- ½ part wheat flour paste.
- Pigment optional.
- Small amounts of chopped straw or mica flakes for decoration and texture in final coat (optional).

Mixing:

1. Make up wheat flour paste (see Chapter 4) and allow to cool.
2. Add roughly 2-3 parts cold water to every 1 part wheat flour paste, to make it liquid enough to enable easy integration of the remaining ingredients.
3. Add mica and clay to wheat flour paste and whisk together, until a creamy, spreadable consistency is achieved like thick cream.
4. Add pigment when well mixed and mix evenly.

Amounts and coverage:

8-10 m² per litre. Coverage may vary depending on the texture and porosity of the wall surface.

Clockwise, from top left: The raw materials: wheat flour paste, fine silica sand, finely sieved clay, water.

Adding water to the wheat flour paste.

Adding silica sand to the water and wheat flour paste.

Adding sieved clay to the other ingredients.

Whisking the ingredients together.

Applying alis clay paint

Two coats should be applied, with the second coat being polished or buffed for a smooth finish.

1. Lightly mist the walls prior to application. Apply when fresh plasters have fully dried.
2. Work the paint well into the surface of the wall, brushing in all directions. For small, curved areas such as niches, it can be mixed thicker and applied by hand.
3. Allow the first coat to thoroughly dry before application of the second coat.
4. Apply the second coat as above.
5. Allow second coat to dry until leather-hard but still damp, then use a damp, well-wrung sponge dipped into clean water (warm water will assist the process). Polish the alis clay paint with the sponge, using tight circular strokes. This should remove brush marks and smooth out the surface. It will also expose flakes of mica or chopped straw if used. Rinse the sponge often to keep a clean edge.
6. If large flakes of mica have been used, a final polish with a dry cloth will further enhance the shine.

Save any leftover material for future repairs. If straw or flour paste have been added, the material should be dried into 'cookies', stored in an airtight container, and rehydrated for future repairs and fresh coats.

Guidelines for test patches:

Testing can be done to assess the quality of the mix and for achieving the desired colouring. Make up as per recipe guideline and apply to the wall substrate (mist wall before applying). Allow it to fully dry and check it with the following in mind:

1. It should not dust off onto clothes or skin. If it does, there is too much sand, not enough clay, or you need to add more wheat flour paste.
2. The finish should be smooth (especially when polished for the final coat). If it is excessively grainy, there is too much sand or the sand is too coarse.
3. If the alis cracks excessively on drying, there is too much clay, not enough sand, it has been applied too thickly, or applied onto a dry, thirsty wall substrate.

The paint should go on the wall smoothly and evenly without lumps and without dripping.

Left: Linseed oil has been used as a stain on an earth plaster to create this beautiful trim detail at the Tower Gallery, New Mexico, USA.
Right: A polished beeswax finish on top of an earth plaster to create a rich, sheeny lustre. Designed by Alison Bunning.

alis clay paint will not stand up well on exposed, external walls. They are therefore not suited for use on external walls unless well protected. Alis clay paints are most suited for use as a decorative and protective internal finish. However, additional ingredients can be used, such as wheat flour paste, mica and fine sand, to improve overall strength and durability. Fine sands can also be used in the base and finishing coats to make a thicker-bodied paint. This can be a useful ingredient for filling in minor cracks and irregularities in the earth plaster finishing coat. If sand is added to the finishing coat, it should be very fine, such as a silica sand, to ensure that a smooth finish is achieved, and so that the wall will not collect dust and dirt. Alis clay paints can also be further protected by being coated with a number of transparent, protective glazes. These include: a casein wash (casein plus water), a linseed oil coating (linseed oil plus citrus thinner), or a 'water-glass' finish (sodium/potassium silicate) – see below for recipes and application methods. An internal, decorative alis can also be enhanced with additional ingredients to create certain effects. Mica, for example, will provide a lustrous and luminous finish, and chopped straw will produce a textured finish. Although alis clay paints are most suited for use on earth plasters, they can also be applied to lime, gypsum, earth walls, plasterboard and clay board. Smooth surfaced walls, such as gypsum or plasterboard, need to be primed first to help adhesion (see Chapter 4).

Adding mica

Mica can be added in the form of a finely ground powder, or as larger flakes, or in a range between the two. A finely ground mica will act more like a sand to give body to the paint, and to make it smooth and easy to work. This smoothness can be attributed to the fact that mica is a clay, and therefore has a flat molecular structure rather than being three-dimensional like sand. A finely ground mica will not add the same luminous shine as larger flakes, but will contribute to making the paint harder and more durable. When finely ground mica is used, it may be necessary to diminish the amount of sand (if used), as the mica will carry out the same functions as the sand. Larger flakes can be added to the finishing coat for an aesthetic effect. When buffed with a sponge and soft cloth it will bring out the shine. If a mixture of fine and large flakes of mica are used, it will be possible to achieve both the aesthetic and functional benefits mentioned above.

Adding wheat flour paste

Flour paste can be added to an alis clay paint in much the same way as it can be added to an earth plaster. It provides similar functions of increasing durability, adhesiveness and workability, and decreasing dusting.

Clear glaze finishes for earth plasters

There are a number of translucent, protective coatings that can be applied directly onto an earth plaster. These will allow for the natural, earth colour to remain whilst providing some protection against the elements (if used in an appropriate external setting) and against general wear and tear. Such a coating will also diminish dusting, and provide an overall rich, lustrous finish. The finishes described work to penetrate into the pores of the plaster without closing them. This ensures that moisture intake is reduced whilst maintaining vapour permeability. Some of these finishes, such as water-glass, can reduce the flexibility of the

plaster, so monitoring for any cracks should be regularly carried out, and repairs made where necessary. These finishes include:

- Colourless casein glaze.
- Potassium or sodium silicate ('water-glass').
- Linseed oil and turpentine glaze and other pre-manufactured oil glazes.
- Beeswax.

For all recipes and methods of application for the following finishes, see p.229.

Colourless casein glaze

For use mainly on internal earth plasters. Can be used outside, but it is not very durable and will therefore need regular reapplication.

Sodium or potassium silicate ('water-glass')

Sodium/potassium silicate, also known as 'water-glass', has been used successfully on earth plasters by numerous natural builders. This finish can increase protection against water, eliminate dusting, and increase durability and hardness. It can also be used to improve the water resistance of lime plasters, protecting them from staining and hardening their surfaces. This is achieved without compromising vapour permeability. When applied onto lime surfaces, the minerals react to create a permanent bond. Sodium silicate or potassium silicate, the raw materials used to make water-glass, are inert minerals, created by being dissolved in water under heat and pressure. Water-glass can be made from either of these (potassium silicate or sodium silicate), depending on the availability of these minerals in different parts of the world. It comes in a liquid solution and can be misted or brushed on in one or two coats.

The finish achieved will be translucent, allowing for the natural, rich colour of the earth to be preserved. Pigments can also be added to create a coloured glaze. Adding quartz dust to the basic solution will create a more opaque paint.

A potassium or sodium silicate solution may need to be diluted with water before being applied. This will take some experimentation and trial and error before you commit to painting the whole wall. Ideally, the mix should be quickly absorbed into the wall, and should brush on smoothly and easily. If adding pigments, a more effective finish will be achieved if an undiluted coat is first applied onto the wall, before the pigmented coat. The pigmented coat should be covered with another undiluted sealant coat. The bond with the wall will be much improved if the finishing coat of plaster contains silica sand (see below).

Linseed oil and turpentine glaze

A simple yet effective coating for earth plasters can be made out of boiled linseed oil, which is brushed onto the surface of the wall with a paint brush. A linseed oil coating will help to repel water without affecting the vapour permeability of the wall, as long as not too many coats are applied over a full wall surface. This kind of finish is useful where earth plasters are being used in areas where water is present, such as around sinks, baths and showers. A linseed oil finish on an earth plaster can also be used decoratively to create interesting effects, such as a wall trim.

To assist with the penetration of the oil into the plaster, the oil can be warmed gently before application, or a natural citrus or pine resin thinner can be added (plant-based turpentine). Adding a thinner is essential if more than one coat is to be applied. The thinner should be added to the first coat in the proportions of 75% beeswax to 25% thinner. If further coats are applied, 50% of each can be added together for the second coat, and 25% beeswax to 75% thinner for the third coat.

Pigments can also be mixed into the linseed oil for a coloured glaze effect. Mix the pigment with a small amount of oil to make a paste first, and then add more oil to make a brushable liquid paint. It is also possible to use pre-manufactured penetrating oils, some of which are already mixed with natural plant thinners (see naturalbuildingresources.com).

Beeswax

A beeswax finish will act in much the same way as a linseed oil finish. It will provide water-repelling properties when on top of an earth plaster, albeit in a more concentrated form. Because it is more concentrated, multiple coats of a beeswax finish will diminish the overall vapour permeability of the wall. It is therefore best used in small areas of the wall as a decorative element, such as a trim or on a fireplace, or in one room of a house, such as in a bathroom.

If applying more than one coat, the beeswax should be thinned with a natural plant thinner in order to enhance its lustre and water-repelling qualities. This will enable the wax to penetrate deep into the body of the plaster, instead of creating a shell on the surface. Beeswax finishes can be made from scratch by melting hard beeswax into a liquid form:

- Place the beeswax in a clean bowl, and sit this in a pan of boiling water until the beeswax melts.
- Add two parts boiled linseed oil to one part beeswax. This is essential for maintaining a workable paste when the beeswax dries (which will happen very quickly).
- The paste should be rubbed in with a rag.
- Add a natural plant thinner if applying more than one coat.
- Natural wax finishes can also be purchased from specialist suppliers.

Silicate mineral paints

Silicate paints are a pre-manufactured version of the water-glass product mentioned above. They are made up of the same potassium or sodium silicate binder (melted quartz sand and potash plus water), and mixed with alkaline-resistant pigments to create a stain, or with inorganic mineral fillers to

make an opaque paint. The potassium or sodium silicate binder reacts chemically with minerals present in the underlying material to create an inseparable permanent coating that is highly resistant to physical and chemical weathering. It is also highly breathable, with a pore structure consisting of holes that are large enough to allow for the free passage of water vapour, but small enough to resist the ingress of moisture from driving rain. They will also flex at the same rate as the underlying mineral material. These attributes make silicate paints ideal for all mineral-based surfaces requiring flexible, breathable and durable protection, such as lime and earth plasters/renders, stone, and brick. These paints make a useful substitute for limewash (which needs to be reapplied every few years), especially on large buildings that require full scaffolding when being painted: they are reputed to only need re-application after a fifteen-year period. Two coats are normally required. Silicate mineral paints are also non-toxic, release no VOCs as they dry, and are fully biodegradable. Their high alkalinity gives them anti-fungal properties.

If applying onto freshly lime plastered/rendered walls, it is necessary to wait for 6-9 months before applying. This is to allow the lime to fully carbonate, which could be hampered by the silicate paint. If some protection is needed on external walls during the waiting time, numerous coats of limewash can be applied in the interim.

Testing home-made paints

Although recipes are provided, all home-made paints should be sampled on the area to be painted before use. This is because raw materials and circumstances will differ from place to place. Please refer to the earlier recipes/instructions pages for information on some of the most common problems and how to deal with them.

Applying home-made paints

Whichever type of home-made paint is used, successful application hinges on carrying out certain steps before, during, and after application of the paint.

General wall preparation
- All walls must be clean, dust-free (use a stiff brush to remove dust) and free of loose particles.
- If applying onto old walls, remove all flaking paint particles and vegetation, and repair walls and old plaster/render where needed.
- Unless otherwise specified, dampen walls lightly with a fine mist sprayer prior to application. This will prevent the wall substrate from sucking moisture out of the paint too quickly, which could lead to poor bonding between the paint and the wall, and excessive cracking.
- Determine the suitability of the paint for the wall substrate before application, and apply a primer if necessary to provide key and/or reduce suction from the substrate.
- Protect floors and woodwork by masking with tape where necessary. Painted wood will clean up easily, whereas raw wood will absorb paints quickly and is liable to stain.
- Do not apply paints in direct sun or when raining. Protect all new work from direct sun, wind and rain.
- Do not apply paints in temperatures of 5⁰C (41⁰F) or below, or above 30⁰C (86⁰F), or when there is a risk of frost within 48 hours of application.
- If the paint appears to be drying too rapidly, spray regularly with a gentle mist sprayer at regular intervals. This will help to prevent cracking, chalking (for lime-based paints), and will assist a limewash to carbonate effectively.

Applying linseed oil and beeswax finishes
Linseed oil finishes, applied onto earth plasters, are simply brushed onto the surface with a paint brush. Heating the oil gently before application will help it to go on smoothly and evenly, and will assist with full penetration into the pores.

Beeswax finishes should be applied with a rag. Once applied, they should be well buffed with a clean, soft cloth. Pre-manufactured natural wax finishes should be applied in the same manner. For a highly decorative, polished, and water-resistant finish, a beeswax polish can be applied on top of several coats of a linseed oil and turpentine finish.

Applying sodium/potassium silicate paints
Make up as described earlier in this chapter, and apply with a paint brush.

Applying pre-manufactured 'eco' paints

Most pre-manufactured 'eco' paints are similar in consistency and texture to synthetic paints, but slightly less thick. Individual manufacturers issue specific application guidelines, and most are applied onto dry walls (not pre-misted), with a normal brush or roller. Spills for most of the water-based paints can be easily cleaned up with water, and contact with the skin is generally not a problem. Wash off with soap and water.

Cleaning brushes
Brushes used to apply above home-made and 'eco' paints require little more than being scrubbed with cold water and a stiff brush. ∎

Lime fresco painting

The term 'fresco' literally means 'fresh' in Italian. This is a style of painting that involves the application of lime-fast pigments, mixed with water or lime-water, onto a wet, freshly laid coat of lime plaster. This process instigates a unique reaction whereby the pigment gets caught up in the carbonation process of the lime. This creates an integral unity between the plaster and the pigment, producing a very stable and long-lasting paint finish. There are many examples of ancient fresco wall paintings which are still intact and vibrant, such as at the ancient Greek temples of Knossos. These date back 3,000 years. The characteristic vividness and clarity of the colour can be attributed to the fact that the pigment is dissolved only in water, and not held within a medium, such as limewash, which will diminish the colour. Although the fresco method has been used throughout the world for thousands of years, it was the famous painters of the Italian Renaissance era, such as Michelangelo and his work at the Sistine Chapel, who really developed the skill and raised it to such a high calibre and status. This is reflected by the fact that it is generally known by its Italian name, 'buon fresco', meaning 'true fresco'.

Fresco painting is a highly skilled craft, and requires training and practice to master. However, a simple fresco can be achieved on a smooth and burnished finishing coat of lime plaster. Experimentation with the technique can prove to be an interesting exercise in creating a unique colour effect on lime-plastered walls.

The standard three coats of lime plaster, as outlined in Chapter 3, should be applied. The finishing coat should be made very smooth with a plastic trowel or special stainless steel trowel. Allow it to firm up for at least one hour (depending on drying conditions). The key to success is that the lime is damp before work commences. Pigment should be mixed with water as per the instructions on p.212. The more water that is added to the pigment, the more watery the colour will appear on the wall.

Application is with a range of different-sized soft-bristled brushes, depending on whether a whole wall is being covered or an intricate pattern created. Every brush stroke is permanent, so it is essential to know exactly what you plan to paint before committing the brush to the wall. ■

Stunning lime fresco finishes created by Cara Campbell.

6

Finishes from around the world

Chapter 6

Most countries around the world have a tradition of finishing their buildings with either lime- or earth-based plasters, renders and paints. This is due to the ubiquitous nature of the raw materials needed: earth, limestone, aggregate, and plant or animal fibres. Every culture has its own specific additives which are used to enhance or amend the performance of the finish, and these are always based on locally available materials. For example, in Japan boiled seaweed is added to lime and earth plasters to improve their binding properties and to impart a glossy sheen to finishing coats.

Through our personal research of lime- and earth-based finishes around the world, it is also evident that many of the materials, recipes and methods used, though similar, vary from region to region and between practitioners. This reinforces the idea that although there are certain principles that need to be observed if a successful outcome is to be achieved, there is no set way to carry out this type of work. Methods have been developed depending on the person carrying out the work, the materials available, cultural preferences, and the prevailing climate of the local area.

Just as these traditional techniques evolved simultaneously around the world, so too are they simultaneously undergoing a revival. This is happening in parts of the world where modern materials and practices have become the norm. This resurgence is occurring as the result of a recognition of the need to carry out less environmentally destructive building practices and to create healthy homes and structures, and an increased desire to create things made by hand. ■

Left: Tadelakt finishes in a Riad in Marrakech, Morocco.
Below: Earth plasters in a Buddhist Retreat Centre by Ben and Jody of 'Naturally Plaster', Colorado, USA.

Marmarino

Paul and Siobhan of P. D. Marlow 'Specialists in Stucco', based in Belfast, Northern Ireland, carry out custom marmorino finishes – highly polished lime plasters originating from Italy. They have helped to raise the overall awareness of this beautiful finish in the United Kingdom. Here they describe what they do . . .

A brief history of marmorino
Lime plaster finishes have been used for thousands of years, and many early civilizations had their own versions, but the most noble of all, in my opinion, is Italian marmorino. Originally, marmorino was valued for its durability; its main purpose was to protect the structure. However, Venetian plasterers developed techniques which transformed marmorino from a purely functional building material to the highly decorative medium it is today, without sacrificing any of the mechanical properties which made it so popular. That is why many of the marmorino exteriors which were finished during the Renaissance can still be viewed today.

The architect best-known for reviving interest in marmorino is Carlo Scarpa. His work during the 1950s and 60s used marmorino extensively, often juxtaposing it with shuttered concrete, glass or stainless steel.

Our materials
Because of the way marmorino is composed, it is extremely durable. Its ingredients are slaked

lime as the binder, marble dust as the aggregate, and linseed oil. So when it has cured, it has the same composition, microstructure and properties as natural marble.

The granulation of the marble dust in marmorino gives it its texture: from a coarse, open grain to a highly refined lustre. We use natural earth or oxide pigments to achieve any colour, and extra depth can be added by including mica, coloured marble dust or *cocciopesto* (brick dust). The final surface is sealed with soap, beeswax, siloxane sealer or potassium silicate.

Techniques

To apply marmorino successfully, it takes considerable skill and experience. An artisan needs to understand how lime and natural pigments work, and be able to produce the most subtle shades in colour and tone. Marmorino is a trowel-applied finish, and it takes real flair to produce a pleasing finish. Slight variations in trowel technique completely alter the final appearance of the surface.
.

Substrates

Marmorino is totally compatible with modern building methods. When used externally, the ideal substrate is lime render – either non-hydraulic lime or natural hydraulic lime – as it will chemically fuse with the marmorino to form one solid layer. For interiors, it's possible to work over virtually any substrate, as long as it is sound.

In design, what gives a space its personality are the finishes, and marmorino is the perfect finish for bringing walls to life. ■

Tadelakt

Tadelakt is a lime-based, polished waterproof plastering technique from Morocco. It was originally developed and used to waterproof cisterns for water collection, and was then used in *Hamams* – the traditional public bathing houses – and later in the bathrooms of private houses.

Tadelakt plaster can be used on sinks, showers, bathtubs, floors and walls because of its waterproof nature. This tradition almost disappeared but has recently (over the last 15 years) undergone a revival and become popular across Europe and in North America. The process of creating a traditional Moroccan tadelakt plaster begins with the application of a specific lime made from the limestone extracted from the foothills of Marrakech. The qualities of this limestone are very particular to the region, and contribute to the individual character of the resulting finish. The limestone contains many impurities, mainly in the form of silica, making it fairly hydraulic, and the burning and slaking processes are not controlled, as is the case with most European lime manufacturing. This produces a less fine, fairly rough lime, making it unnecessary to add an aggregate to the lime mix. This produces a material rich in lime binder, which creates the inherent micro-fissures that are found in authentic Moroccan tadelakt plasters, and which has been likened to old earthenware. It is these micro-fissures that create its unique beauty.

The rest of the process for creating a tadelakt finish in Morocco varies considerably from one craftsperson to the next. Each *mallam* (master craftsperson) has his own unique procedure and set of specialist tools; however, the basic principles remain consistent. After a minimum of two coats of lime plaster have been applied to the substrate, the second coat is well scoured with a wood float before drying completely. The lime is then smoothed out with a plastic trowel or a strong piece of plastic. A metal trowel is generally not used for smoothing, unless it is a high grade steel, because of the tendency for the metal to leave burnish marks on the lime. Once the lime has been smoothed and has dried for at least one day, a special soap known as *savon noire* (black soap) is applied. The traditional Moroccan *savon noire* is made out of olive oil and fish bone, produced in a town by the sea called Safi. The black soap reacts with the lime to not only create the waterproofing, but also to produce the beautiful lustrous shine that tadelakt is so famous for. The black soap is diluted with water for ease of application. It is spread on with a paint brush in small sections, and then immediately followed by vigorous, tight circular polishing with a special tadelakt stone.

This stone is chosen to fit neatly into the hand, and must have a flat polishing surface (usually ground down). The stone must be hard, such as a granite, so that it can resist the pressure of the polishing. This polishing action with the stone serves to further tighten the lime mix to eliminate voids, thus closing the pores and contributing to its ability to resist water. The polishing also helps to feed the soap into the lime so that they become fully integrated. Areas that will be continually coming into contact with water, such as a bath or sink, require roughly five applications of the black soap. It usually requires reapplication once a year.

The vibrant colours of tadelakt plasters are achieved by incorporating lime-fast pigments into the lime. Traditionally, Moroccan tadelakt plasters were

"The secret of tadelakt is in the time you put into it and the passionate nature of application." - Malam Said Chaarawi, Marrakech

either red from the red pigments found in the surrounding areas, or a grey/buff colour from the unpigmented lime. Modern renditions utilise a wide variety of colours, from the more natural earth pigments to the brightly coloured synthetic pigments. The act of polishing the plaster with the stone creates an irregular colour tone within the final finish. This is due to the differential compression that will naturally occur over the wall surface. Where more pressure is applied, a darker tone will develop. This creates the natural varied patina that makes authentic tadelakt appear so uncontrived and at ease with its environment.

To create a tadelakt plaster it is possible to import lime direct from Marrakech, but to avoid the implications associated with the long transport, many people have successfully adapted local limes to allow it to behave and look the same as an authentic Moroccan tadelakt. A natural hydraulic lime (NHL 2 or NHL 3.5) is best, especially when applied to a bathroom area and when there will be direct contact with water. It is also possible to use a non-hydraulic lime with a pozzolan added. Unlike Moroccan lime, which contains within it a proportion of under- and over-cooked lime particles which act as the aggregate, the finer European limes must be blended with an added aggregate. This is so that the fine balance can be achieved between creating the decorative micro-fissures that make tadelakt so unique, and not creating large cracks that will jeopardize the integrity of the plaster and will certainly make it lose its waterproofing qualities. Without these micro-fissures, it is said that you simply create something more akin to an Italian polished 'marmorino' plaster. To achieve this balance, a fine aggregate such as marble powder is normally added (well graded, less than 1mm) in the proportion of 1 part lime : 2 parts aggregate. Master plasterer Bruno Bengamra of D'Ocres, in the south of France, recommends this mix, although as with all lime mixes, it is necessary to test and adjust the mix according to the lime being used. ∎

Litema

Ms Carina Mylene Beyer is a lecturer in photography at the School of Design Technology and Visual Art, Central University of Technology, Free State in Bloemfontein, South Africa. She is involved in a community service and research project focusing on 'litema', and has compiled a photographic book documenting this ancient art form as it is being practiced in contemporary South Africa. Here are her thoughts and photos on the subject . . .

Litema is the tradition whereby Basotho women (from South Africa) apply elaborate decorations to the freshly plastered walls of their mud dwellings. For centuries the tradition of litema has been associated with Basotho women only. Nowadays the practice extends itself across cultural as well as regional borders. Zulu and Xhosa women, either married to Basotho spouses or living in the vicinity of practising litema artists have, in the past two or three decades, also favoured the tradition. The art is only practised in Lesotho (where it originates from) and in the Free State province of South Africa. Some decorated homes may, however, be found in areas bordering the Free State and Lesotho, such as Kwazulu Natal and the Eastern Cape.

It involves four basic techniques: engraving, painting, mosaicing and relief-moulding.
- Engraving is done in the wet plaster using sticks, fingers, forks and combs.
- Paint is mostly applied to dry plaster, and very occasionally it is done *al fresco* style (on wet mud). Usually water-based paints, such as PVA, are used – the desired colour tones are achieved by mixing dyes (called *marello* in Sesotho) into the white paint. A more traditional approach to painting involves simply applying different tones of earth during the plaster process.
- Mosaicing is done by embedding small pebbles or stones into the wet plaster. Peach trees are

synonymous with the Free State province of South Africa. As a result, peach kernels (stones) are often used instead of stones.

- Relief-moulding involves sculpting mud patterns onto the existing plaster. Shelves, displaying the most treasured items in a household, are created in the same manner (no support is used besides the mud!). This is probably the most difficult of all application processes, and is therefore very seldom found.

Plaster material consists of a mixture of earth/clay and cow dung. Often the earth from ant heaps is also added – its excellent binding properties (due to the saliva of the ants) are much desired.

With regards to the designs, symmetry is probably the most significant feature in traditional litema. A pattern is usually outlined in a square, which is then copied into adjacent squares, either in reverse or in a mirror image. These 'cells', consisting of four squares, are then repeated across a wall in the same manner.

The patterns or colours used have no significance other than the purpose of beautifying the women's homes. It serves as an extension of the Basotho woman's identity and, as long as this woman and artist is able to assert her identity in this way, she will continue the practice.

Engravings mostly mimic the furrow lines of ploughed fields (a type of bird's eye view). Basotho women have always played a very important role in agriculture, and significance may therefore be found in these engravings.

Patterns are generally representative of the natural world. Flowers, petals and leaves feature most commonly – not only in shape, but also in colour. Litema is very much a seasonal phenomenon. Decorating tones more than often mirror the surrounding landscape, with bright and colourful tones dominating in summer and spring, and more natural tones in autumn and winter. More modern design inspiration comes from the images seen on household utilities and packaging. Visual media (magazines and television) also serve as a design source. Furthermore, there is a definite copying of patterns found on the traditional Basotho blanket.

The craft, although declining in sightings at an alarming rate (factors such as westernization and urbanization may be blamed), is still alive. It is also transforming itself into a more modern rendition of a traditional art. ∎

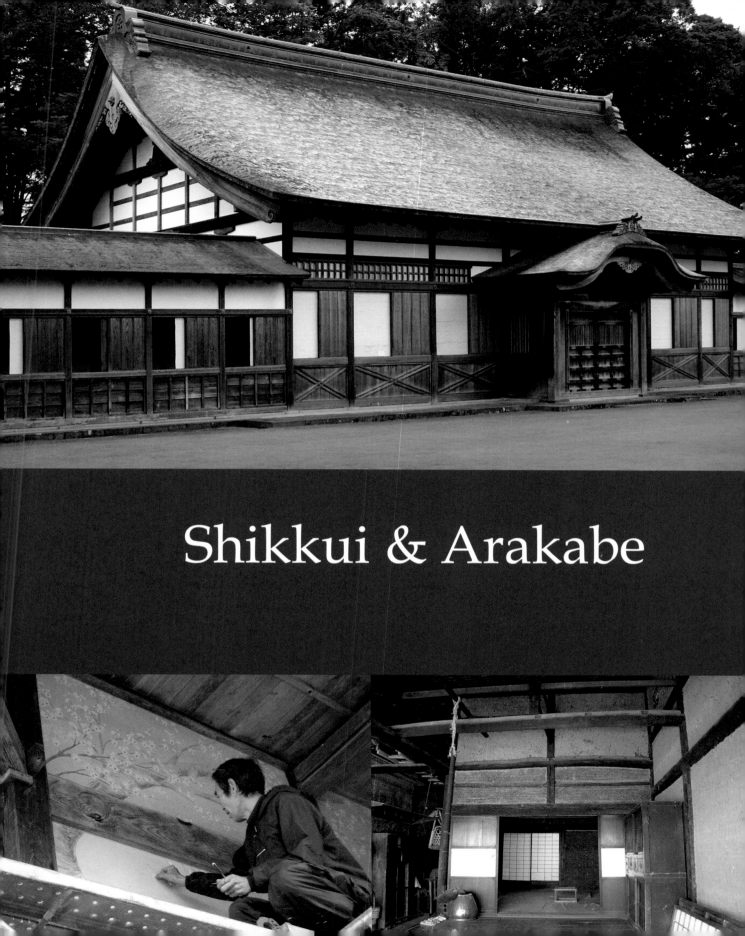

Shikkui & Arakabe

Japan has rich traditions of both lime- and earth-based finishes. The traditional mud wall, known as 'arakabe', consists of packing several coats of a clay, aggregate and straw mix onto a bamboo lath framework between post and beams. It is similar to the traditional British wattle and daub walling system. The daub mixture is generally applied in three consecutive coats on either side of the lath. The clay and aggregates become finer, and the fibres (usually rice or oat straw) shorter, as the coats proceed. The final coat often contains an additive made from boiled 'nori' seaweed, which produces a high gloss finish. The materials were traditionally sourced locally, and the mix made up on-site. This mix was always left to steep for a couple of weeks for the straw to soften and for the mud to achieve the desired consistency. These days, a ready-mixed material can be purchased.

The traditional Japanese lime-based finish is known as 'shikkui'. The name is derived from the Chinese word 'suk-wui', which means a slaked lime. Shikkui plaster consists of slaked lime, aggregate, natural fibres, and boiled nori seaweed extract as an additional binder. In ancient times rice starch was used instead of seaweed, but this was a precious and therefore expensive commodity. For this reason shikkui plasters were confined to use on important buildings, such as temples, shrines and houses of the nobility. During the sixteenth century there was a castle-building boom, at which time the technology was developed to replace rice starch with seaweed. This made the use of shikkui more widespread and accessible. Prior to 1963, at which time a bagged shikkui plaster became available, the shikkui plasterer would also make up the materials on site – boiling the seaweed and mixing it together with the slaked lime, aggregates and fibre.

There is currently a renewed interest in Japan in both forms of traditional finishes - the arakabe mud plaster (mud wall), and the shikkui lime plaster. This is due to the recognition of 'sick building syndrome' in industrial Japan, brought on by the use of toxic building materials which are trapped within increasingly air tight buildings. It is also due to the awareness of the impact of many modern materials on the environment, as well as a desire to maintain vernacular building practices.

This information was provided through an interview with shikkui expert Nobuyoshi Yukihira.

Photos are of lime and earth finishes from Japan: 'shikkui' (lime) and 'arakabe' (earth). ■

San Francisco de Asís

Adobe earth plasters

"How can one describe our church? It needs to breathe; it gets old, wrinkles and cracks; it needs to be cared for; it loves to be washed by the rain, and to feel the touch of women's hands applying the mud plaster to conceal and heal the cracks of weather and time. Our church is almost human. Our church 'is' human. The link and bond between an adobe church and its people are strong and require commitment: we keep the church together, and the church keeps us together." (Father Michael O'Brien, Pastor of San Francisco de Asis Church (1979), New Mexico).

"For the Spanish colonists, the adobe re-mudding of their homes and their church was as much a part of their yearly ritual as sowing and harvesting.

Following the old Indian tradition, the women did the replastering. They used fleeces of sheepskin or their hands to smooth the thick clay over a year's stresses and cracks, leaving the walls' coating of butterscotch earth pale and unblemished once again. So it had been with the Ranchos de Taos church since the days of its creation. But today we have other demands on our time, other commitments." (Wolfgang Pogzeba, Ranchos de Taos, San Francisco de Asis Church).

In 1979 the San Francisco de Asis church in Taos, New Mexico, was falling apart. The church was built 200 years before, with traditional adobe construction, by the hands of Spanish settlers and their Pueblo Indian neighbours. Up until 1967, the church had

Above: This thousand-year-old earth-plastered Pueblo in Taos, New Mexico, is still inhabited today.
Below: Different-coloured micaceous clay alis finishes.

been lovingly cared for by its community with annual repair sessions using the traditional mud plasters. In 1967 the parish council took the decision that there was no longer time for this, and that the church would be covered with the seemingly more permanent solution of cement onto wire meshing. Covered with cement from head to foot, it was now unable to breathe and within one year the cement had cracked, allowing water in, which was then unable to escape. For the first time in 200 years, the church was literally melting from within. It was Father O'Brien who took the initiative to instigate the removal of the cement from the church, and reinvigorate the yearly mudding sessions with the community. The church still stands healthy and strong with a vibrant and active community, who still gather once a year – women, men and children – to re-plaster the church with mud.

The Taos Pueblo, a native American community in New Mexico, boasts thousand-year-old multi-storeyed earth buildings that have been kept healthy by being covered with mud plasters. The earths used to make these plasters are mined from designated areas in the surrounding hillsides. It is the women 'enjarradoras' (mud plasterers) who know which muds to use, and who have been passing on these skills to the next generation for millennia. Among these special muds are micaceous clays (clay with mica), designated to make a finishing seal ('alis'). This was painted onto the earth plasters, making them more impervious to water. These clays come in different colours, such as 'tierra amarilla' (yellow earth), 'tierra blanca' (white earth), and 'tierra colorada' (pink earth). These special clay washes were rubbed onto the walls regularly with sheepskin (tanned, with the wool left on it), and sometimes polished with hard agate stones. There are many modern-day 'enjarradoras' (and men), practicing these traditions on new and old adobe structures, cob buildings and those built out of straw bales. ∎

Resources and suppliers

There has never been a time in history when we have had at such a large variety of excellent resources for lime and earth finishes, as well as for all types of traditional and ecological building works.

For this reason, we have decided to create an online database to present this information to our readers. Within this database you will find information relating to materials suppliers, courses, organisations and practitioners. This information will cover the UK and Ireland primarily, but we are also including resources within the USA, Australasia and much of Europe. Having this data presented online will also enable us to regularly update the material. This is important because of the way that the current burgeoning interest in traditional and ecological building is fuelling the rapid growth of businesses relating to these areas. We would like to be able to reflect this rapid growth by providing information that is always up-to-date and relevant. For an extensive resources section for all things relating to earth and lime finishes (and more), please go to:

www.naturalbuildingresources.com

Bibliography

BOOKS

Adobe Conservation (2006)
by Cornerstones Community
Partnerships, Sunstone Press
ISBN 0865345279

The 'Amiriya in Rada': The History
and Restoration of a 16th Century
Madrasa in the Yemen (1997)
by Selma Al-Radi,
Oxford University Press
ISBN 0197280234

Applied Artistry (1995)
by Jocasta Innes, Bulfinch
ISBN 0821222422

An Architecture for the People:
The complete works of Hassan
Fathy (1997)
by James Steele, Thames and Hudson
ISBN 0823002268

The Art of Natural Building (2002)
by Joseph Kennedy, Micheal
G. Smith and Catherine Wanek
New Society Publishers
ISBN 0865714339

The Beauty of Straw Bale Homes (2000)
by Bill and Athena Steen, Chelsea
Green Publishing Company
ISBN 1890132772

Building with Awareness (2005)
by Ted Owens, Syncronos
Design Incorporated
ISBN 0977334317

Building with Cob:
A Step by Step Guide (2006)
by Adam Weismann and
Katy Bryce, Green Books
ISBN 1903998727

Building with Earth:
A Handbook (2001)
by John Norton
ITDG Publishing
ISBN 18533393371

Building with Earth:
Design and Technology of a
Sustainable Architecture (2006)
by Gernot Minke
Birkhauser Publishing
ISBN 9783764374778

Building Green (2005)
by Clarke Snell and Tim
Calahan, Lark Books
ISBN 1579905323

Building with Hemp (2006)
by Steve Allin, Seed Press
ISBN 0955110904

Building with Lime,
A Practical Introduction (1997)
by Stafford Holmes and Michael
Wingate, Intermediate
Technology Publications
ISBN 1853393843

Building with Straw Bales: A practical
guide for the UK and Ireland (2003)
by Barabara Jones, Green Books
ISBN 1903998131

Built by Hand: Vernacular
Buildings Around the World (2003)
by Bill and Athena Steen, Gibbs Smith
ISBN 158685237X

Cahier de recettes de la Marchande
de Coleurs: Chaux, Pigments,
Liants, Charges, Outils (2005)
by Anne Marie and Jean
Claude Misset, Massin
ISBN 2707204528

Caring for Old Houses (2002)
by Pamela Cunnington
Marston House
ISBN 1899296174

Cave Painting: Movements
in World Art (1963)
by Roxane Cuvay and
translated by Margaret Shnefield,
Crown Publishers Inc.

Ceramic Houses and
Earth Architecture:
How to build your own (2000)
by Nader Khalili
Cal Earth Press
ISBN 1889625019

Classic Paints and
Faux Finishes (1993)
by Annie Sloan and Kate
Gwynn, Readers Digest
ISBN 0895778971

Clay and Cob Buildings (2004)
by John McCann
Shire Publications Ltd
ISBN 0747805792

Cob Buildings,
A Practical Guide (2004)
by Jane Schofield and Jill
Smallcombe, Black Dog Press
ISBN 0952434156

Colors of the World:
a geography of color (2004)
by Jean Phillipe and Dominique
Lenclos, Norton
ISBN 0393731472

Cottage Building in Cob, Pise,
Chalk and Clay (1913)
by Clough Williams-Ellis
Country Life

The Charm of the English
Village (1985)
by P. H. Ditchfield, Bracken Books
ISBN 0946495297

Colour, Making and
Using Dyes and Pigments (2002)
by Francois Delamare and
Bernard Guineau
Thames and Hudson
ISBN 05003011026

Design of Straw Bale Buildings (2006)
by Bruce King, Green Building Press
ISBN 09764911117

Discovering Your Old House: How to Trace the History of Your Home (1997) by David Iredale and John Barrett, Shire Publications
ISBN 0747801436

Earth Building: Methods and Materials, Repair and Conservation (2005) by Laurence Keefe, Taylor and Francis, *ISBN 0415323223*

Earth: The Conservation and Repair of Bowhill, Exeter: Working with Cob (1999) by Ray Harrison, English Heritage/ James and James
ISBN 1873936648

Earth Construction: A Comprehensive Guide (2003) by Hugo Houben and Hubert Guillard, ITDG Publishing, *ISBN 185339193X*

Earth Plasters for Straw Bale Homes (2000) by Keely Meagan, Self Published
ISBN 0615116485

Earth Structures and Construction in Scotland: A Guide to the recognition and Conservation of Earth Technology in Scotland (1996) by Bruce Walker and Christopher McGregor, Historic Scotland
ISBN 1900168227

Earth to Spirit: In Search of Natural Architecture (1994) by David Pearson, Gaia Books
ISBN 0811807029

Ecohouse 2: A Design Guide (2005) by Sue Roaf, Architectural Press
ISBN 0750657340

EcoNest: Creating Sustainable Sanctuaries of Clay, Straw and Timber (2005) by Paula-Baker Laporte and Robert Laporte, Gibbs and Smith
ISBN 158685691X

The Ecology of Building Materials (2003) by Bjorn Berge, Arhitectural Press
ISBN 07560633948

Exterior Details (1990) by Jocasta Innes, Simon and Schuster
ISBN 0671725769

Fresco Painting: Modern methods and techniques for painting in fresco and secco (1947) by Ollie Nordmark American Artists Group Inc.

Green Building Handbook, Volume One (1997) by Wooley, Kimmins, Harrison and Harrison, SPON Press
ISBN 0419226907

The Green Imperative (1995) by Victor Papanek, Thomas and Hudson
ISBN 0500278466

The Hand Sculpted House: A Practical and Philosophical Guide to Building a Cob Cottage (2002) by Ianto Evans, Michael G. Smith and Linda Smiley, Chelsea Green Publishing
ISBN 1890132349

Home-made Homes: Dwellings of the Rural Poor in Wales (1988) by Eurwyn Williams, The National Museum of Wales, *ISBN 0720002202*

Home Work: Handbuilt Shelter (2004) by Lloyd Kahn, Shelter
ISBN 0936070331

Hydraulic Lime Mortar: for stone, brick and block masonry (2003) by The Foresight Research Team, Donhead Publishing
ISBN 1873394640

Introduction to Permaculture (2000) by Bill Mollison with Reny Mia Slay, Tagari Publications
ISBN 0908228082

Lime and Lime Mortars (1927 and 1998) by Ad Cowper Donhead Publishing
ISBN 1873394292

Lime in building: A Practical Guide (1997) by Jane Schofield, Black Dog Press
ISBN 0952434121

Mortars, Plasters and Renders in Conservation, Second Edition (2002) by John Ashurst, Ecclesiastical Architects and Surveyors Association

The Mud Wall in England (1984) by J. Harrison, Ancient Monuments Society

The Natural House (2000) by Daniel D. Chiras Chelsea Green Publishing Company, *ISBN 1890132578*

The Natural Paint Book: The Complete Guide to natural paints, recipes and finishes (2002) by Lynn Edwards and Julia Lawless, Kyle Cathy Ltd.
ISBN 1856264327

The Natural Plaster Book: Earth, Lime and Gypsum Plasters for Natural Homes (2003) by Cedar Rose Guelberth and Dan Chiras, New Society Publishers
ISBN 00865714495

The Nature of Order: An Essay on the Art of Building and The Nature of the Universe (2005) by Christopher Alexander, Centre for Environmental Structure
ISBN 0972652930

Ocres et Finitiions a la Chaux: Enduits decoratifs, stucs et tadelakt (2004) by Vincent Tripard, Edisud
ISBN 27449004066

Ocres et Peintures Decoratives
de Provence (2006)
by Vincent Tripard, Edisud
ISBN 27449001903

Out of Earth II: National Conference
on Earth Buildings (1995)
by Linda Watson and
Rex Harries (editors)
University of Plymouth
ISBN 0905227409

Paint Alchemy (2001)
by Annie Sloan, Collins and Brown
ISBN 185585886X

Petit Anthologie de l'ocre (1999)
by Callixte Cocylima, Equionoxe
ISBN 2841331491

Places of the Soul (1990)
by Christopher Day
The Aquarian Press
ISBN 0850308801

Plastering (1951 and 2007)
by J. T. Sawyer, Donhead Publishing
ISBN 9781873394830

Plastering (1990)
by J. B. Taylor, Pearson Longman
ISBN 0582056349

Plastering: Plain and
Decorative (1897 and 1998)
by William Millar, Donhead Publishers
ISBN 1873394306

Rammed Earth: Design and
construction guidelines (2005)
by Peter Walker, Rowland Keable,
Joe Martin and Vasilios Maniatidis
BRE Bookshop
ISBN 1860817343

Shelter (1973)
by Lloyd Kahn, Shelter Publications
ISBN 0936070110

A Shelter Sketchbook (1997)
by John S. Taylor, Chelsea Green
Publishing Company
ISBN 1890132020

The Spell of the Sensuous (1996)
by David Abram Vintage Books
ISBN 0679776397

Strawbale Building (2000)
by Chris Magwood and Peter Mack,
New Society Publisers
ISBN 0865714037

The Strawbale House (1994)
by Athena and Bill Steen, David
Bainbridge with David Eisenberg,
Chelsea Green Publishing Company
ISBN 0930031717

Le Tadelakt: Un deco a la chaux (2005)
by Solene Delahousse, Massin
ISBN 2707204765

Terra Britannica (2000)
by John Hurd and Ben Gourley
(editors), James and James
ISBN 1902916131

Village Buildings of Britain (1991)
by Matthew Rice, Time Warner
ISBN 0316726257

Wattle and Daub (2006)
by Paula Sunshine, Shire Publications
ISBN 0747806527

The Whole House Book (2005)
by Cindy Harris and Pat Borer, Centre
for Alternative Technology Publications
ISBN 1902175220

MAGAZINES AND JOURNALS

**Appropriate Plasters, Renders and
Finishes for Cob and Random Stone
Walls in Devon (2nd ed)**
by Paul Bedford, Bruce and and Liz
Induni and Larry Keefe, Devon Earth
Buildng Association (DEBA)

**The Cob Buildings of Devon: Repair
and Maintanence (Volume 2, 1992)**
by Larry Keefe, The Devon Historic
Buildings Trust (DHBT)

**The Last Straw Journal
(Issue 33, Spring 2001)**

**The Last Straw Journal
(Issue 43, Fall 2003)**

**Straw Bale Construction Details:
A Sourcebook (2000)**
by Ken Haggard and Scott
Clark(Editors), California Straw Bale
Association (CASBA)

**Charlestown limeworks:
Research and Conservation (2006)**
by The Scottish Lime Centre, Historic
Scotland

**Technical Advice Note 1: Preparation
and Use of Lime Mortars (2003)**
by The Scottish Lime Centre,
Historic Scotland

**Technical Advice Note 2:
Conservation of Plasterwork (2002)**
by The Scottish Lime Centre,
Historic Scotland

**Technical Advice Note 15: External
Lime Coatings on Traditional
Buildings (2001)**
by The Scottish Lime Centre,
Historic Scotland

**The Journal of the Building Limes
Forum (Volume 8, 2001)**

**The Journal of the Building
Limes Forum (Volume 9, 2002)**

**The Journal of the Building
Limes Forum (Volume 10, 2003)**

**The Journal of the Building
Limes Forum (Volume 11, 2004)**

**The Journal of the Building
Limes Forum (Volume 12, 2005)**

**The Journal of the Building
Limes Forum (Volume 13, 2006)**

**Lime: A Guide to the Use of
Lime in Historic Building**
by the South Somerset District Council

Adobe Builder (Issue 11, 2003)

Index

Page numbers in *italic* refer to illustrations.

A

additives, for earth plasters 161–3, 189
adhesion coats 45, 76–7, *174*, 174–5
clay slip bonding coats 182, 190
adobe *14*, 15, *248–52*, *249–51*
pinning out (rajuela system) 75–6
aggregates *80*, 81–7, *84*, *86*, 93, *106–7*, 172
making up lime-aggregate mixes 111–19, *114*, *116–17*
mix for earth plasters *155*, 172
mixers for *see* cement mixers
pozzolanic 82, *86*, 105–7
sedimentation test 86, *153*, 153–4
selection for lime renders/plasters 107
alis clay paint *218*, 219–27, *223–5*
silica in *87*
alkalinity testing 103
animal dung 158, 161–2, 173
animal hair 107–9, 113–14, *114*
arakabe *245–7*, 246

B

ball dropping test *152*, 152
Bau-Biologie 10
beach sands 83
beeswax finishes 229, 231
Beyer, Carina Mylene 243
boards, building 20–2, 73
borax 221
box test 153
BREAM 9
bricks 19
moisture and 23
British Standard for lime 9
brushes *54*, 55–6, 231
brushing 71, *75*
buckets 58
building boards 20–2, 73
see also specific types of

board
building design 35–46
building materials
environment and 5–7
health and 7–9
using lime and earth finishes in the modern world 9–10
wall systems 14–22
building principles 4–10
building regulations 9
breathing finishes and 33
building sites 79
siting a building 37–8
burlap 43
burnishing 70
burnt sand mastic *40*

C

calcium carbonate 89, *92*, 93–4, 101–2
see also limestone
calcium hydroxide *92*, 94–5, 102, 109, 163
carbon emissions 5, 201
carbon sinks 16, 20
carbonation 75, 85, *92*, 98, 101–3, 105
aided by scouring 68
of limewash 213
casein paints 216–19, *217*, 220–1
casein primer 220
casein wash 220, 226
colourless casein glaze 227
limewash with casein 210, 216
making casein curds from skimmed milk 210
cavity walls 25
cement 5–7, 26, 90–1, 93
moisture and cement finishes 29, 30
cement mixers 56, *57*
mixing earth plasters with 176–8, *178*
mixing natural hydraulic lime mortars with 115–16, *116*
mixing non hydraulic lime putties with 114
clat 15
clay
alis clay paint *87*, *218*, 219–

27, *223–5*
applying clay/lime slip onto straw bale walls with render gun 64–5
as a binder 154
burlap strips and clay slip 43
chemistry of 144–7
clay slip and straw stuffing mix 174
clay slip bonding coat 182, 190
clayboard *19*, 22, 134
clays to avoid 157
dry clay and aggregate mix for earth plasters 155
fired clay honeycomb insulating blocks *19*, 19
kaolin 106, *155*, 157, *162*, 219
light clay *15*, 16
locating clay 157
mixing bagged clays 179
mixing pre-manufactured clay plasters 179
moisture and clay rich earth plasters and renders 29–30
preparation *155*, *168*, *170–1*, 170–2
restriction in aggregates 82
sieving *155*, *168*, 170–2
and soil formation 143–4
wall systems 15
clay plasters *see* earth plasters and renders
clear glaze finishes 226, 227–9
clob 15
clom 15
clunch 15
coat systems
for alis clay paints 222, 224
for earth plasters 181–4
for lime plasters/renders 121–2, 132, 136–7
see also specific coats
cob 15, *103*
cob block 15, *18*
moisture and 23
comb scratchers 52, *53*, 66
concrete blocks 19–20
counterlathing 43–5
coverage rates
earth plaster 190
lime-aggregate 119
cracking (dry shrinkage)

in earth plasters 166–7
reduction through aggregates 81
Crews, Carol 219
Crocker, Ed 156

D

damp problems 23, 27, 34
see also moisture
damp-proof courses 27
darbies 55, 67, *68*
detail trowels 52, *53*
devil floats 55, 67, 125
doors: wall reinforcements around openings 46–7
drainage
roof design and 38–9
surface drainage and foundations 39–41
dung 158, 161–2, 173
dusting (resistance to abrasion) 167

E

earth plasters and renders
additives and stabilisers 161–3, 173–5
adobe *see* adobe
advantages of 142–3
aftercare 191–2
aggregates 157, 172 *see also* aggregates
application 131–2, 181–92, *183*, *187–8*
arakabe *245–7*, 246
clay and 143–8, 157 *see also* clay
clear glaze finishes 226, 227–9
composition 150, 154–8
coverage rates 190
customised mixes 167–9
fibre reinforcement 158–60
health and safety issues when working with 163
history of use 141–2
material preparation 169–75
mechanisms as a wall finish 147–8
mixing *165*, 175–9

257

By the same authors:

Building with Cob: a step-by-step guide
ISBN 9781903998 72 4   £25.00 paperback

For our complete booklist, see
www.greenbooks.co.uk